Object-Relations Theory and Clinical Psychoanalysis

OBJECT-RELATIONS THEORY AND CLINICAL PSYCHOANALYSIS

Otto F. Kernberg, M.D.

A JASON ARONSON BOOK

ROWMAN & LITTLEFIELD PUBLISHERS, INC.
Lanham • Boulder • New York • Toronto • Oxford

A JASON ARONSON BOOK

ROWMAN & LITTLEFIELD PUBLISHERS, INC.

Published in the United States of America
by Rowman & Littlefield Publishers, Inc.
A wholly owned subsidiary of The Rowman & Littlefield Publishing Group, Inc.
4501 Forbes Boulevard, Suite 200, Lanham, Maryland 20706
www.rowmanlittlefield.com

PO Box 317
Oxford
OX2 9RU, UK

First softcover edition 1995
First Rowman & Littlefield edition 2004

British Library Cataloguing in Publication Information Available

Library of Congress Cataloging-in-Publication Data

ISBN 0-87668-247-6 (cloth : alk. paper)
ISBN 1-56821-612-2 (pbk : alk. paper)
Library of Congress Catalog Card Number: 75-42548

Printed in the United States of America

To the Memory of Herman van der Waals

About the Author

Otto F. Kernberg, M.D., F.A.P.A., is Associate Chairman and Medical Director of The New York Hospital-Cornell Medical Center, Westchester Division, and Professor of Psychiatry at the Cornell University Medical College. He is also Training and Supervising Analyst of the Columbia University Center for Psychoanalytic Training and Research. In the past, Dr. Kernberg served as Director of the C.F. Menninger Memorial Hospital, Supervising and Training Analyst of the Topeka Institute for Psychoanalysis, and Director of the Psychotherapy Research Project of the Menninger Foundation. More recently, he was Director of the General Clinical Service of the New York State Psychiatric Institute, and Professor of Clinical Psychiatry at the College of Physicians and Surgeons of Columbia University. Dr. Kernberg is a Vice-President of the International Psychoanalytic Association, and President of the Association for Psychoanalytic Medicine. He is also Book Editor of the *Journal of the American Psychoanalytic Association*. He was awarded the 1972 Heinz Hartmann Award of the New York Psychoanalytic Institute and Society, the 1975 Edward A. Strecker Award from the Institute of Pennsylvania Hospital, the 1981 George E. Daniels Merit Award of the Association for Psychoanalytic Medicine, the 1982 William F. Schonfeld Memorial Award of the American Society for Adolescent Psychiatry, the 1986 Van Gieson Award from the New York State Psychiatric Institute, the 1987 Teacher of the Year Award from The New York Hospital-Cornell Medical Center, Westchester Division, and the 1990 Mary S. Sigourney Award for Psychoanalysis. He is the author of 6 books: *Psychotherapy and Psychoanalysis: Final Report of the Menninger Foundation's Psychotherapy Research Project* (with other authors), *Borderline Conditions and Pathological Narcissism*, *Object Relations Theory and Clinical Psychoanalysis*, *Internal World and External Reality: Object Relations Theory Applied*, *Severe Personality Disorders: Psychotherapeutic Strategies*, and *Aggression in Personality Disorders and Perversion*. He is also author (with Michael Selzer, Harold W. Koenigsberg, Arthur Carr, and Ann Appelbaum) of *Psychodynamic Psychotherapy of Borderline Patients*, and guest editor of the volume *Narcissistic Personality Disorder* in the *Psychiatric Clinics of North America* Series.

Contents

Acknowledgments

The late Dr. Herman van der Waals, who was director of the Topeka Institute for Psychoanalysis and the C. F. Menninger Memorial Hospital and to whom this book is dedicated, first opened to me the perspectives of a structural model of the mind which centered on the internalization of object relations. I owe to Dr. John Sutherland, former editor of the *International Journal of Psycho-Analysis* and senior consultant to the Menninger Foundation, the orientation toward recent thinking within psychoanalytic object-relations theory and the awareness of the importance of the psychoanalytic understanding of affects for further metapsychological analyses.

My colleagues and friends at the Menninger Foundation, particularly those involved with me in the work of the Topeka Institute for Psychoanalysis and the Psychotherapy Research Project of the Menninger Foundation, provided a continuing source of encouragement, a critical yet supportive review of my concepts as they were developing, and the stimulation to apply my theoretical formulations to new areas. I am particularly indebted to Drs. Robert Wallerstein, Gertrude Ticho, Ann Appelbaum, Stephen Appelbaum, Leonard Horwitz, Ramon Ganzarain and Peter Hartocollis. I am very grateful to Dr. Ernst Ticho for his stimulating exploration of my theoretical formulations from the viewpoint of contemporary ego psychology. His penetrating clarification of many issues has been invaluable to me.

Dr. Edith Jacobson's contributions have crucially influenced my theoretical as well as my clinical thinking, and in many ways my theoretical model is based on the developmental model formulated in her book *The Self and the Object World*. I am also greatly indebted to

Drs. Margaret Mahler, Harold Blum, John Frosch, Nathaniel Ross, Martin Wangh, and Donald Kaplan for their encouragement and help at various stages of this work.

I thank Mrs. Virginia Eicholtz, managing editor of the *Bulletin of the Menninger Clinic* for her skill and dedication in editing the papers included in this volume.

Finally, I wish to express my deep gratitude to Mrs. Mary Patton, chief secretary of the Menninger Foundation Psychotherapy Research Project and later my secretary when I was director of the C. F. Menninger Memorial Hospital, and to Mrs. Jean Thomas, senior secretary of the General Clinical Service of the New York State Psychiatric Institute, for their extremely precise and efficient work with the many versions of the chapters included in this book.

Preface

In the course of attempting to develop a systematic analysis of the borderline conditions, their psychopathology, diagnosis, prognosis, and treatment, I was faced with many unresolved and controversial issues in psychoanalytic metapsychology. Because I felt that a clear metapsychological frame of reference was important in developing an integrative conception of borderline conditions, I first tried to arrive at operational definitions of some psychoanalytic terms in order to conceptualize my material. Chapter 1 is the product of this early effort. In the process, however, I was tempted to examine more systematically some current concepts within psychoanalytic metapsychology, particularly those regarding early development, in the light of my clinical findings with patients presenting borderline personality organization. This resulted in a theoretical framework which seems suited to the clinical data and constitutes a special formulation of psychoanalytic object-relations theory in terms of ego psychology. Chapters 2, 3, and 4 outline this new theoretical frame.

I was then able to apply this theory to a general classification of character pathology and to place the borderline conditions in that classification: Chapter 5 contains that effort. Chapter 6 summarizes and updates my treatment approach to borderline personality organization. Chapters 7 and 8 describe a special study, the application of psychoanalytic object-relations theory to normal and pathological love relations. Finally, in Chapter 9, I attempt to apply this general theory to the study of group processes and administrative theory, particularly as they apply to treatment in psychiatric hospitals.

PART I

THEORY

one

Structural Derivatives of Object Relations

This chapter begins with the observation of some peculiar defensive operations in patients suffering from severe character disorders and so-called "borderline" conditions (Knight, 1954). There is a kind of "selective" impulsivity shown by many borderline patients, especially those suffering from "acting out" character disorders with some borderline features. I am referring here to the observation that the apparent lack of impulse control of these patients is often of a particular, selective kind. Some patients may present very good impulse control in all but one area. In this one area, there may exist, rather than lack of impulse control, activation of contradictory manifestations of the patient of such an impressive nature that one comes to feel that there is a compartmentalization of the entire psychic life of the patient. For example, a patient showed constant switching between severe fears in regard to sexual activity and an impulse-ridden sexual behavior, the alternating conditions being temporarily ego syntonic during their respective appearances. Another patient appeared to be lying "impulsively" at times; at other times he gave the impression of feeling guilty or ashamed of lying. He insisted that lying was no longer a problem for him and angrily accused other people (the therapist) of lying. What was striking was the complete separation of the "impulsive" lying from the times the patient remembered the lying but did not feel emotionally connected with it and, on the contrary, was strongly convinced that lying was not or at least was no longer part of his psychic reality. This patient presented good impulse control in other areas of his life, and it finally appeared that both the lying and the "anti-lying" episodes were psychic manifestations of one global, rigid characterological pattern.

In more general terms, in these patients there was an alternating expression of complementary sides of a conflict, such as the acting out of the impulse at some times and of the specific defensive character formation or counterphobic reactions against that impulse at other times. The patients were conscious of the severe contradiction in their behavior; yet they would alternate between opposite strivings with a bland denial of the implications of this contradiction and showed what appeared to be a striking lack of concern over this "compartmentalization" of their mind.

It has to be pointed out that these observations do not seem to fit with what we conceptualize as the defensive operations of isolation and denial. In isolation, it is the specific affect which is kept separate from the ideational representation of the impulse, and these two do not appear in consciousness together. By contrast, in the kind of patients I mentioned, there is a complete, simultaneous awareness of an impulse and its ideational representation in the ego. What are completely separated from each other are complex psychic manifestations, involving affect, ideational content, subjective and behavioral manifestations. In denial there is a tendency to eliminate from consciousness a sector of the external or subjective reality, a sector which appears in contradiction to what the synthesizing function of the ego dictates as ego syntonic. By contrast, in the observations I mentioned, there exists what we might call mutual denial of independent sectors of the psychic life. Actually, we might say that there exist alternating "ego states," and I use the concept "ego state" as a way of describing these repetitive, temporarily ego syntonic, compartmentalized psychic manifestations.

There is no doubt that this state of affairs represents an ego weakness, but it also shows itself as a most rigid kind of structure. I came to wonder whether the alternating activation of contradictory ego states might not reflect a specific defensive organization, perhaps characteristic of borderline patients. Freud's (1927, 1938) comments on splitting of the ego as a defensive operation, and Fairbairn's (1952) analysis of splitting as a characteristic and crucial defensive operation in schizoid personalities appeared to be of special interest in this connection.

Freud (1938) mentioned in his paper "Splitting of the Ego in the Process of Defence" the case of a child who solved his conflict by alternately enacting opposite reactions, representing on the one hand his awareness and consideration of reality, and on the other his unwillingness to accept reality. Freud commented that this "success" was achieved at the expense of a rupture in the ego that would not cure but would enlarge, and he added that these two opposite reactions to the conflict remained as the nuclei of this split in the ego. In the *Outline of Psycho-Analysis*, Freud (1940) stated that splitting of the ego may represent a general development in the psychoses and other psychopathological conditions, among which he mentioned fetishism. He defined splitting of the ego as the lifelong co-existence of two implicitly conscious contradictory dispositions which did not influence each other.

My next observation was that each of these mutually unacceptable "split" ego states represented a specific transference disposition of the patient of a rather striking kind. It was as if each of these ego states represented a full-fledged transference paradigm, a highly developed regressive transference reaction in which a specific internalized object relationship was activated in the transference.

I gradually assumed that these phenomena appeared with impressive regularity and that one might actually describe the difference between the typically neurotic and the borderline personality organization in something like the following terms: In neurotic patients, the unfolding of internalized object relations in the transference occurs gradually, as regression develops and the secondary autonomy of character structure dissolves in actualized transference paradigms. For example, "depersonified" superego structures (Hartmann and Loewenstein, 1962; Jacobson, 1964) gradually crystallize into specific internalized parental objects. In borderline patients, by contrast, the highest level depersonified superego structures and autonomous ego structures are missing, and early, conflict-laden object relations are activated prematurely in the transference in connection with ego states that are split off from each other. The chaotic transference manifestations that borderline patients typically present might be understood as the oscillatory activation of these ego states, representing "nonmetabolized" internalized object relations.

Before going into the analysis of the mutual relationship between persistence of early, pathological object relations in a nonmetabolized state on the one hand and splitting of the ego on the other, I shall illustrate all these characteristics of borderline patients with an example. The patient was a man in his late thirties who had been referred to me with the diagnosis of a borderline, paranoid character structure and with the recommendation for expressive psychotherapy. In the third interview, the patient started violently accusing me of having seen him on the street and not greeted him. In the first two sessions we had talked about his main fear, namely, that people might think that he was a homosexual and that a woman with whom he had not been able to achieve intercourse might revengefully be spreading that rumor too. The sudden outbreak of his anger toward me in the third session was of a rather high intensity, and the implications of his accusations were that I was depreciating him for what he had told me about himself and that, while I was willing to listen to him as long as I was sitting in my office, in my life outside the treatment situation I would have only contempt and disgust for people like him. This was clear to him from my not greeting him.

It soon became apparent that the intensity of his anger had to do not only with his feeling attacked and depreciated by me but also with his impotent rage at feeling that I was becoming very important to him, that he needed me very much, and that, in spite of this anger, he would not be able to stop his therapy. After constantly expressing his anger at me in verbal attacks over the next few sessions, he suddenly changed his attitude again. I was seeing him three sessions per week, and after approximately a week and a half of the attitude just described, he apologized emphatically for his hostile behavior and expressed intense feelings of gratefulness because I had been patient with him and not thrown him out as he feared I might. He said that what was painful now was that he had such an intense positive feeling for me that it would be impossible really to convey it to me, and that any distance from me would be hard to stand. With tears in his eyes he expressed his profound admiration for me, his gratitude, and the painful longing to see me which would make the time between sessions seem excessively long. A few weeks later he reverted to the attitude and feelings related to his first angry outburst. He again expressed intense hatred toward me, attacked me verbally with a sadistic, derogatory attitude, and appeared at this point to be completely unable to be aware of any good feeling or opinion he formerly professed to hold about me. During the time he expressed the intense feelings of love and longing for me he was completely unable to be aware of any negative feeling, in spite of preserving perfect memory of the days in which his feelings were completely opposite to his present state of mind. The same was true in regard to his good feelings on the days when he was only able to express bad feelings about me.

This patient remembered having bad periods in which absolutely opposite feelings to the present ones occupied his mind, but this memory had no emotional reality at all for him. It was as if there were two selves, equally strong, completely separated from each other in their emotions although not in the patient's memory and alternating in his conscious experience. It was this successive activation of contradictory ego states which I would refer to as an example of splitting of the ego. It is important to point out that this patient showed nothing of this kind of lack of impulse control in his daily work and activities, where he was emotionally controlled and his behavior was quite stable and socially appropriate. In other words, he did not present simply lack of impulse control as an expression of ego weakness, but specific, well-structured alternation between opposite, completely irreconcilable affect states.

One other striking feature of this patient was that any effort on my part to question his idealization of me during the time he had only good feelings and to remind him at that point of how critical and angry he had felt with me at other times would bring about intense anxiety. The same was true for any effort on my part to bring to his awareness, at times at which there were only bad feelings for me, the unrealistic nature of his verbal attacks, by reminding him of how he had in the past also seen some good qualities in me. I inferred that what we have called splitting of the ego in this case served an essential function of protecting the patient against anxiety, and I could repeat this observation in most cases in which splitting seemed prominent. *Splitting, then, appeared to be not only a defect in the ego but also an active, very powerful defensive operation.*

I would like to examine now the transference implications of the contradictory ego states of this patient. The premature intensity of the transference feelings, their explosive, rapidly shifting nature, the lack of impulse control in regard to these affects in the transference, the weakening of his reality testing in connection with these feelings are all typical borderline characteristics. Characteristics such as these tend to give the therapeutic situation a chaotic nature, but even under these circumstances, as one's knowledge of the patient increases, specific transference patterns can be detected. In the case of this patient, I came gradually to understand that the depreciative, harsh, and haughty image of me that he had in times of intense anger corresponded to one image of his mother, while the image of the all-forgiving, all-loving and understanding therapist that he had during the times of positive feelings toward me reflected that of a fused ideal mother and weak but protective father image. In intimate relationship with these two images were self-images of, respectively, the rejected, depreciated, attacked little boy (this is how he felt in his relationship with his harsh and rejecting mother) and the longing, guilt-ridden child (which represented his feeling about both parents together, seen as the kind, weak, forgiving keepers of the home that he had lost). All of these self- and object-images had to do with rather early, severe pathology in his object relations. The affect states of impotent rage and guilt in the transference related to these two constellations of early conflicts. The fact that rage and guilt could never merge or modify each other and that, as long as these affects could be completely separated from each other, anxiety was not prominent was an important overall characteristic of this patient.

In more general terms, I inferred that the defensive function of splitting of the ego consisted precisely in keeping contradictory primitive affect states apart—but *not* the affect states alone: these contradictory affects were inseparably linked with corresponding internalized, pathological object relations. I concluded that whatever the origin of this predisposition for splits in the ego, they constituted a defensive mechanism attempting to deal with early pathological object relations. I also felt that the persistence of these internalized object relations in a rather "nonmetabolized" condition within the psychic apparatus might be a consequence of the splitting operations.

Fairbairn's (1952) analysis of splitting appeared to be of special interest at this point because he had observed these phenomena in patients displaying schizoid tendencies which usually fall into the "borderline" field. He stated:

> In a word "impulses" cannot be considered apart from the endopsychic structures which they energize and the object-relationships which they enable these structures to establish; and, equally, "instincts" cannot profitably be considered as anything more than forms of energy which constitute the dynamic of such endopsychic structures.

Sutherland (1963), in summarizing Fairbairn's formulations, states that "such a split involves a division of the pristine ego into structures each of which contains (a) a part of the ego, (b) the object that characterizes the related relationships, and (c) the affects of the latter."

While in what follows some important differences between Fairbairn's formulations and my own will become clear, his observations provide a fertile background for the structural model of internalization of object relations that I will suggest.

I next asked myself about the origin of splitting, the predisposition of the ego toward this defensive operation, the relationship between splitting on the one hand and other defensive operations—especially repression—on the other, and, finally, the relationship between the split-off ego states and the more general mechanisms of introjection and identification. I actually assumed that these "nonmetabolized" ego states, with a self-image component, an object-image component, and both of these components linked with an early affect, were the pathologically fixed remnants of the normal processes of early introjection.

What follows is a tentative model linking the mechanisms of internalization of object relations, on the one hand, with the vicissitudes of instinctual drive derivatives and of ego formation, on the other. In summary, I formulate the following main propositions:

1. Introjections, identifications, and ego identity are three levels of the process of internalization of object relations in the psychic apparatus; all three will be referred to comprehensively as *identification systems*. All these processes of internalization bring about psychic precipitates or structures for which we will use exactly the same term as for the respective mechanism. Introjection, for example, will be considered to be both a process of the psychic apparatus and, as a result of that process, a structure.

2. All these processes of internalization consist of three basic components: (a) object-images or object-representations, (b) self-images or self-representations, and (c) drive derivatives or dispositions to specific affective states.

3. Organization of identification systems takes place first at a basic level of ego functioning in which splitting is the crucial mechanism for the defensive organization of the ego. Later a second, advanced level of defensive organization of the ego is reached at which repression replaces splitting as the central mechanism.

4. The degree of ego, as well as superego, integration and development depends on the degree to which repression and its allied mechanisms have replaced splitting and its allied mechanisms.

REVIEW OF PERTINENT LITERATURE

I have already referred to Freud's introduction of the concept of splitting and his contributions in this regard. Fairbairn's work has also been mentioned. Melanie Klein (1946), who has further developed the concept of splitting, relates it specifically to the "paranoid-schizoid position," that is, the earliest level of ego development within her frame of reference, preceding the higher level of ego integration characteristic of the "depressive position." She has stressed the intimate relationship between aggression and splitting and the central importance of excessive splitting in severe psychopathology. Segal (1964), on the other hand, has stressed the normal functions of splitting as an early mechanism of the ego and contrasts it with pathological development characterized by excessive splitting.

Klein's failure to consider structural factors in her theories and her lack of precision in the use of her own terminology, specifically in regard to splitting which she appears to use for all kinds of dissociated or repressed material creates very serious difficulties for her formulations. I believe that, if it is to be used at all, the term "splitting" should be used in a clearly defined, restricted sense.

Fairbairn's (1952) efforts to connect Klein's mechanisms with a consistent structural model interested me very much, as did his related analysis of the vicissitudes of early object relations; I have already mentioned Sutherland's (1963) analysis and would now add Guntrip's (1961) as two elaborations on Fairbairn's theories which directly stimulated my thinking. Nevertheless, the lack of emphasis on drives, and especially what appeared to me to be an underestimation of the importance of aggression in Fairbairn's formulations, did not seem to correspond to the clinical observation of severely regressed patients. Also, Fairbairn's implication that only "bad" object relationships are introjected seems questionable. Fairbairn's suggestion to replace impulse-psychology by a new psychology of dynamic structures (of the ego) is interesting, but I do not feel that the conceptualization of the ego as composed of such dynamic structures invalidates Freud's instinctual theories of libido and aggression.

Hartmann's (1939, 1950) analysis of the primary autonomous structures of the ego and their relationship with conflict-determined structures and ego autonomy in general was an indispensable instrument for studying the origin and development of defensive structures. His concept of the "self" as the organization of self-representations, giving rise to a fundamental structure within the ego, clarified a central problem: the relationship between self and ego.

Jacobson's (1964) and Erikson's (1950, 1956) contributions to the study of early object relations and their influences on the organization, integration, and development of ego structures were extremely helpful bridges between metapsychological and especially structural analysis of the psychic apparatus, on the one hand, and the clinical study of the vicissitudes of object relations, on the other. Jacobson has pointed out the importance of differentiating the self and object representations of early introjections and has crucially clarified the development of these structures. The definition of introjection suggested in this chapter differs from Jacobson's, but the analysis of introjective and projective processes, described in what follows, derives in many respects from her observations. The way in which introjection, identification, and ego identity are conceptually linked here stays quite close to Erikson's conceptualization. Nevertheless, Erikson does not differentiate between the organization of self-representations and object-representations and, as Jacobson (1964) has pointed out, tends to move in the direction of a sociological conceptualization of ego identity, a direction in which she and I do not follow him.

The concept of introjection as used here implies that it is a crucial mechanism of early development of the ego and is in this regard somewhat related to Klein's (1946) formulation. Klein, however, throughout her writings shifts the meaning of that term, ending with a broad, puzzlingly comprehensive concept. Also, as Heimann (1966) points out, Klein sees introjection as a consequence of the mode of oral incorporation, or an id-derived oral metabolic principle, a conceptualization with which Heimann and I disagree. I will consider introjections as independent psychic structures, mainly growing out of primary autonomous functions (perception and memory) as they are linked with early object relations; and, although introjections will be seen as strongly influenced by oral conflicts, they will not be seen as growing out of them.

Menninger's and his colleagues' (1963) conception of mental illness as a unitary process and of the different forms of psychopathology as related to specific orders or levels of defensive organization stimulated the present effort to clarify two levels of defensive organization of the ego. His and Mayman's (1956) description of periodic ego rupture as a specific order of dyscontrol used for defensive purposes and defining one level of mental illness is relevant to the present analysis: there are clinical forms of the mechanism of splitting which may appear as episodic dyscontrol. Menninger *et al.* (1963) describe the occurrence of chronic, repetitive aggressive behavior and of episodic, impulsive violence, and state: "The functional episodic dyscontrol, acute or chronic, is presumed to be the adverting of greater failure, a more catastrophic disintegration." They stress the dynamic importance of severe aggression and paranoid mechanisms and denial as underlying this condition.

Glover's (1956) hypothesis of a multinuclear primitive ego structure, the partial autonomy of ego nuclei in the earliest phases, and the decisive influence of the original state of nucleation of the ego on its later strength or weakness is another important source, as is Spitz's (1965) analysis of development during the first year of life.

INTROJECTION, IDENTIFICATION, EGO IDENTITY

When giving the example of the borderline patient who shifted between contradictory ego states, I stressed that these ego states represented an affect linked with a certain object-image or object representation of the patient while in that affective state. I have said that this represented a "nonmetabolized," internalized object relation, which in the neurotic patient would develop only over a period of time out of the depersonified ego and superego structures, but in the borderline patient was available in a relatively free state very early in the treatment. This also implies that in all these patients (neurotics, character disorders, and borderline personality organization) eventually the same kind of "units" can be found; namely, internalized early object relations represented by a certain affect, object-representation, and self-representation. I would now add that, even in rather regressed patients whose rapidly shifting transference dispositions tend to give the therapeutic situation a chaotic nature, these "units" of affective state, object-representation, and self-representation can be seen in the transference. It was this kind of observation which led me to conceptualize all processes of internalization of object relations as referring to such units or constellations of them. The earliest fully developed introjections probably represent these units in the purest form and thus imply a relatively simple affect, object-image, and self-image linked together.

Introjection is the earliest, most primitive, and basic level in the organization of internalization processes. It is the reproduction and fixation of an interaction with the environment by means of an organized cluster of memory traces implying at least three components: (i) the image of an object, (ii) the image of the self in interaction with that object, and (iii) the affective coloring of both the object-image and the self-image under the influence of the drive representative present at the time of the interaction. This process is a mechanism of growth of the psychic apparatus, and it is also used for defensive purposes by the ego. Introjection, then, depends on perception and memory (that is, on apparatuses of primary autonomy), but it transcends these not only by a complex and specific organization of perceptions and memory traces but also by linking "external" perception with the perception of primitive affect states representing drive derivatives.

In the earliest introjections, object and self-image are not yet differentiated from each other (Jacobson, 1964), and the definition of introjection suggested really corresponds to a somewhat later stage in which successive differentiations, refusions, and redifferentiations of the self- and object-images have finally crystallized into clearly delimited components. The "reciprocal smiling response" at around three months of age that Spitz (1965) has described and considered an indicator of the first organizer of the psyche, probably corresponds to this crystallization.

The affective coloring of the introjection is an essential aspect of it and represents the *active valence* of the introjection, which determines the fusion and organization of introjections of similar valences. Thus, introjections taking place under the *positive valence* of libidinal instinctual gratification, as in loving mother-child contact, tend to fuse and become organized in what has been called somewhat loosely but suggestively "the good internal object." Introjections taking place under the *negative valence* of aggressive drive derivatives tend to fuse with similar negative valence introjections and become organized in the "bad internal objects."[1]

In the process of the fusion of introjections of the same valence, homologous components of introjection tend to fuse, self-image with other self-images and object-image with other object-images. Since by this fusion more elaborate self-images and object-images are being "mapped out," this process contributes to the differentiation of self and object and to the delimitation of ego boundaries.[2] This, in turn, further organizes and integrates the apparatuses of perception and memory; thus, later introjections contain an ever growing complexity of information about both the object and the self in any particular interaction.

Identification is a higher-level form of introjection which can only take place when the perceptive and cognitive abilities of the child have increased to the point that it can recognize the role aspects of interpersonal interaction. Role implies the presence of a socially recognized function that is being carried out by the object or by both participants in the interaction. For example, when mother does something with the child (such as helping it to get dressed), she is not

1. The term "aggression" throughout this chapter is restricted to the direct instinctual drive derivatives, as typically related to early, primitive rage reactions; it refers to aggression as opposed to libido; it does not refer to the broader conceptualization of aggression which includes exuberant motor discharges or even all active, explorative behavior of the child.

2. The terms "self-image" and "self-component" refer to what is generally called "self-representations," and these three terms are used interchangeably here.

only interacting with it but also actualizing in a certain way the socially accepted role of mother (giving clothes, protecting, teaching). Also, the affective component of identification is of a more elaborate and modified character than that characteristic of introjection because of the moderating effects of various developing ego apparatuses and the decrease in splitting mechanisms, to which we will return.

The psychic derivatives of drives, as they enter into object relations, are integrated into identifications as well as into introjections, and, in more general terms, it is suggested that the original penetration of the psychic apparatus with drive derivatives is achieved through these internalization processes. The cluster of memory traces implicit in identification comprises then: (i) the image of an object adopting a role in an interaction with the self, (ii) the image of the self more clearly differentiated from the object than in the case of introjection (and possibly playing a complementary role), and (iii) an affective coloring of the interaction of a more differentiated, less intense quality than in the case of introjection. Identification is also considered to be a mechanism of growth of the psychic apparatus which may be used for defensive purposes, and identifications fuse in a way similar to introjections. Actually, introjections form the core of similar, related identifications.

Since identifications imply the internalization of roles as defined above, behavioral manifestations of the individual, which express one or both of the reciprocal roles of the respective interaction, become a predominant result of identification; the behavioral manifestations of introjections are less apparent in interpersonal interactions. The child learns his own, at first more passively experienced roles as part of his self-image component of the identification. He also learns mother's roles (as part of mother's object-image) and may at some time re-enact those roles. Long-term storage and organization are typical of role actualization in ego identity. Identifications ordinarily first appear during the last few months of the first year but become fully developed only during the second year of life. Behavior manifestations of the child which are imitative of mother's behavior are indicators of the matrix of identifications.

Ego identity represents the highest level in the organization of internalization processes, and Erikson's (1956) conceptualization is followed here closely. Ego identity refers to the overall organization of identifications and introjections under the guiding principle of the synthetic function of the ego. This organization implies:

1. a consolidation of ego structures connected with a sense of continuity of the self (the self being the organization of the self-image components of introjections and identifications) to which the child's perception of its functioning in all areas of its life and its progressive sense of mastering the basic adaptational tasks contribute significantly (Murphy, 1964);

2. a consistent, overall conception of the "world of objects" derived from the organization of the object-image components of introjections and identifications and a sense of consistency in one's own interpersonal interactions, the behavioral aspects—that is, general consistency in the behavior patterns—being even more important aspects of ego identity than those of identifications; and

3. a recognition of this consistency in interactions as characteristic of the individual by his interpersonal environment and, in turn, the perception by the individual of this recognition by the environment ("confirmation").

There is one important difference between ego identity and the subordinate processes of introjection and identification. Introjections and identifications are structures of the psychic apparatus in general, and I shall mention direct introjection into the superego later on, and also refer to introjection when talking about the organization of the id. Ego identity, by contrast, is a structure characteristic of the ego, a fundamental outcome of the synthetic function of the ego. Ego identity also represents that specialized part of the ego which has awareness of and control over those drive derivatives which determine by their organization the modified matrix of affect dispositions available to the ego (I shall refer later on to one aspect of how affect modification is achieved). Different childhood periods determine different integrations of ego identity, and the general integration of ego identity stemming from all these partial ego identities normally operates as an attempt to synthesize them into an overall harmonious structure (Erikson, 1950).

I have implied that ego identity is the highest level organization of the world of object relations in the broadest sense, and also of the self. This is a very complex development because, while object relations are continuously internalized (such internalizations take place at gradually higher, more differentiating levels), at the same time the internalized object relations are also "depersonified" (Jacobson, 1964) and integrated into higher level ego and superego structures, such as the ego ideal, character constellations, and autonomous ego functions. Simultaneously with these processes of internalization and depersonification, internalized object relations are organized into persistent object-images, which come to represent internally the external world as experienced by the developing ego. This corresponds roughly to what Sandler and Rosenblatt (1962) have called the "representational world." It has to be stressed, however, that this internal world of object representations as seen in conscious, preconscious, and unconscious fantasies never reproduces the *actual* world of real people with whom the individual has established relationships in the past and in the present; it is at most an approximation, always strongly influenced by the very early object-images of introjections and identifications. It should also be stressed that the "world of inner objects," which, as used by Klein, gives the impression of remaining free-floating object-images in the psychic apparatus rather than being related to any specific structures, does not do justice to the complexity of integration of object relations. Organization of object-images takes place both in the sector of depersonified ego structures and in the sector of developing ego identity. Those object-images which remain relatively unmodified in the repressed unconscious are less affected by structuralization; in this sense, very primitive, distorted object-images certainly continue to exist in the unconscious mind. Nevertheless, by far the greater part of internalized object-images is normally integrated into higher level structures, and those which remain as object-representations experience important modifications over the years under the influence of ego growth and later object relations. The normal outcome of identity formations is that primitive identifications are gradually replaced by selective, partial, sublimatory identifications in which only those aspects of object relations are internalized which are in harmony with the individual identity formation. Actually, the enrichment of one's personal life by the internal presence of such selective, partial identifications representing people who are loved and admired in a realistic way without indiscriminate internalization constitutes a major source of emotional depth and well-being. The normal process of individualization is marked by the shift from identifications to partial, sublimated identifications under the influence of a well-integrated ego identity. One might say that *depersonification* of internalized object relations, *reshaping* of part of them so that they come to resemble more the real objects, and *individualization* are closely related processes (Ticho, 1965).

The world of object representations, then, gradually changes and comes closer to the "external" perceptions of the reality of significant objects throughout childhood and later life without ever becoming an actual copy of the environmental world. Intrapsychic "confirmation" is the ongoing process of reshaping the world of object representations under the influence of the reality principle, of ego maturation and development, and through cycles of projection and introjection. *The persistence of "nonmetabolized" early introjections is the outcome of a pathological fixation of severely disturbed, early object relations,* a fixation which is intimately related to the pathological development of splitting. Splitting, in turn, interferes with the integration of self- and object-images and the depersonification of internalized object relations in general. Under these pathological circumstances, early nonintegrated object-images come to the surface; but even then, as is being stressed throughout this chapter, we never do have "free-floating" internal objects but always confront specific ego structures into which they have crystallized.

Keeping in mind our reservations about the concept of the "representational world" as a close reproduction of the external world of objects, we might say that ego identity is the highest level organization of the world of object relations in the broadest sense, and comprises the concept of the representational world, on the one hand, and that of the self, on the other.

EARLY STAGES OF EGO DEVELOPMENT

Let us start by focusing on the affect components of introjections. Several authors (e.g. Brierley, 1937; Rapaport, 1954, 1960) have stressed the many difficulties in clarifying this issue. For our purpose, what is important is the intense, overwhelming nature of early affect and its *irradiating* effect on all other perceptual elements of the introjection. Intense "negative" affect states related to aggressive drive derivatives create perceptual constellations entirely different from those generated by intense "positive" affect states under the influence of libidinal strivings in external circumstances that are not too different. This overwhelming nature of early affective states is the cause of the *valence* of the introjection and of the kind of fusion and organization which will take place involving it. Introjections with positive valence and those with negative valence are thus kept completely apart. They are kept apart at first simply because they happen separately and because of the ego's incapacity to integrate introjections not activated by similar valences, but then *gradually, in response to anxiety, because of the ego's active use of this separation for defensive purposes.* This is actually the origin of splitting as a mechanism of defense.

Introjections, the earliest form of identification systems, may be considered as precipitants around which ego nuclei consolidate. It is suggested that the fusions of similar positive introjections constitute such ego nuclei and that they have an essential function in directing the organization of perception, memory, and, indirectly, other autonomous ego functions, such as those outlined by Murphy (1963): the general level of psychomotor activity; control over delay; orientation and planning of activities; flexibility in shifting attention; differentiation of all kinds of stimuli; and integration of experience and actions (skill).

At what point does the ego come into existence? Certain ego structures, and functions connected with them, exist from the beginning of life: perception, the capacity to establish memory traces, and the other functions just mentioned. These are essentially functions of the primary autonomous apparatuses (Hartmann, 1939). On the other hand, the capacity to establish introjections represents a higher level of inborn capacity, intimately linked with the "perceptualization" of drive derivatives.

It is suggested that the ego as a differentiated psychic structure, in the sense of Freud's (1923) description, comes about at the point when introjections are used for defensive purposes, specifically in an early defensive organization against overwhelming anxiety. We could describe a stage, brief as it may be, of "forerunners of the ego" during which a certain development and organization of introjections have to take place in order for these defensive operations to function. As stated above, introjections with positive valence under the influence of libidinal strivings are built up separately from introjections with negative valence under the influence of aggressive strivings. What originally was a lack of integrative capacity is gradually, in the presence of overwhelming anxiety, used defensively by the emerging ego and maintains introjections with different valences dissociated or split from each other. This serves the purpose of preventing the anxiety arising at the foci of negative introjections from being generalized throughout the ego and protects the integration of positive introjections into a primitive ego core.

The first ego state is probably one in which the "good internal objects" (the early positive introjections with mostly undifferentiated and fused self- and object-images) and the "good external objects" (such reality aspects of external objects which are really "part-objects") constitute the earliest defensive organization of the ego (the "purified pleasure ego"), while all negative introjections are "ejected" (Jacobson, 1964) and considered "not me." One might also say that by the act of this ejection "me" is established (Sandler, personal communication).

Later, under the influence of maturing perception, motor control, and memory organization, when external objects come to be differentiated more from the internal psychic world, a typical tripartite situation exists: (i) the ego is organized around the positive introjections ("good internal object"); (ii) a positive, libido-invested aspect of reality is acknowledged as "external reality" in intimate relation with the ego, and self- and object-images are being differentiated in this interaction; (iii) an entity of "bad external objects," representing both realistically frustrating or threatening external objects and the projected, negative, early introjections completes the picture.

This active separation by the ego of positive and negative introjections, which implies a complete division of the ego and, as a consequence, of external reality as well, is, in essence, the defensive mechanism of *splitting*. In the earliest stage of the ego when active splitting operations start, the ego only presents fused positive introjections, within which object- and self-images are also fused, and early "positive part-objects." There is as yet no ego boundary between the positive external part-objects and their mental representations. Negative introjections (within which self- and object-images, internal and external objects are also fused) are ejected, and active splitting keeps the purified pleasure ego dissociated from the "not me." At the later stage which we have mentioned, reality is more acknowledged by the ego, both in the awareness of the difference between good external "part-objects" and good object representations, and in the growing separation within the ego of object- and self-images. This stage also implies the beginning delimitations of ego boundaries in the area of positive object relations, the beginning of reality testing. Splitting is now maximally present and permits the complete projection of negative introjections ("bad internal objects") onto the outside. Introjection is now also used as a defensive mechanism in that an intensification of positive interactions, the development of dependent strivings, takes place not only in relation to libidinal drive derivatives but also as a protection against anxiety and helplessness, especially when these are increased by the fear of projected, bad external objects. Spitz's (1965) description of the "eighth-month anxiety" that appears when the child is approached by a stranger explains this reaction as a consequence of the infant's now being able to differentiate his mother from other people and the infant's interpreting the situation as an indication that mother has left him. It may well be that this specific anxiety is also related to the mechanism of splitting, to the defensive use of mother's "good" image as a protection against fear of (projected) bad external objects, the "stranger."

Splitting as an active defensive process can come into existence only after introjections have fully developed. Splitting processes probably begin around the third and fourth month of life, reach a maximum between the sixth and twelfth months, and gradually disappear in the second and early part of the third year.

In summary, the maturation and development of primary ego apparatuses give rise, at one point, to introjections, which in turn become an essential organizer of what is going to be the ego as an integrated structure. After some development of introjections as psychic structures, a point is reached when introjections are actively kept apart or split for defensive purpose. Now the ego as a centralizing, synthetic function (in the sense of overall organizational purpose) and as a definite organizational structure comes into existence. Thus, introjections, the earliest point of convergence of object relations and instinctual drive representatives, may be visualized as an essential "switch" bringing the ego into operational readiness. Later development of all ego structures and functions then contributes to the development of the specific ego structures which we have called identification systems. These ultimately determine ego identity, the highest level of the ego's synthetic functions.

The mechanism of splitting may be considered an outgrowth of what was primarily a "physiological" lack of integrative capacity in the psychic apparatus. It becomes an essential defensive operation of the early ego, and splitting in this regard is splitting of the global, poorly differentiated ego. Later on, however, splitting becomes a mechanism especially involved in the organization and in the pathology of identification systems, the object relations-determined structures of the ego (that is, the self, the representational world, and ego identity in general). In these later stages of development, the integrity of the ego is less interfered with by splitting mechanisms; secondary autonomy is partially maintained even with severe regression and with splitting of the self and the representational world. By contrast, excessive, pathological early splitting threatens the integrity of the ego at that point and also the future developmental capacity of the ego as a whole. It has to be stressed that in the active keeping apart of introjections of opposite valence, what is split is not only affect states of the ego but also object-images and self-images. Excessive, pathological splitting, therefore, interferes not only with the integration of affects but also with integration of the self and with the development of the representational world. Because of the fundamental importance of early introjections in the organization and integration of the ego as a whole, pathological splitting carries over into splitting of the ego as an organization.

The present model of early ego development is based on Hartmann's (1939, 1950) assumption of an undifferentiated phase of development, a matrix common to the ego and the id. It specifies a certain stage in which the ego may be considered, for the first time, an integrated structure, although, of course, oscillations back and forth from that point have to be assumed. Object relations are seen as an essential ego organizer long before self and objects are differentiated. A word may be in order here contrasting this model with the object-relations orientations of Fairbairn (1952) and Melanie Klein (Heimann, 1943-44; Klein, 1952). Our model implies a disagreement with their assumption that an ego exists from birth. As mentioned before, introjection is not seen as derived from oral incorporative fantasies but from primary autonomous apparatuses of perception and memory. Here Fairbairn's criticism of Klein is relevant:

> Melanie Klein has never satisfactorily explained how fantasies of incorporating objects orally can give rise to the establishment of internal objects as endopsychic structures—and, unless they are such structures, they cannot be properly spoken of as internal objects at all, since otherwise they will remain mere figments of fantasy.

I also agree with Jacobson's (1964) criticism of Klein's lack of differentiation of self-images from object-images in her concept of "inner objects." The assumption that inner reality can be differentiated from outer reality from the beginning of life is clearly rejected by our model. With all these reservations, I would agree with Klein's (1952) formulation that the drive toward integration and synthesis, the establishment of defenses against anxiety, the development of processes of introjection and projection, the development of object relations and the mechanism of splitting are all essential conditions for the ego to come into full operation.

LATER STAGES OF STRUCTURAL DEVELOPMENT

The next stage in normal development is a crucial one for this discussion. The maturation of autonomous ego apparatuses, the delimitation of ego boundaries, and the gradual development of higher forms of introjection (identification) in the area of positive object relations make splitting more difficult because the reality of "negative" interactions and their "contamination" of purely positive introjections can no longer be eliminated and kept from the synthetic processes of the ego. Sometimes, given certain types of pathology in the parental figures, the environment may reinforce splitting mechanisms (Murphy, personal communication). But normally, at a certain point, the stage is reached in which the synthetic processes bring positive and negative introjections and identifications together, and a radically new situation develops.

At this point, the positive self-images of positive introjections are connected with the negative self-images of negative introjections and the positive object-images are connected with the respective negative object-images. At the same time, the negative, aggressively determined affects and the positive, libidinally determined affects are also brought together, and a typical situation arises which probably corresponds to what Klein (1939, 1940) has described as the "depressive position." Tension between contradictory self-images develops, with the appearance of guilt and concern (Winnicott, 1955) because of the acknowledged aggression of the self toward the object which before appeared to be bad but is now seen as part of a "total object" which is both good and bad. Guilt, concern, and mourning over the good object, which is felt partly lost by this synthesized integration and partly endangered, are new affective dispositions which strongly develop in the ego at this stage (Winnicott, 1955).[3]

The fusion of positive and negative introjections implies a fusion and concomitant modification of their affect components. The irradiating effect of purely positive and purely negative affective states diminishes, and the mutual compenetration of libidinal and aggressive drive derivatives fosters a broader spectrum of affect dispositions of the ego. This development, essential for normal psychic growth, also triggers off an additional development of the intrapsychic life: the image of an *ideal self* representing the striving for reparation of guilt and for the reestablishment of an ideal, positive relationship between self and object. The image of an *ideal object* which represents the unharmed, all-loving, all-forgiving object completes the picture (Jacobson, 1964; Sandler *et al.*, 1963).

Anxiety constitutes a basic motive for defensive operations of the ego at all levels of development. Guilt feelings, an ego state arising under the influence of the fusion of identification systems of opposite valences and the real self/ideal self tensions which originate in this process, later become the typical motive of defense prompted by superego demands. In other words, the superego uses the capacity of the ego for experiencing guilt for its own purposes.

3. There may, of course, be important physiological and psychological "forerunners" of these affects (as in the case of anxiety), but this is not essential for our discussion here.

The success of repeated fusions of positive with negative introjections in numerous introjections and identifications depends on the different areas in which they occur. There exists a tendency to fusion and defusion of positive and negative introjections, in the course of which regression to earlier states with strong splitting or progression to higher synthesized ones reflect reality testing and the work of the synthetic function of the ego (Nunberg, 1955) at the level of the self and object representations. While, when it succeeds, fusion takes place at the levels of early introjections as well as later ones, it is probable that it reaches its definite crystallization into a new "four unit system" composed of object, self, ideal object and ideal self only with later identification systems.

From here on, synthetic processes show an accelerated development. Integrative processes combining all kinds of introjections and identifications into the ego identity take place, and this expands and solidifies all structures of the ego. Ego boundaries are further delimited, and the ego extends its centralized control over perception and motility. "Pockets" of intolerable, severely negative introjections are dissociated from the ego core and lose their previous free access to perception and motility: from now on, negative introjections may be directly repressed.

It is suggested that this consolidation of the ego establishes repression as the central defensive operation, in contrast to the splitting of the earlier ego. In fact, this developmental step brings about a fundamental difference between early and later ego development, and I will come back to a discussion of splitting and repression as two basic mechanisms of ego defense at different levels of development and the energic conditions related to this change.

The continuing processes of introjection and projection now also permit the internalization of previously feared, dangerous, frustrating objects (especially prohibitive parental images), and fusion takes place between these introjected prohibitive parental images and the guilt-determined ideal objects which were mentioned above. The product of this fusion is partly integrated into the ego and partly repressed, and these nuclei of fused ideal object/prohibitive parental images constitute forerunners of the superego. Fusions between the ideal self and the ideal objects come to constitute the ego ideal (Jacobson, 1964), again part of which is integrated into the ego and part of which is repressed and synthesized like other forerunners of the superego and later contributes with them to the definite formation of the superego.

At this point, a change occurs in the patterns of growth of the ego through the development and integration of identification systems. Henceforth, drive derivatives entering the psychic apparatus are partially repressed before they penetrate the ego core, and become directly part of the rejected identification systems which constitute the dynamic unconscious in its definite form. On the other hand, intense guilt feelings, derived from the tensions between self and ideal self and from the "prohibitive parent/ideal object" pressures on the ego, may be projected onto the outside and reintrojected directly into the superego. Guilt is projected in the form of accusations or threats attributed to parental figures, and this projection determines the reinforcement of introjection of prohibitive parental images into the superego.

The next step is the fusion of the superego nuclei and the development of an organized superego, which gradually becomes abstracted and "depersonified." We refer here to the comprehensive analysis of Jacobson (1964), who has described how the superego is integrated and systematized, incorporating early forerunners derived from archaic, projected, and reintrojected object-images; the major aspects of the ego ideal; and the later internalization of more realistic parental prohibitions and demands. Hartmann and Loewenstein's (1962) and Sandler's (1960) analyses are also relevant here.

A tentative consideration of the time frame of this model may be of interest at this point. All these processes take place over the first two or three years of life, and certainly do not crystallize in the first six months as Melanie Klein thought. I have suggested that splitting as an active mechanism comes into operation around the third month and reaches its maximum several months later, only to disappear gradually in the second and early part of the third year. The later developments of the ego that have been described presuppose an overcoming, to an important degree, of splitting processes and cannot crystallize earlier than the second and third years. Superego formation is a later and more complex structure-building process than early ego formation—although I question whether its essential phases occur as late as in classical theory and suggest that its main components are built up from the second through the fifth years. I have already mentioned the close relationship between higher-level ego structures, such as the ideal self, the ideal object, and the intimately connected ego ideal, on the one hand, and the formation of superego components, on the other. The definite integration of all the superego components probably takes place mainly between the fourth and sixth years, and depersonification and abstraction of the superego become quantitatively significant between the fifth and seventh years. Jacobson (1964) has pointed out that even under ideal circumstances superego integration is not completely accomplished by that time.

One consequence of this model of structural development of the psychic apparatus is the conceptualization of the dynamic unconscious as a system composed of rejected introjection and identification systems. In other words, the repressed portion of the id would possess an internal organization, as well as specific structures composed of self-image, object-image, and unacceptable impulse components. One might consider displacement, condensation, and other primary process operations as the result of "temporary circuits" in the id linking different repressed identification systems to each other under the guiding principle of a common affective valence. At the 1951 symposium on the mutual influences in the development of ego and id, van der Waals (1952) ended his discussion with a related idea: "We would have to conclude that the repressed portion of the id is not pure id, but an ego id, just like the undifferentiated phase in the early part of psychic life."

As mentioned before, I am suggesting that both libido and aggression make their appearance in the psychic apparatus as part of early introjections and thus are intimately connected with object relations in the context of definite early ego structures.

SPLITTING AND REPRESSION AS CENTRAL MECHANISMS

Let us now contrast splitting and repression as defensive operations. Freud (1915) stated that "the essence of repression lies simply in turning something away, and keeping it at a distance, from the conscious."

Anna Freud (1936) states, in a comment on Freud's (1926) reference to repression in *Inhibitions, Symptoms and Anxiety,* that "repression consists in the withholding or expulsion of an idea or affect from the conscious ego. It is meaningless to speak of repression where the ego is still merged with the id."

It is true, of course, that when repression is combined with other mechanisms, as with isolation in the case of obsessive-compulsive symptom formation, the ideational content of what is repressed may become conscious, but the impulse continues to be kept outside consciousness. In fact, generally, in typically neurotic or normal mechanisms such as rationalization, intellectualization, isolation, displacement, and "higher-level" character defenses (especially reaction formations and inhibitory types of character traits), drive derivatives in the form of specific affects and the ideational representation of the respective impulse do not appear in consciousness together. The complete, simultaneous awareness of an impulse and its ideational representation are kept out of the ego (Madison, 1961). By contrast, complete consciousness of the impulse may exist at a "lower level" of characterological defenses, such as those seen in severe "acting out" and impulse-ridden characters and in the defenses characteristic of borderline personality structures, such as early forms of projection and especially projective identification and denial. All of these are closely related to splitting.

Splitting, it has been suggested here, is a mechanism characteristic of the first stages of development of the ego. It grows out of the naturally occurring lack of integration of the first introjections and is used as a defensive mechanism to protect positive introjections, thereby indirectly fostering ego growth. Splitting consists in dissociating or actively maintaining apart identification systems with opposite valences (conflicting identification systems) without regard to access to consciousness or to perceptual or motor control. The drive derivative attains full emotional, ideational, and motor consciousness but is completely separated from other segments of the conscious psychic experience. In other terms, in the process of splitting, the ego protects itself against anxiety connected with early intrapsychic conflicts (represented by conflicts between introjections of opposite valences) by a regressive nucleation. As stated before, splitting is typically a mechanism of the early ego in which identification systems have not crystallized into higher organizations such as the self or the representational world, but it can persist pathologically at higher levels of ego organization. In this case, it characteristically affects the self and ego identity in general. Hopefully, this clarifies the question whether what is split is the ego or the self. The crucial intervention of the mechanism of splitting occurs before the self has differentiated within the ego, so that what is split is the ego. Later, when the self has consolidated as a definite structure (a substructure of ego identity), what is typically split with excessive use of this mechanism (for example, in severe character disorders) is the self and no longer the ego.

Repression, by contrast, is a central defensive mechanism of the ego at a later stage and consists in the rejection of an impulse or its ideational representation, or both, from the conscious ego. Just as splitting, at a more primitive level of development, is reinforced by projection, denial, and other typical primitive defenses, repression, on its higher level of ego development, is reinforced by mechanisms such as isolation, displacement, and other typical neurotic or normal defensive operations. Repression consolidates and protects the core of the ego and contributes crucially to the delimitation of ego boundaries. At the time when splitting properly prevailed, and, under pathological conditions, when it continues to do so over the years, the ego protects itself against anxiety by a defensive nucleation, which necessarily exacts a high price in regard to the ego's synthetic functions and reality testing. After repression has become predominant and in the less severe forms of psychopathology (mainly the neuroses and moderate character disorders), the ego protects itself against the anxiety connected with intolerable conflicts by eliminating these conflicts from consciousness. Repression is thus a much more effective defensive operation, but it requires strong countercathexes because, unlike splitting, it is characterized by the blocking of discharge (Sandler, personal communication). Moreover, in order for it to become established, important energic preconditions have to be met.

As stated before, the normal fusion of positive and negative introjections at the time when repression comes into existence implies a fusion and consequent modification of their affect components. Actually, it is suggested that neutralization (Hartmann, 1955; Menninger, 1938) takes place quite decisively at this point of combination of libidinal and aggressive affects. *The synthesis of identification systems neutralizes aggression and possibly provides the most important single energy source for the higher level of repressive mechanisms to come,* and, implicitly, for the development of secondary autonomy in general. One consequence of pathological circumstances in which splitting is excessive is that this neutralization does not take place, or takes place very insufficiently; and thus an important energy source for ego growth fails. *Splitting, then, is a fundamental cause of ego weakness. Since splitting also requires less countercathexis than repression, a weak ego falls back easily on splitting, and a vicious circle is created by which ego weakness and splitting reinforce each other.*

SOME CLINICAL APPLICATIONS OF THIS MODEL

I mentioned in the introduction to this chapter that in some severe character disorders the alternating expression of complementary sides of a conflict, such as the acting out of the impulse at some times and of the specific defensive character formations against that impulse at other times, is an expression of splitting. This creates special technical problems. As I said there, the patient may be conscious of severe contradiction in his behavior, but he can alternate between opposite strivings with a bland denial of this contradiction and with what is, seen from outside, a striking lack of concern over it. The analyst may try to interpret "directly" the implication of each of the two sides of the conflict as it presents itself, only to realize after some time that what appeared to be a "working through" of conscious, deep conflicts, was really a repetitive, oscillating acting out of that conflict without any intrapsychic change. The conflict is not "unconscious" in the strict sense connected with repression, and, as long as the rigid barrier between contradictory ego states is maintained, the patient is free from anxiety. Only the attempts to bridge these independently expressed, conflicting ego nuclei bring about severe anxiety, mobilize new defensive operations, and may bring about changes in the intrapsychic conflicts. In short, an important consequence of this formulation for psychotherapeutic techniques is the active focus on the mechanism of splitting as a primary defensive operation to be overcome before any further changes can be achieved in such patients.

In some severe character disorders, the mechanism of splitting is reflected in what appears on the surface as simple lack of impulse control rather than in alternating expression of complementary sides of a conflict. Such "lack of impulse control" is often of a highly selective, specific kind and represents the emerging into consciousness of a split identification system. The episodic character of this lack of impulse control, the typical ego syntonicity of the impulses expressed during the time of emotional contact between that part of the patient's personality and the rest of his self-experience, and, finally, the bland denial secondarily defending the contradictions between his usual feelings and behavior and his behavior during the specific episodes all reflect the presence of strong splitting operations.

For example, a patient presented episodic sexual promiscuity, in contrast to her usually rigid, inhibited, puritanical sexual and social life. She showed no lack of impulse control in other areas of her personality. The consistent interpretation of the rigid dissociation between the episodes of sexual promiscuity and her usual self, rather than direct efforts to "strengthen her impulse control" or to interpret "deeper meanings" of her acting out (such as unconscious guilt, which could effectively be brought to the surface only much later on), proved an effective way of overcoming her pseudo lack of impulse control. In general, a consistent interpretation of the patient's efforts to keep two areas of his experience completely separated from each other may bring about, for the first time, more deeply felt anxiety and guilt and may mobilize the conflict specifically in the transference.

A classification of character disorders according to the degree of splitting versus repressive mechanisms present implicitly in the characterological structure might prove clinical meaningful. We might rate character disorders from a lower limit, represented by the chaotic and impulse-ridden characters in whom splitting tends to be predominant to the milder "avoidance trait" characters at the other extreme, with the classical reaction formation types of character structures somewhere in the middle.[4]

4. The model proposed might be of interest also in the study of the hysterical dissociative states, in which some severe form of ego splitting seems to occur. It is interesting to note that in the exploration of some of these cases underlying schizophrenic reactions can be detected (Stross), and these patients probably represent one form of borderline personality organization.

The observations and formulations in this chapter stem to a great extent from the clinical study of the so-called borderline (Knight, 1954) personality disorders. I propose to denominate this broad variety of psychopathology *borderline personality organization* rather than "borderline states" or simply "borderlines," because it appears that these patients represent not only acute or chronic transitional states between the neuroses on one side and the psychoses on the other, but a specific and remarkably stable form of pathological ego structure. I would suggest that one of the main features of ego structure in these cases is the predominance of splitting mechanisms and related defensive operations, with the concomitant failure of the normal processes of development and integration of identification systems. Such a pathological failure of early ego development can occur because of a constitutional defect or retardation in the development of the apparatuses of primary autonomy which underlie the operation of introjection and identification processes. In this case, one might say, the non-object-relations-determined substructures of the ego are defective and interfere with the development of internalized object relations. Actually, this state of affairs is probably more characteristic of psychotic states than of borderline personality organization and is characterized by regressive fusion of the earliest self- and object-images and a concomitant lack of development of ego boundaries (Jacobson, 1964). More characteristic for the borderline personality organization may be a failure related to a constitutionally determined lack of anxiety tolerance interfering with the phase of synthesis of introjections of opposite valences. The most important cause of failure in the borderline pathology is probably a quantitative predominance of negative introjections. Excessive negative introjections may stem both from a constitutionally determined intensity of aggressive drive derivatives and from severe early frustrations. From a clinical point of view, severe aggressive and self-aggressive strivings in the patient, and severe family pathology are consistently related to borderline personality organization; and, whatever the origin of this aggression, once it operates as part of early introjections, a number of pathological sequences are set in motion.

First of all, the painful nature of the object relation under such an all-out negative valence increases anxiety and the need to project aggression in the form of projection of negative introjections, which then become "bad external objects." Under these circumstances, splitting is reinforced as a fundamental protection of the positive introjections and a general protection of the ego against diffusion of anxiety. The need to preserve good internal and outer objects leads not only to excessive splitting but also to a dangerous "primitive idealization" (seeing the external objects as totally good in order to make sure that they cannot be contaminated, spoiled, or destroyed by the projected "bad external objects"). Primitive idealization creates unrealistic all-good and powerful object-images and, later on, a corresponding hypercathected, blown-up, omnipotent ego ideal, which is quite typical of borderline patients. The high degree of projection of aggressive self- and object-images of negative introjections perpetuates a dangerous world of persecuting objects. This world of extremes, of "all good" and "all bad" self- and object-images is at first a consequence of excessive splitting but then itself reinforces splitting. Excessive splitting also interferes with the strengthening of ego boundaries because of its interference with fusion of similar introjections and, therefore, with the normal, gradual mapping out of the self and objects. With relatively frail ego boundaries, the mechanism of projection remains at a rather primitive, inefficient level. Confusingly, what is projected outside is still, in part, felt inside, with the additional need to exert control over external objects onto whom aggression has been projected. All of this is characteristic of "projective identification" (Kernberg, 1965; Klein, 1946; Rosenfeld, 1963), an early form of projection that is typically present in patients in whom splitting operations are very strong and who present the early form of idealization which we have called primitive idealization.

Later forms of idealization are of a different kind, typically involve a reaction formation against unconscious guilt toward the object, and are not protective devices against fear of attack by bad objects. I am hinting here at the more general observation that numerous defensive mechanisms change their characteristics with ego development and the shift from predominance of splitting to the predominance of repression.

The pathological state of affairs that I have described in regard to borderline personality organization also determines the superego pathology typical of these patients. The internalization of extremely idealized early object-images creates impossible internalized demands; catastrophic fusions between these unrealistic ideal objects and other superego components, such as threatening, demanding, "external persecutors," induce the formation of sadistic superego nuclei which interfere with the normal internalization of more realistic parental prohibitions and demands and with the integration of the superego itself. One other consequence of all these developments is that both excessive splitting and the lack of superego integration interfere with further synthesis of the ego core. Mutual reinforcements of ego weakness and splitting end up in a pathologically fixated personality organization in which early drive derivatives, as part of split-up ego states, persist dangerously close to consciousness and to directly influencing all aspects of psychic life.

I have attempted to sketch briefly the differences between borderline personality organization, on the one hand, and the more normal development of the ego and superego compatible with the development of neurosis and normality, on the other. The differences between borderline personality organization and psychotic regression or fixation are another field of investigation which might be illuminated by the suggested conceptualization. It is possible that in psychotic reactions the main common psychopathological factor (in addition to persistence of splitting mechanisms) is the lack of differentiation between self- and object-images in the earliest stages of ego development, or a regressive fusion of those early self- and object-images under the impact of pathogenic factors which, in milder situations, induce excessive splitting only and not refusion of self- and object-images. Lack of differentiation of self- and object-images in the earliest introjections interferes with the differentiation between self and object and therefore with the delimitation of ego boundaries. Interesting related questions might consider to what extent primary autonomous ego apparatuses, especially perception and memory, influence the degree to which self- and object-images can be differentiated. Quantitative factors involving the degree of aggressive drive derivatives, the degree of objective deprivation and frustration, and the degree of the early ego's anxiety tolerance may also be crucially involved.

What is the relationship between the degree to which primary or secondary thought processes predominate and the degree to which splitting or repressive mechanisms predominate? I have suggested elsewhere (1963) that identification systems might be visualized as precipitates of the ego around which cognitive functions and adaptive aspects of defensive functions construct a secondary, stable "interstitial web." This "interstitial web" gives strength to the whole ego structure, preserves the delimitation of early object relations and contributes further to the delimitation of ego boundaries. On a higher level of organization, these interstitial structures then emancipate themselves toward independent structures. We might say that secondary autonomy of thought processes presupposes such emancipation of thought processes from their connection with early identification systems. The modification of affective dispositions available to the ego also indirectly fosters the emancipation of thought processes because the irradiating effect of earlier "pure" affective states exerts a powerful regressive pull in the direction of primary process thinking, which decreases when modification of affects occurs. The emancipation of cognitive functions is, of course, always a relative one, but rather severe failure of such an independent development occurs in the borderline personality organization. Under these circumstances, thought processes remain strongly linked to "nonmetabolized" identification systems, abstraction and generalization are interfered with, and the regressive pull of "pure" affective states influences thought processes. Finally, insufficient neutralization, related to lack of fusion of positive and negative introjections, deprives the ego of an important part of the energic factors which permit thought processes to develop secondary autonomy. In general terms, excessive splitting interferes with the later differentiation of apparatuses of primary autonomy and with the full development of secondary autonomy. It also inhibits the development of the ego core and weakens the concomitant capacity for repression and related defensive operations of the higher level.

REFERENCES

Brierley, M. (1937). Affects in theory and practice. In: *Trends in Psychoanalysis*. London: Hogarth, 1951, pp. 43-56.

Erikson, E. H. (1950). Growth and crises of the healthy personality. *Psychological Issues* 1:50-100.

———(1956). The problem of ego identity. *Journal of the American Psychoanalytic Association* 4:56-121.

Fairbairn, W. D. (1952). *An Object-Relations Theory of the Personality*. New York: Basic Books.

Freud, A. (1936). *The Ego and the Mechanisms of Defense*. New York: International Universities Press, 1946, pp. 30-32.

Freud, S. (1915). Repression. *Standard Edition* 14: 141-158.

———(1923). The ego and the id. *Standard Edition* 19: 19-27.

———(1926). Inhibitions, symptoms and anxiety. *Standard Edition* 20: 87-175.

———(1927). Fetishism. *Standard Edition* 21: 149-157.

———(1938). Splitting of the ego in the process of defence. *Standard Edition* 23: 141-207.

———(1940a). An outline of psycho-analysis. *Standard Edition* 23: 141-207.

Glover, E. (1956). *On the Early Development of Mind*. New York: International Universities Press.

Guntrip, H. (1961). *Personality Structure and Human Interaction*. London: Hogarth Press.

Hartmann, H. (1939). *Ego Psychology and the Problem of Adaptation*. New York: International Universities Press, 1958.

———(1950). Comments on the psychoanalytic theory of the ego. In: *Essays on Ego Psychology*. London: Hogarth Press; New York: International Universities Press, 1964, pp. 113-141.

———(1955). Notes on the theory of sublimation. In: *Essays on Ego Psychology*. London: Hogarth Press; New York: International Universities Press, pp. 215-240.

———, and Loewenstein, R. (1962). Notes on the superego. *Psychoanalytic Study of the Child* 17: 42-81.

Heimann, P. (1943-44). Certain function of introjection and projection in early infancy. In *Developments in Psycho-Analysis*, ed. Klein *et al*. London: Hogarth, 1952, pp. 122-168.

———(1966). Discussion of the present paper. *International Journal of Psycho-Analysis* 47: 254-260.

Jacobson, E. (1964). *The Self and the Object World*. New York: International Universities Press.

Kernberg, O. (1963). Discussion of Sutherland (1963).

———(1965). Notes on countertransference. *Journal of the American Psychoanalytic Association* 13.

———(1965). Countertransference. In: *Borderline Conditions and Pathological Narcissism*. New York: Jason Aronson, 1975, pp. 69-109.

Klein, M. (1939). A contribution to the psychogenesis of manic-depressive states. In: *Contributions to Psycho-Analysis.* London: Hogarth Press, pp. 282-310.

———(1940). Mourning and its relation to manic-depressive states. In: *Contributions to Psycho-Analysis.* London: Hogarth Press, 1948, pp. 311-338.

———(1946). Notes on some schizoid mechanisms. In: *Developments in Psychoanalysis,* ed. Klein *et al.* London: Hogarth Press, 1952, pp. 292-320.

———(1952). Discussion of the mutual influences in the development of ego and id. *Psychoanalytic Study of the Child* 7: 51-53.

Knight, R. P. (1954). Borderline states. In: *Psychoanalytic Psychiatry and Psychology,* ed. Knight and Friedman. New York: International Universities Press. pp. 97-109.

Madison, P. (1961). *Freud's Concept of Repression and Defense.* Minneapolis: University of Minnesota Press.

Menninger, K. (1938). *Man Against Himself.* New York: Harcourt Brace.

———, and Mayman, M. (1956). Episodic dyscontrol: a third order of stress adaptation. *Bulletin of the Menninger Clinic* 20: 153-165.

———, Mayman, M., and Pruyser, P. (1963). *The Vital Balance.* New York: Viking.

Murphy, L. (1963). From a report presented to Topeka Psychoanalytic Institute Research Seminar, May 15, 1963. Unpublished.

———(1964). Adaptational tasks in childhood in our culture. *Bulletin of the Menninger Clinic* 28: 309-322.

Nunberg, H. (1955). *Principles of Psychoanalysis.* New York: International Universities Press.

Rapaport, D. (1954). On the psychoanalytic theory of affects. In: *The Collected Papers of David Rapaport,* ed. M. M. Gill. New York: Basic Books, 1967, pp. 476-512.

———(1960). *The Structure of Psychoanalytic Theory.* New York: International Universities Press.

Rosenfeld, H. (1963). Notes on the psychopathology and psychoanalytic treatment of schizophrenia. In: *Psychotic States.* London: Hogarth Press, 1965. pp. 155-168.

Sandler, J. (1960). On the concept of the superego. *Psychoanalytic Study of the Child* 15: 128-162.

———, and Rosenblatt, B. (1962). The concept of the representational world. *Psychoanalytic Study of the Child* 17: 128-145.

———, Holder, A., and Meers, D. (1963). The ego ideal and the ideal self. *Psychoanalytic Study of the Child* 18: 139-158.

Spitz, R. A. (1965). *The First Year of Life*. New York: International Universities Press.

Stross, L. Personal communication.

Sutherland, J. D. (1963). Object-relations theory and the conceptual model of psychoanalysis. *British Journal of Medical Psychology* 36: 109-124.

Ticho, E. (1965). Personal communication.

van der Waals, H. G. (1952). Discussion of the mutual influences in the development of ego and id. *Psychoanalytic Study of the Child* 7: 66-68.

Winnicott, D. W. (1955). The depressive position in normal emotional development. *British Journal of Medical Psychology* 28: 89-100.

two

Normal and Pathological Development

My efforts to clarify the psychopathology, diagnosis, and treatment of patients with borderline personality organization and narcissistic personalities (Kernberg, 1967, 1968, and 1970) led me to explore psychoanalytic object-relations theory as a major theoretical frame of reference for understanding the origin and structural characteristics of these patients. In attempting to clarify some of its basic concepts from an operational viewpoint, I developed some formulations of my own, in addition to integrating those of various authors in the field. Chapter 1 and my paper "Early Ego Integration and Object Relations" (1972) reflect these earlier efforts. In Chapter 1, I suggested two general levels of ego organization (centering, respectively, on the mechanisms of splitting and repression) and proposed that primitive units of affect state, object-representation, and self-representation constitute the basis of later structuring of internalized object relations. I reexamined the concepts of introjection, identification, and ego identity from this viewpoint and, using these formulations, outlined a tentative developmental model. In the paper just mentioned, I developed these formulations further, relating them to the work of other authors—particularly Bowlby, Erikson, Fairbairn, Jacobson, Melanie Klein, Mahler, and Talcott Parsons—and suggested a more specific set of normal and pathological states of development of internalized object relations.

In this and the following two chapters, I will examine psychoanalytic object-relations theory in terms of the broader issues of psychoanalytic metapsychology and focus particularly on the "boundary" or "interface" regions relating intrapsychic structures to biological, and especially neurophysiological, structures, on the one hand, and to the interpersonal, psychosocial field, on the other. I will later examine some of the clinical implications of psychoanalytic object-relations theory, particularly the implications of this theory for the diagnosis and treatment of borderline conditions, the psychoanalytic understanding of love relations, the classification of normal and pathological character structures, and hospital treatment.

A PROPOSED DEFINITION

In broadest terms, psychoanalytic object-relations theory represents the psychoanalytic study of the nature and origin of interpersonal relations, and of the nature and origin of intrapsychic structures deriving from, fixating, modifying, and reactivating past internalized relations with others in the context of present interpersonal relations. Psychoanalytic object-relations theory focuses upon the internalization of interpersonal relations, their contribution to normal and pathological ego and superego developments, and the mutual influences of intrapsychic and interpersonal object relations. This broad definition may be narrowed down in three, progressively more restricted ways.

1. Object-relations theory may refer to the general theory of the structures in the mind which preserve interpersonal experiences and the mutual influences between these intrapsychic structures and the overall vicissitudes of expression of instinctual needs in the psychosocial environment. In this broad definition, psychoanalytic object-relations theory would include all the vicissitudes of the relationship between the intrapsychic and the interpersonal fields. One might even say that psychoanalysis as a general theory constitutes an object-relations theory. This would make a distinct theory of object-relations within psychoanalysis unnecessary, except, perhaps, as a general focus or approach occupying an intermediate ground between psychoanalytic metapsychology proper (Rapaport and Gill, 1959) and clinical analyses of normal and pathological functioning. Psychoanalytic object-relations theory, thus defined, has been referred to as a "middle language" between the metapsychological and the clinical ones (Mayman, personal communication, 1963). Two recent significant overviews of psychoanalytic object-relations theory have used this broad conceptualization, integrating it with contemporary ego psychology. I am referring to *Aspects of Internalization* by Schafer (1968) and *Object Love and Reality* by Modell

(1968). Schafer's book presents probably the most comprehensive analysis to date of identification processes from an ego psychological viewpoint, and Modell stresses the importance of the vicissitudes of internalized object relations in the examination of borderline and psychotic conditions.

2. Object-relations theory can also refer to a more restricted approach within psychoanalytic metapsychology stressing the buildup of dyadic or bipolar intrapsychic representations (self- and object-images) as reflections of the original infant-mother relationship and its later development into dyadic, triangular, and multiple internal and external interpersonal relationships. This second, more restricted definition of object-relations theory stresses the simultaneous buildup of the "self" (a composite structure derived from the integration of multiple self-images) and of object-representations (or "internal objects" derived from the integration of multiple object-images into more comprehensive representations of others). The terminology for these "self" and object" components varies from author to author, but what is important is the essentially dyadic or bipolar nature of the internalization within which each unit of self- and object-image is established in a particular affective context. In this conceptualization, the self-object-affect "units" are primary determinants of the overall structures of the mind (id, ego and superego). Authors who adopt this approach deal with the questions this structural model raises regarding the interrelationships of instincts, affects, and object relations in various ways. This second definition of psychoanalytic object-relations theory implies, in contrast to the first one, a more circumscribed approach to psychoanalytic metapsychology, but includes authors with very different viewpoints regarding instinct theory, structural models of the mind, and treatment approaches. It encompasses the ego psychological approaches of Erikson (1956), Jacobson (1964), and Mahler (1968); the British schools of Fairbairn (1952), Winnicott (1955, 1960, 1963), Bowlby (1969), and Melanie Klein (1934, 1940, 1946); to some extent, Harry Stack Sullivan (1953); and the exploration of psychoanalytic theories by Talcott Parsons (1964a, 1964b).

3. A still more restricted definition of psychoanalytic object-relations theory limits the term to the specific approach of the so-called "British psychoanalytic school" of Melanie Klein and Fairbairn

(and approaches related to Fairbairn's, such as those of Winnicott [1955, 1963], Wisdom [1963, 1971], Guntrip [1961, 1971], and Sutherland [1963]). This has been the ordinary understanding of object-relations theory, and it has traditionally been counterposed to contemporary ego psychology.

For theoretical and clinical reasons, I prefer the second definition. It limits itself to what is specific to object-relations theory within psychoanalytic theory at large and includes a common type of "unit of internalization" which permits relating the works of authors of different schools to one other. It also allows one to bring together findings and conceptualizations which at times have been artificially separated because of the difficulties of communication between various psychoanalytic groups. As I see it, object-relations theory, already implied in Freud's writings, transcends any particular psychoanalytic school or group and represents a general psychoanalytic development to which authors of very different orientations have contributed significantly.

The term "object" in object-relations theory should more properly be "human object", since it reflects the traditional use of this term in psychoanalytic metapsychology for relations with others. To counter the occasional misunderstandings in psychoanalytic literature which consider object-relations as examining only interpersonal relations, it needs to be stressed that psychoanalytic object-relations theory is particularly concerned with the intrapsychic field, the intrapsychic structures representing the primary dyadic relationship which later expands in many directions. Psychoanalytic object-relations theory, as circumscribed in the second definition, represents, in my opinion, a major integrative framework which can link the psychosocial approach to and the subjective, experiential nature of human life, on the one hand, with the intrapsychic structures comprehended in general metapsychology, on the other.

Having offered a definition and circumscribed the field of object-relations theory, I would now like to discuss the usefulness of this psychoanalytic approach. Object-relations theory has contributed significantly to: (a) our understanding of severe types of psychopathology, such as borderline conditions, psychoses, regressive types of character pathology with problems of identity, and chronic types of marital conflicts; (b) a better knowledge of ego and superego formations and their mutual relationships; (c) the clarification of various processes of internalization; (d) the psychoanalytic examination of small group processes; (e) and the discovery of a link between individual psychopathology and pathological group behavior. Object-relations theory has also raised new questions in the complex field of psychoanalytic instinct theory; and, as I suggested in an earlier paper (Kernberg, 1972), internalized object relations may be considered a crossroad where instinct and the social system meet and contribute crucially to the development of the personality of the individual. Finally, this approach focuses upon such special criteria for mental health and normality as: (1) the depth and stability of internal relations with others; (2) the tolerance of ambivalence toward loved objects; (3) the capacity for tolerating guilt and separation and for the working through of depressive crises; (4) the extent to which the self-concept is integrated; and (5) the extent to which behavior patterns correspond to the self-concept.

NORMAL AND PATHOLOGICAL DEVELOPMENT OF INTERNALIZED OBJECT RELATIONS AND THEIR CLINICAL IMPLICATIONS

In what follows I will outline a general theory of (1) the origin of the basic "units" (self-image, object-image, affect disposition) of internalized object relations, (2) the development of four basic stages in their differentiation and integration, (3) the relationship between failure in these developments and the crystallization of various types of psychopathology, and (4) the implications of this sequence of phases for general structural developments of the psychic apparatus. In order to present an integrated overview, I will repeat findings from earlier work. However, my main stress here will be on providing an integrative framework which will relate my work to that of various other authors. In the process I will illustrate the usefulness of psychoanalytic object-relations theory for a general developmental analysis and a structural theory of psychopathology.

Stage 1: Normal "Autism" or Primary Undifferentiated Stage. This earliest stage of development precedes the consolidation of the "good" undifferentiated self-object constellation built up under the influence of pleasurable, gratifying experiences of the infant in interactions with his mother. This phase covers the first month of life, and a pathological arrest, failure or fixation of development at this stage would be reflected in the lack of development of the undifferentiated self-object image and the consequent incapacity to establish a normal "symbiotic" relationship with the mother—a condition characteristic of autistic psychosis (Mahler, 1968). Throughout this stage there is a gradual buildup of the normal, primary, undifferentiated self-object representation.

Stage 2: Normal "Symbiosis" or Stage of the Primary, Undifferentiated Self-Object Representations. The consolidation of the pleasurable or rewarding or "good" self-object image signals the beginning of this stage, which extends from the second month of life to somewhere between the sixth and eighth months of age. This is the basic "good" self-object constellation, which will become the nucleus of the self system of the ego and the basic organizer of integrative functions of the early ego. I am including in this phase the symbiotic phase of development in the strict sense described by Mahler and the differentiation sub-phase of the separation-individuation process described by her (1971, 1972). The reasons for including the differentiation subphase in stage 2 of the development of internalized object relations are the relative incompleteness of the differentiation of self and object representations from each other and, more importantly, the persisting tendency for defensive regressive refusion of "good" self and object images when severe trauma or frustration determine pathological development of this stage. This is in contrast to later defensive organizations in which splitting mechanisms operate while boundaries between self- and object-images remain stable (borderline personality organization). Pathological fixation of or regression to stage 2 of development of internalized object relations is clinically characterized by the failure in—or loss of—the differentiation of ego boundaries, which is characteristic of symbiotic psychosis of childhood (Mahler, 1968), most types of adult schizophrenia (Jacobson, 1954), and depressive psychoses (Jacobson, 1966). Jacobson (1971) has proposed basic structural differences between depressive and schizophrenic psychoses. In the case of depressive psychosis, ego-superego boundaries are preserved in spite of the refusion of self- and object-images within the ego and the superego; in the case of schizophrenia, a more generalized refusion of self- and object-images takes place, with the disintegration of the overall psychic structures and the pathological fusion of fragments of self- and object-representations, so that fantastic, new units are created in the process.

Stage 2 in the development of internalized object relations comes to an end when the self-image and the object-image have been differentiated in a stable way within the core "good" self-object representation. I mentioned before that the primary, undifferentiated "good" self-object representation is built up under the influence of pleasurable, gratifying experiences involving the infant and his mother. Simultaneously with the development of this "good" self-object representation, another primary, undifferentiated self-object representation is formed, integrating experiences of a frustrating, painful nature: the "bad" self-object representation, centering on a primitive, painful affective tone. It needs to be stressed that the "good" and the "bad" primary intrapsychic structures are organized separately under different affective circumstances, determining two separate constellations of "affective memory" (see also chapter 3).

Because of the crucial importance of this stage for the theory of instinctual development, the relationship between affective and cognitive development, and all later developmental stages, a detailed examination of the processes involved in its establishment is appropriate at this point.

Evidence has been accumulating in recent years which indicates that homeostatic disturbances reflecting physiological disequilibrium related to hunger, thirst, temperature changes, etc., activate the hypothalamic-hypophyseal axis and the hypothalamic structures that provide these processes with either a painful or punishing affective tone or a rewarding or pleasurable affective tone. MacLean (1969) has discussed the role of the limbic forebrain-hypothalamic-limbic midbrain formation in the control of visceral activity and emotion and has designated it as "visceral brain." Morgane (1972) has reviewed the relationship of the hypothalamus with the hippocampal and limbic complexes, concluding that all information from the internal and external environment feeds into the ascending reticular system which, in turn, relays into the limbic forebrain and hypothalamic and hippocampal fields, whose main function is to develop and organize the behavioral and affective aspects of "drive" or motivated behavior. He suggests that "primal needs activate appropriate drive mechanisms in the brain which themselves are apparently established by natural selection and expressed through inherited neural patterns of reactions. Affective desire or motivation might then be thought of as the subjective experience of the behavioral drive in such a schema for a neurological mechanism of motivation" (p. 302).

Thus, homeostatic disturbances impinging on the visceral brain would activate simultaneously: (1) generalized arousal (that is, alertness reflecting a diffuse, nonspecific arousal mechanism mediated predominantly by the ascending reticular formation), (2) inborn behavior patterns, such as the orienting reflex and the various inborn attachment behaviors of sucking, crying, clinging, etc. (Bowlby, 1969). MacLean (1969) has reported evidence indicating that particular striatal areas are the centers controlling such inborn behavior patterns; and (3) subjective affect experiences of a "rewarding" or pleasurable and "punishing" or painful type controlled by the hypothalamic and other "reward" centers (Olds, 1960).

As a consequence of these processes, the following developments would take place: (1) increased arousal and general alertness would lower perception thresholds and facilitate the infant's perception of touch, smell, and of those intraceptive and proprioceptive sensations included in the nonspecific or "coenesthetic" constellation of stimulus modalities (Freedman, 1972, and Spitz, 1945); arousal would also increase the scanning of the environment and "external" perception; (2) the activation of inborn attachment patterns (particularly crying) would, in an average, expectable environment, bring about mothering behavior, which in turn would provide, in addition to food intake and its direct physiological changes, a crucial sensorial enrichment and modification of the sensory input; and (3) all the information contained in the various components mentioned so far would be stored in the infant as its total perceived situation, presumably in the form of primitive "affective memory" (Arnold, 1970a, 1970b).

Primitive affect, conceived as the earliest subjective experience of pleasure or unpleasure, thus constitutes the basic organizing element bringing together into a common memory trace fixating that experience the primitive perception of bodily states, of activated inborn behavior and the corresponding "external" (environmental) responses "mixed" with it. In short, various inborn physiological, behavioral, affective, and perceptive structures are internalized jointly as a first unit of intrapsychic structure. Cognition and affect are thus two aspects of the same primary experience. Although the neurophysiological structures responsible for affective experience and for (cognitive) storage capability of this experience are different, their integration in the earliest affective memory (Arnold, 1970a, 1970b) establishes, in my opinion, a common structure (pleasurable or unpleasurable primitive experience) out of which cognition and affect will evolve in diverging directions. This has relevance for psychoanalytic instinct theory.

Affects gradually differentiate in the context of the development of the undifferentiated self-object representations. The earliest undifferentiated pleasurable affects will evolve into more specific pleasure with oral satiation, excitement of various erotogenic zones, gratification of exploratory behavior, and, above all, with evolving interpersonal experiences (and their intrapsychic derivatives). The same is true with the primitive painful affects, which gradually evolve into anxiety, fear, and rage, as well as the more elaborate and toned down derived affects of the "unpleasure" series. Eventually, in stage 4 of development, when "good" and "bad" self- and object-images are integrated, more complex fusion of various affects will become possible, thereby fostering the higher level development of affects related to depression.

Experiences which activate the gratifying self-object representation also activate attention and motivate learning; both gratification and limited frustration (which also activates attention and learning) contribute to gradual differentiation of the self components from the object components in the infant's perception of interaction with its mother. This gradual differentiation is powerfully supported by the maturation of primary autonomous ego functions such as perception and memory and by cognitive developments occurring in the context of the infant-mother relation. In contrast, excessive activation of the "bad" self-object representation under the influence of frustration or deprivation brings on generalized anxiety, whose disorganizing effect interferes with the early differentiation of self and object components.

Later, efforts are made to "expel" the "bad" self-object experience, while the "good" self-object representation becomes the nucleus of the ego. The expelling of the "bad" self-object representation to the "periphery" of psychic experience originates a motivated conception of the "out there," but, as a more realistic exploration and perception of the external environment occurs in the context of self-object differentiation in the "good" self-object realm, the "bad" nucleus of self-experience is ascribed to "uncanny," disturbing, or frightening experiences and is subject to later projective mechanisms.

Differentiation of the self and the object components of the undifferentiated "good" self-object representation probably begins in the third or fourth month of life and is probably completed between the sixth and the ninth month. The developmental series of "good" self-object representations become the intrapsychic structures originally invested with libido, while the series of "bad" self-object representations become those invested with aggression. From a clinical viewpoint, one might say that the evolving affect states and affect dispositions actualize, respectively, libidinal and aggressive drive derivatives. From a theoretical viewpoint, this formulation requires further examination of the relationship among psychoanalytic instinct theory, object-relations theory, and the role of affect states, a subject to which I will return in Chapter 3.

Stage 3: Differentiation of Self- from Object-Representations. This stage begins with the completion of the differentiation of the self-representation from the object-representation within the core "good" self-object representation, and includes the later differentiation of self- from object-representation within the core "bad" self-object representation. It ends with the eventual integration of "good" and "bad" self-representations into an integrated self-concept, and the integration of "good" and "bad" object-representations into "total" object-representations, that is, the achievement of object constancy. This stage begins between the sixth and the eighth month of life and reaches completion between the eighteenth and the thirty-sixth month. This stage, with the exclusion of the differentiation sub-phase, corresponds roughly to the separation-individuation stage of development of Mahler (1972, 1973), who has also stressed that borderline conditions relate to pathological resolution of the rapproachment subphase of separation-individuation. The differentiation of self and object components determines, jointly with the general development of cognitive processes, the establishment of stable ego boundaries; there is not yet an integrated self or an integrated conception of other human beings (so that this is a stage of "part object-relations"). Pathological fixation and/or regression to this stage of development of internalized object relations determines borderline personality organization (Kernberg, 1967).

In my work with borderline patients (Chapter 1, 1967, and 1968), I found that they actively sought to separate ego states with opposite affective colorings. What at first seemed to be chaotic manifestations of multiple primitive transference dispositions and an immediate availability of primary process material in consciousness turned out to reflect not a weakness of these patients' defensive structures but a specific primitive defensive organization. This organization was responsible for the fact that they could calmly discuss conscious sexual fantasies regarding their parents, polymorphous sexual interests, primitive forms of aggression, etc., while they became extremely anxious when I attempted to relate material presented within one affective context to material they had presented in a different, usually opposite, affective context. These patients manifested splitting or primitive dissociation as a major defensive operation separating contradictory ego states, along with other, related defenses, such as primitive forms of projection (especially "projective identification"), omnipotence, denial, primitive forms of idealization, and devaluation.

These findings led me to propose an early constellation of defenses of the ego centered on splitting and its related mechanisms characteristic of borderline personality organization, which contrasts with the higher level of defensive organization (primarily repression and its related defensive mechanisms) characteristic of non-borderline character pathology and symptomatic neuroses (the pathology of Stage 4 within the present classification). The psychoanalytic exploration of borderline patients consistently revealed that the several ego states which were actively kept separate from one another represented the activation of past (real or fantasied) relationships with significant persons or a combination of such real or fantasied relationships and fantasy formations geared to protect the individual from real or imaginary dangers in those relationships. Such internalized object relations always presented at least three components: a self-representation; an object-representation in some kind of interaction with the self-representation; and an affective state, usually of a strong, diffuse, overwhelming quality (rage, fear, idealized love, etc.). One does not see in neurotic patients or in normal individuals the preservation of primitive, past internalized object relations in such an unaltered condition. However, in the course of any psychoanalysis repressed, past object relations with a primitive self- and object-representation linked by a primitive affect can be observed at points of deep regression and analyzed.

In the development of Stage 3, the recognition of mother marks the beginning of the delimitation of self and nonself, of self and external objects. This delimitation, in turn, permits the building up of different kinds of self-representations and corresponding object-representations under varying circumstances of predominantly pleasurable, libidinally invested or derived affective conditions. In other words, a multiplication of libidinally invested self-representations and object-representations occurs, with a gradual reshaping of the early self-concept in connection with the reshaping of object-representations, which are gradually differentiated from one another. This differentiation powerfully reinforces the perceptual and cognitive developments which differentiate self from nonself.

At first, ego boundaries are fluctuating and fragile, and refusion of self- and object-representations of a good (and, gradually, idealized) type can easily occur as an early defense against bad, frustrating, or anxiety-producing situations (Jacobson, 1954). Severe frustrations and the consequent predominance of bad self-object representations, which become invested with aggressive drive derivatives, interfere with the development of ego boundaries insofar as they determine excessive defensive refusion of primitive, "all-good" self- and object-representations.

Later, self and object components are also differentiated in the area of frustrating, anxiety-producing, or hostile interactions; at first, under these new circumstances, the infant perceives his own hostility as naturally justified by what he experiences as hostility from a "bad" external mother. As self- and object-representations become further differentiated in both libidinally and aggressively invested interactions, ego boundaries expand and consolidate. At first, during Stage 3, good and bad self-representations and good and bad object-representations (at first only representing mother, and then also father, siblings, etc.) coexist without being integrated into a comprehensive self-concept and a comprehensive concept of others, respectively.

During this stage the separation of libidinally invested and aggressively invested self- and object-representations becomes strengthened by active utilization of the mechanism of splitting, which is geared to protect the ideal, good relationship with mother from "contamination" by bad self-representations and bad representations of her. Normally, splitting mechanisms gradually decrease; but, under pathological circumstances, splitting may actually increase. The main objective of the defensive constellation centering on splitting in borderline personality organization is to keep separate the aggressively determined and the libidinally determined intrapsychic structures stemming from early object relations. The price the patient pays for this defensive organization is twofold: the inability to integrate libidinally and aggressively invested self-representations into a self-concept which more truly reflects the actual self and to integrate libinally invested and aggressively invested object-representations and so to understand in depth other people. Together, these characteristics determine the syndrome of identity diffusion.

Stage 4: Integration of Self-Representations and Object-Representations and Development of Higher Level Intrapsychic Object Relations-Derived Structures. This stage begins in the latter part of the third year of life and lasts through the entire oedipal period. It is characterized by the integration of libidinally invested and aggressively invested self-representations into the definite self system and of libidinally invested and aggressively invested object-images into "total" object-representations. Ego, superego, and id, as definite, overall intrapsychic structures, are consolidated in this phase. The typical psychopathology of Stage 4 is represented by the neuroses and the "higher level" of organization of character pathology, particularly hysterical, obsessive-compulsive, and depressive-masochistic characters (Chapter Five). Pathogenic conflicts typically occur between the ego and a relatively well-integrated but excessively strict and punitive superego. One type of character pathology, the narcissistic personality, is characterized by an abnormal condensation of new intrapsychic structures which appear at this stage, along with a regression to the organization of stage 3 (Kernberg, 1970, 1974). In essence, I have proposed that the structure of narcissistic personalities is characterized by (1) a pathological condensation of real self, ideal self, and ideal object structures; (2) repression and/or dissociation of "bad" self-representations; (3) generalized devaluation of object-representations; and (4) blurring of normal ego-superego boundaries. The end result is the development of a grandiose self (Kohut, 1971) embedded in a defensive organization similar to that of borderline personality organization (Kernberg, 1974).

Cognitive maturation is crucial for the integration of self-representations and object-representations reflecting affectively opposite perceptions and experiences; however, the continuing pathological predominance of primitive defensive operations, particularly splitting, related to severe pregenital conflicts may interfere with integrative processes to such an extent that, in spite of adequate cognitive integration of external objects, the normal integration of object relations at this stage breaks down.

The integration of affectively opposite self-representations gives rise to the developmental phase described by Melanie Klein as the "depressive position" (Klein, 1934, 1940), which, according to Winnicott (1955, 1963), is the developmental phase where guilt feelings and concern appear. I disagree with Melanie Klein's timetable for this developmental phase, with her assumption of superego functions in the first year of life, and with other metapsychological assumptions of hers to which I will come back later. Earlier (Chapter 1, 1972), I outlined how this integration of opposite self-representations brings about a general deepening and broadening of affective potentials, a modulation of affects, and particularly a broadening and deepening of the capacity for guilt feelings, which is later utilized by the developing superego. I also stressed how, in contrast to the new, more realistic self- and object-representations, there develop other representations of an ideal self and an ideal object reflecting in fantasy the now "lost" ideal state of the "all good" self- and object-representations. The ideal self represents a wishful, ideal state of the self which would make the individual acceptable to, close to, and, in the last resort, symbolically re-fused with the ideal object (the unharmed, all loving, all forgiving early mother image).

Joffe and Sandler (1965) suggest that the depressive response constitutes an affect representing the fundamental psychobiological disposition activated when there is a feeling of being unable to restore a wished-for, ideal state. This response is activated in the dynamic tension that develops between the real self and the ideal self (which incorporates the sought-for ideal state). The tension between the integrated self-representation (the real self) and the ideal self leads to a regressive activation of a primitive depressive affect disposition in the ego, while the tension between the real self and the real object (the integrated object-representation) sets in motion more progressive, realistic trends. The child now realizes that his "badness" is expressed toward the same object (mother) that he loves, and the depressive affect released in the context of this developmental stage reflects both a primitive affect disposition and a higher level of depression linked with feelings of guilt and concern toward the object. The general implication is that cognitive development, affective development, and the development of structures representing internalized object relations are intimately linked.

I have suggested that all these integrative processes reduce the utilization of splitting mechanisms and that, some time in the third year of life, repression (reinforced by related mechanisms such as isolation, undoing, and reaction formation) becomes the main defensive operation of the ego. Insofar as the operation of repression from now on separates id from ego, one might say that the id as a psychic structure (Hartmann, et al., 1946) comes into existence only at this point. This formulation implies the differentiation of the id out of a common matrix from which ego and id develop (Hartmann, 1950); the id now integrates functions which previously existed "separately" or, rather, as part of early, mutually dissociated or split systems of internalized object relations. Thus, primitive aggressive and libidinal drive derivatives or their respective affective states have access to consciousness before the integration of the id. Primary process thinking (or, rather, primitive cognitive processes intimately linked with primitive affect states) was previously expressed in the context of affect-determined "linkages" of self- and/or object-representations under the sway of pleasure and unpleasure tensions without regard to reality. It is only now, after repression sets in as a major defensive operation, that the id integrates these functions. Van der Waals

(1952), in a pioneering examination of this issue, stressed that the clinical examination of manifestations of the id always reveals repressed object relations; he suggested that the repressed portion of the id is not a pure id but an ego id, just like the undifferentiated phase in the early part of psychic life. The conclusions derived from Schur's (1966) careful analysis of the concept of the id point in the same direction. The characteristics of both the ego and the id are on a quantitative and qualitative continuum. He suggests that there are evolutionary and developmental aspects of the id as well as of the ego.

In short, in the context of this developmental analysis of internalized object relations, I propose that the predominance of repression over earlier defenses organized around splitting consolidates the id as an overall intrapsychic structure containing the sum of those internalized object relations which are unacceptable because of the dangerous, anxiety- and guilt-producing experiences involved in the respective intrapsychic and interpersonal interactions. Thus, the most frightening and disturbing units involving self- and object-images under the influences of primitive affect are repressed, and this interferes with their ultimate differentiation and integration within the total personality. Primitive, unrealistic self- and object-representations remain relatively unchanged in the id, and so do their correspondingly primitive, overwhelming affect dispositions. In the id, therefore, primitive cognitive constellations of self- and object-representations and their associated primitive affect dispositions persist. This accounts for many of the characteristics of the id, such as displacement and condensation (of primitive self- and object-representations), and the primitive nature of the aggressive and libidinal drive derivatives involved.

Stage 4 of development also marks the beginning of the integration of the superego as an independent intrapsychic structure. My conceptualization attempts to integrate various contributions (Hartmann and Loewenstein, 1962; Sandler and Rosenblatt, 1962; Sandler, Holder and Meers, 1963) with Edith Jacobson's formulations (1964). Since Jacobson has already greatly clarified this area, I will summarize this development in the context of the earlier developmental stages of internalized object relations described before.

The earliest superego structure derives from the internalization of fantastically hostile, highly unrealistic object-images reflecting "expelled," projected, and reintrojected "bad" self-object representations. These images probably originate at a time when self- and object-representations are already differentiated in the area of "good" self- and object-representations and reflect primitive efforts of the infant to protect the good relationship with the idealized mother by turning the aggressively invested images of her (fused with the respective self-images) against himself. These early, sadistically determined superego forerunners probably correspond to Melanie Klein's primitive, sadistic superego and to Fairbairn's anti-libidinal object. The stronger the pregenital frustration and aggression, the more predominant are these sadistic superego forerunners.

The second superego structure is derived from the ego's ideal self and ideal object representations (which have been mentioned before as coming into operation at the time of the integration of libidinal and aggressive self- and object-representations). The condensation of such magical, wishful, ideal self and ideal object representations constitutes the kernel of the ego ideal. The sadistically determined superego forerunners and the early ego ideal formation (which probably reaches the height of its development early in stage 4) are then integrated. Thus, the superego has to repeat the process that has already started in the ego, namely, the integration of internalized object relations of libidinal and aggressive characteristics. When this step in superego integration is achieved, a "toning down" of the absolute, fantastic nature of primitive idealization (the early ego ideal) and of the sadistic forerunners within the superego occurs, along with a decrease in the processes of projection of such sadistic and idealized superego nuclei. The decrease of these projective processes (which were previously utilized as a protective device against excessive pressures from the primitive superego) leads to still another level of superego structures, namely, internalizations of the more realistic demands and prohibitions of the parental figures during the oedipal period of development.

Failure of superego integration may occur at various levels. First, failure to integrate the preoedipal superego forerunners interferes with the internalization of more realistic oedipal parental images and perpetuates the primitive, sadistic, and unintegrated quality of the superego. This, in turn, fosters excessive reprojection of superego nuclei (with the potential for developing paranoid defensive character traits) and also interferes with higher levels of integration and development of internalized value systems. Second, failure of superego integration may take the form of a pathological integration of sadistic and idealized superego nuclei eventually dominated by aggressive features, with the result that the "ideal" object-representations acquire characteristics of sadistic demands for perfection. In this case, superego integration occurs under the predominance of sadistic characteristics and brings about excessive repression of instinctual needs, thereby establishing a classic precondition for neurotic symptom formation.

When, under ideal circumstances, sadistic and primitive ego ideal forerunners are integrated and (later) realistic images of the parents are introjected at the height of the oedipal period, a further, integrative step in development can take place.

In Chapter 1, I defined introjection, identification, and ego identity as a sequence in the organization of the processes of internalization of object relations. I defined ego identity as the overall organization of identifications and introjections under the guiding principle of the synthetic function of the ego. The establishment of ego identity occurs during Stage 4 of development and includes the integration of self-representations into an integrated self (or self-concept), an overall integration of the inner world of objects derived from the integration of "part" object-representations into "total" object-representations, and the ongoing processes of "confirmation" (Erikson, 1956). These formulations are largely based upon the work of Erikson (1950, 1956), Hartmann (Hartmann et al., 1946, and Hartmann, 1950) and Sandler and Rosenblatt (1962). Thus, ego identity includes a consolidated self-concept and a consolidated world of object representations.

Stage 5: Consolidation of Superego and Ego Integration. Stage 5 begins with the completion of the integration of all the levels of superego. Gradually, the sharp opposition between superego and ego decreases. An integrated superego also fosters further integration and consolidation of ego identity. Here, ego identity continues to evolve by means of an ongoing reshaping of the experiences with external objects in the light of internal object-representations, and of these object-representations in the light of real experiences with others. The self-concept, in turn, undergoes continuous reshaping on the basis of real experiences with others and experiences with the internal world of objects. An integrated self, a stable world of integrated, internalized object-representations, and a realistic self-knowledge reinforce one another. The more integrated the self-representations, the more self-perception in any particular situation corresponds to the total reality of the person's interactions with others. The more integrated the object-representations, the greater the capacity for realistic appreciation of others and reshaping one's internal representations on the basis of such realistic appraisals. A harmonious world of internalized object-representations, including not only significant others from the family and immediate friends but also a social group and a cultural identity, constitutes an ever growing internal world providing love, reconfirmation, support, and guidance within the object relations system of the ego. Such an internal world, in turn, gives depth to the present interaction with others. In periods of crisis, such as loss, abandonment, separation, failure, and loneliness, the individual can temporarily fall back on his internal world; in this way, the intrapsychic and the interpersonal worlds relate to and reinforce each other.

In more general terms, the internal resources that an individual has in the face of conflict and failure are intimately related to the maturity and depth of his internal world of object relations. Perhaps the most dramatic example of this situation is incurable illness and the prospect of imminent death: persons who have been able to love other human beings in a mature way retain images of them which provide love and comfort at points of danger, loss, and failure. Clinical observation shows how much trust in one's self and one's goodness is based upon the confirmation of love from internalized good objects. In this regard, one aspect of regression in the service of the ego is a reactivation in fantasy of past good internalized object-relations which provide "basic trust" to the self. Basic trust, of course, ultimately derives from the first internalization of a gratifying, reliable mother-representation in relation to a loving, gratified self-representation.

In contrast, the most striking example of failure of normal development of internalized object relations is given by narcissistic personalities who have difficulty evoking not only real people in their past but their own self experiences with such people. The dual absence of libidinally invested, integrated object-representations and of a libidinally invested, integrated self-concept determines the experience of emptiness so characteristic of borderline patients and particularly of narcissistic personalities, regardless of whether they function within the borderline range. Such an experience of emptiness creates for patients a need to focus exclusively on immediate present interpersonal experiences in an effort to understand interpersonal situations. Narcissistic personalities often are aware of their incapacity to judge others and themselves as perceived by others beyond the immediate behavioral cues of the actual interaction (Kernberg, 1970, 1974).

The processes of integration, depersonification, and individualization represent structural outcomes of the internalization of object relations not only in the superego but in the ego as well. I have already referred to the integration of self- and object-representations in the ego as part of the establishment and consolidation of ego identity. Depersonification may also be applied to the "adaptive generalization" (Sutherland, 1966), that is, the attempt to coordinate and integrate our viewpoints with others' in the context of our interpersonal relations under the influence of the need to share thinking and communicate our thoughts and feelings with other people. Thus, general attitudes emerge expressed by generalizations about human life and experience. Individualization includes the gradual replacement of primitive introjections and identifications with partial, sublimatory identifications fitting into the overall concept of the self. Emotional maturity is reflected in the capacity for discriminating subtle aspects of one's own self and of other people and in an increasing selectivity in accepting and internalizing the qualities of other people. Mature friendships are based on such selectivity and the capacity to combine love with independence and emotional objectivity.

The character structure represents the automatized, predominantly behavioral aspects of ego identity. A reciprocal relationship exists between the self-concept and the character structure: the more integrated the former, the more consistent and harmonious the latter, and, conversely, the more integrated the character structure, the closer the correspondence between the self-concept and the actual behavior and personality as they are experienced by others. The character structure is also under the influence of intrapsychic and actual relations with others; the activation of self and/or object aspects by means of character traits in interacting with others implies the attribution of reciprocal roles to such persons. A rigid, pedantic, obsessive person forces persons with whom he interacts to adopt reciprocal attitudes (of submission to such perfectionism, of angry opposition to it, etc.). Significant others who do not let themselves be forced into such reciprocal roles may, under certain circumstances, influence the individual's character structure: this is, of course, maximally true in the systematic analysis of character in the context of a neutral psychoanalytic relationship.

In more general terms, the internal world not only shapes the perception of the external one but influences, by means of the character structure, the individual's interpersonal field. Some people have the capacity to bring out the best in others; other people bring out the worst. Human growth also involves to a great extent the reshaping of the internal world on the basis of interpersonal experience; the deeper the knowledge of the self, the deeper the knowledge of others. This phenomenon can be seen dramatically in the course of a psychoanalysis, when the distorted images of the past are changed gradually into a more realistic perception of the parents and an understanding in depth of their values and frailties. It is perhaps even more dramatic to see realistic reconstruction of the past occur after working through of the fantastic, highly distorted internal world of patients with borderline conditions.

INTERNALIZATION PROCESSES REVIEWED

In Chapter 1, I suggested that all processes of internalization of object relations refer to the internalization of units of affective state, object-representation, and self-representation. Following Erikson (1956), I considered introjection, identification, and ego identity as a progressive sequence of such internalization processes. In the case of introjection, object- and self-representations are not yet fully differentiated from each other, and their affect is primitive, intense, and diffuse. In the case of identification, not only is there a well-established separation between self- and object-representations, but there is an internalization of a role aspect of the relationship, that is, of a socially recognized function that is being actualized in the self-object interaction. The affective state is less intense, less diffuse, and, as self- and object-representations with, respectively, libidinal and aggressive investments are integrated, the spectrum of affect dispositions is broadened and deepened. In the case of ego identity, a more definite structuring of the internal world of objects takes place, as outlined above under stages 4 and 5.

Within this conceptualization, internalization is the broadest concept, encompassing the subordinate ones of introjection, identification, and ego identity. (Incorporation refers to the orally determined content of primitive fantasy formation implied in early introjections, but not to a specific process and structure in itself.) This view of introjection contrasts with its definition as a relatively advanced mechanism involved particularly in setting up the higher level superego structures or introjects. A review of the various definitions of all these terms throughout the psychoanalytic literature would go beyond our scope; the main reason for selecting the particular terminology derived from Erikson is its applicability to the basic definition of units of internalization I have proposed and to the developmental continuity of internalization processes.

Within this conceptualization, identification is at the same time the major process and its derived structure determining the vicissitudes of internalized object relations. Introjections may be considered primitive or immature types of identification, while ego identity may be thought of as the supraordinate integration of identifications into a dynamic, unified structure. In the broadest sense of the term, identification refers to a modeling of the self after an object. However, on the basis of the stages of development described, it appears that the modeling of the self after an object is the highly sophisticated, complex outcome of various processes in the intrapsychic and interpersonal fields.

First, identification presupposes an actual object relation in which the individual experiences himself as the subject interacting with another person. This relationship may be perceived in more or less fantastic or distorted ways, and it is under the impact of some predominant affective state linking subject and object. Libidinally or aggressively determined affect states constitute the primary motive for the internalization of this relationship, and, as noted before, affects and object relations are integrated as units in the internalization process.

Second, the internalization of the experienced interpersonal relation implies the building up of a self-representation and an object-representation linked by an affect disposition within the ego, and, at times, simultaneously within the superego. The shape of these object-and self-representations depends upon previous self- and object-representations and the extent to which such previous representations have been integrated. Thus, for example, an internalization occurring under the predominance of splitting mechanisms will be less discriminative than a later one occurring under an integrated self. Crude, dissociated "imitations" of the object may signal the completion of an identification embedded in a primitive ego structure, in contrast to the subtle, discreet modification of the self-concept with few behavioral manifestations characteristic of identification at a stage of greater ego integration.

Third, identification involves a modification of the self-representation under the influence of the object-representation: this phase accords with the definitions of Jacobson (1964) and Sandler et al. (1963). This aspect of identification depends not so much on the nature of the actual object relation and of the perception of self and object that is internalized as upon the extent to which the particular self-representation fits into the individual's overall self-concept. The pressure for radical modification of the self in terms of the object-representation may be greatest when splitting mechanisms are operative and intensive efforts are underway to preserve an ideal state of the self in the face of dissociated, aggressively invested object relations.

Fourth, identification involves the modification of ego functions and ego structures, particularly of characterological patterns constituting the behavior aspects of the self under the influence of the internalized object relation. In short, identification processes depend upon the stage of development of internalized object relations and the extent to which ego, superego, and id have crystallized as definite structures. They also involve a sequence of operations which may have various degrees of normal or pathological outcome.

Pathological identifications may involve one or several of the following developments. In regard to the first phase of identification processes, the projection onto the object of primitive superego forerunners or of repressed drive derivatives may affect the object relation to such an extent that a crudely distorted version of it is internalized. This is extremely important in the case of patients with severe superego pathology stemming from alterations in stages 3 and 4 of the development of internalized object relations. In the case of pathological refusion of self- and object-images characteristic of psychotic identifications (Jacobson, 1954), there may be a distortion of the second phase of identification. In this case, identifications are replaced by regressive introjections of an "all good" or "all bad" type, and, according to the degree of superego integration achieved at the time when such pathological internalization occurs, the preconditions for depressive or schizophrenic psychosis are thus established. The third phase of identification, namely, the modeling of the self-representation after the object-representation, depends, of course, on the normality or pathology of the first and second phases. A global modification of the self-representation under the influence of the object-representation, in sharp contrast to other, split-off aspects of the self-concept, is typical for borderline conditions. The consequence is the establishment of global primitive identifications often characterized by behavior which imitates the object, with the magical implication of maintaining or reestablishing an idealized (or persecutory) relationship. Pathology of the fourth phase of identification again depends on the vicissitudes of the earlier phases and is reflected in the development of behavior patterns and character traits of a conflictual nature. If superego integration has proceeded to a point where character formation very much reflects ego-superego compromises, a rigid reaction formation may ensue; if superego integration has not been achieved, contradictory character traits reflecting overidentification with certain models may ensue, side by side with acting out of opposite tendencies.

Normal identification implies (1) a partial modification of the total self-concept under the influence of a new self-representation, (2) some degree of integration of both self- and object-representations into autonomous ego functioning in the form of neutralized character traits, and (3) some degree of reorganization of the individual's behavior patterns under the influence of the newly introduced identificatory structure. "Behaving" like one's identificatory model depends on complex factors, perhaps the most crucial of which is the degree of integration of the self-concept prior to the particular identification involved. Behavior which simply "imitates" that of an external model is therefore not necessarily an indication of either normal or pathological identification with that model. Imitating behavior may reflect pseudoidentifications represented by "magical mimicry" of the object or primitive identifications—introjections—stemming from unconscious incorporative fantasies of properties of the object appropriated through the imitative behavior. In general, crude imitations of an object usually reflect primitive ego and superego conflicts in the context of the predominance of splitting operations in the ego, so that "foreign" behavior patterns can be copied without any real integration within the ego.

The final outcome of pathological identification processes is character pathology. The more rigid and neurotic the character traits are, the more they reveal that a past pathogenic internalized object relation (representing a particular conflict) has become "frozen" into a character pattern. Psychoanalytic exploration and resolution of character traits as they become transformed into active transference dispositions consistently reveal the activation of units of self- and object-representations linked by a particular affect disposition. At some times, while projecting a parental object-representation onto the analyst, the patient reactivates a self-representation in the interaction with that transference figure; at other times, while projecting the self-representation onto the analyst, the patient identifies himself with the corresponding parental representation. In addition, psychoanalytic exploration of character pathology frequently reveals that the internalized object relation is expressed not so much in the relationship of the patient with the analyst as in the intrapsychic relationship that arises between the patient's ego and superego.

For example, a hysterical patient, struggling with a conflictual identification with the powerful, domineering, threatening mother "introject" (a superego identification), is forced to repeat in her own interactions with her husband and children the same controlling and domineering attitude she hates in her mother. Under these circumstances, character traits of a domineering, controlling, sadistic quality may become activated in the transference, and the patient then appears to identify herself with her mother, treating the analyst as she felt her mother had treated her. At the same time, in behaving like her mother, she also actualizes a submission on the part of her ego to her mother image internalized in the superego. In this regard, it is the patient's superego introjection which now treats the patient's self as her mother had treated her. The establishment of character traits which are an imitation of this aspect of her mother represents an internalized submission to the superego, one aspect of the classical identification with the aggressor (A. Freud, 1936).

From this viewpoint, exploring the ego syntonicity or dystonicity of pathological character traits may be helpful in indicating the extent to which the organization of the self has been distorted by pathological superego pressures, the extent to which pathological splitting operations predominating within the ego permit contradictory identity formation to persist, and the extent to which the patient's self-concept corresponds to his actual behavior.

REFERENCES

Arnold, M. B. (1970a). Brain function in emotion: a phenomenological analysis. In: *Physiological Correlates of Emotion*, ed. P. Black. New York: Academic Press, pp. 261-265.

———(1970b). Perennial problems in the field of emotion. In: *Feelings and Emotions*, ed. M. B. Arnold. New York: Academic Press, pp. 169-185.

Bowlby, J. (1966). *Maternal Care and Mental Health*. New York: Schocken Books.

———(1969). *Attachment and Loss. Vol. I: Attachment*. New York: Basic Books.

Erikson, E. H. (1950). Identity and the life cycle. *Psychological Issues*. New York: International Universities Press, 1959, 1: 50-100.

———(1956). The problem of ego identity. *Journal of the American Psychoanalytic Association* 4: 56-121.

Fairbairn, W. D. (1952). *An Object-Relations Theory of the Personality*. New York: Basic Books.

———(1963). Synopsis of an object-relations theory of the personality. *International Journal of Psycho-Analysis* 44: 224-225.

Freedman, D. A. (1972). On the limits of the effectiveness of psychoanalysis—early ego and somatic disturbances. *International Journal of Psycho-Analysis* 53: 363-370.

Freud, A. (1936). *The Ego and the Mechanisms of Defense*. New York: International Universities Press, 1946, pp. 117-131.

Guntrip, H. (1961). *Personality Structure and Human Interaction*. London: Hogarth Press.

———(1971). *Psychoanalytic Theory, Therapy, and the Self*. New York: Basic Books.

Hartmann, H. (1950). Comments on the psychoanalytic theory of the ego. In: *Essays on Ego Psychology*. London: Hogarth Press; New York: International Universities Press, 1964, pp. 113-141.

———, Kris, E., and Loewenstein, R. (1946). Comments on the formation of psychic structure. *Psychoanalytic Study of the Child* 2: 11-38.

———, and Loewenstein, R. (1962). Notes on the superego. *Psychoanalytic Study of the Child* 17: 42-81.

Jacobson, E. (1954). Contribution to the metapsychology of psychotic identifications. *Journal of the American Psychoanalytic Association* 2: 239-262.

———(1964). *The Self and the Object World*. New York: International Universities Press.

———(1966). Differences between schizophrenic and melancholic states of depression. In: *Depression*. New York: International Universities Press, 1971, pp. 264-283.

———(1971). *Depression*. New York: International Universities Press.

Joffe, W. G., and Sandler, J. (1965). Notes on pain, depression, and individuation. *Psychoanalytic Study of the Child* 20: 394-424.

Kernberg, O. (1967). Borderline personality organization. In: *Borderline Conditions and Pathological Narcissism*. New York: Jason Aronson, 1975, pp. 3-47.

———(1968). The treatment of patients with borderline personality organization. In: *Borderline Conditions and Pathological Narcissism*. New York: Jason Aronson, 1975, pp. 69-109.

———(1970). Factors in the psychoanalytic treatment of narcissistic personalities. In: *Borderline Conditions and Pathological Narcissism*. New York: Jason Aronson, 1975, pp. 227-262.

———(1972). Early ego integration and object relations. *Annals of the New York Academy of Sciences* 193: 233-247.

———(1974). Further contributions to the treatment of narcissistic personalities. In: *Borderline Conditions and Pathological Narcissism*. New York: Jason Aronson, 1975, pp. 263-314.

Klein, M. (1934). A contribution to the psychogenesis of manic-depressive states. In: *Contributions to Psycho-Analysis, 1921-1945*. London: Hogarth Press, 1948, pp. 282-310.

———(1940). Mourning and its relation to manic-depressive states. In: *Contributions to Psycho-Analysis, 1921-1945*. London: Hogarth Press, 1948, pp. 311-338.

———(1946). Notes on some schizoid mechanisms. In: *Developments in Psychoanalysis*, eds. M. Klein, P. Heimann, S. Isaacs, and J. Riviere. London: Hogarth Press, 1952, pp. 292-320.

Kohut, H. (1971). *The Analysis of the Self*. New York: International Universities Press.

MacLean, P. D. (1969). The hypothalamus and emotional behavior. In: *The Hypothalamus*, eds. W. Haymaker, E. Anderson, and W. J. H. Nauta. Springfield, Ill.: Charles C Thomas, pp. 659-678.

Mahler, M. S. (1968). *On Human Symbiosis and the Vicissitudes of Individuation. Vol. 1: Infantile Psychosis*. New York: International Universities Press.

———(1972). On the first three subphases of the separation-individuation process. In: *International Journal of Psycho-Analysis* 53: 333-338.

———(1973). Personal communication.

Mayman, M. (1963). Personal communication.

Modell, A. H. (1968). *Object Love and Reality*. New York: International Universities Press.

Morgane, P. J. (1972). Panel Discussion. *Annals of the New York Academy of Sciences* 193: 302-304.

Olds, J. (1960). Differentiation of reward systems in the brain by self-stimulation techniques. In: *Electrical Studies on the Unanesthetized Brain*, eds. Ramey and O'Doherty. New York: Harper and Row, pp. 17-51.

Parsons, T. (1964a). Social structure and the development of personality: Freud's contribution to the integration of psychology and sociology. In: *Social Structure and Personality*. London: The Free Press, pp. 78-111. Also in: *Psychiatry*, 1958, 21: 321-340.

———(1964b). The superego and the theory of social systems. In: *Social Structure and Personality*. London: The Free Press, pp. 17-33.

Rapaport, D., and Gill, M. (1959). The points of view and assumptions of metapsychology. In: *The Collected Papers of David Rapaport*, ed. M. Gill. New York: Basic Books, 1967, pp. 795-811.

Sandler, J. and Rosenblatt, B. (1962). The concept of the representational world. *Psychoanalytic Study of the Child* 17: 128-145.

Sandler, J., Holder, A., and Meers, D. (1963). The ego ideal and the ideal self. *Psychoanalytic Study of the Child* 18: 139-158.

Schafer, R. (1968). *Aspects of Internalization*. New York: International Universities Press.

Schur, M. (1966). *The Id and the Regulatory Principles of Mental Functioning*. New York: International Universities Press.

Spitz, R. (1945). Diacritic and coenesthetic organizations: the psychiatric significance of a functional division of the nervous system into a sensory and emotive part. *Psychoanalytic Review* 32: 146-161.

Sullivan, H. S. (1953). *The Interpersonal Theory of Psychiatry*. New York: Norton.

Sutherland, J. D. (1963). Object relations theory and the conceptual model of psychoanalysis. *British Journal of Psychology* 36: 109-124.

———(1966). Psychoanalytic object-relations theory applied to the analysis of psychological tests. Presented to the Topeka Psychoanalytic Society, April, 1966. (Unpublished).

van der Waals, H. G. (1952). Discussion of the mutual influences in the development of ego and id. *Psychoanalytic Study of the Child* 7: 66-68.

Winnicott, D. W. (1955). The depressive position in normal emotional development. *British Journal of Medical Psychology* 28: 89-100.

———(1960). Ego distortion in terms of true and false self. In: *The Maturational Processes and Facilitating Environment*. New York: International Universities Press, 1965, pp. 140-152.

———(1963). The development of the capacity for concern. *Bulletin of the Menninger Clinic* 27: 167-176.

Wisdom, J. O. (1963). Fairbairn's contribution on object-relationship, splitting and ego structure. *British Journal of Medical Psychology* 36: 145-159.

———(1971). Freud and Melanie Klein: Psychology, ontology, and Weltanschauung. In: *Psychoanalysis and Philosophy*, eds. C. Hanly & M. Lazerowitz. New York: International Universities Press, pp. 327-362.

three

Instincts, Affects, and Object Relations

Has the time come to reexamine the possibility of relating psychoanalytic concepts regarding instincts and affects to new findings in such fields as ethology, neurophysiology, psychophysiology of affect, and general learning theory? My answer would be a cautious yes, with the hope that exploring the boundaries of psychoanalytic instinct theory may stimulate further developments in psychoanalytic scientific thinking and new ways of looking at clinical phenomena. This does not mean that recent findings (and fashions) in other fields should lead us prematurely to modify or abandon basic psychoanalytic hypotheses regarding instincts derived from what is now a long history of clinical findings. Also, such an exploration of boundaries should certainly not fall into the trap of relating physical findings to psychological phenomena in a mechanistic way.

My approach in this regard is an application of systems thinking, particularly that aspect of it which focuses upon the boundaries of hierarchically related systems (Miller, 1969). This conceptualization implies that biological systems are composed of dynamically organized subsystems and, in turn, constitute component systems of higher level or suprasystems. I propose that the units of internalized object relations constitute subsystems on the basis of which both drives and the overall psychic structures of ego, superego, and id are organized as integrating systems. Instincts (represented by psychologically organized drive systems) and the overall psychic structures then become component systems of the personality at large, which constitutes the suprasystem. In turn, the units of internalized object relations themselves constitute an integrating system for subsystems represented by inborn perceptive and behavior patterns, affect dispositions, neurovegetative discharge patterns, and nonspecific arousal mechanisms.

In order to avoid misunderstandings, it needs to be stressed that I am not proposing a neurophysiological model of the mind or a mechanical model of body-mind equivalence; on the contrary, the general implication of this formulation is that, at one point, neurophysiologically based functions constitute physiological units or "building blocks" which are integrated into a higher system represented by purely intrapsychic structures, namely, the primitive units of internalized object relations (self-object-affect units) referred to in Chapter 2. These units, in turn, constitute higher level "building blocks" for the hierarchy of purely intrapsychic structures, so that there is no simple mechanistic biological determination of behavior or simple body-mind parallelism involved in this formulation.

In what follows, I will examine the implications of psychoanalytic object-relations theory for the psychoanalytic theory of instincts and, in this process, attempt a reformulation of Freud's dual instinct theory. This reformulation will also attempt to integrate concepts of instincts developing within the biological sciences and recent findings regarding affects in psychoanalysis and general psychology with the vicissitudes of internalized object relations. This analysis will necessarily be sketchy and condensed but will, I hope, illustrate how psychoanalytic object-relations theory may contribute to the clarification of various crucial but not fully mapped areas in psychoanalytic theory.

There is a growing tendency in the field of ethology and neuropsychology to consider instincts as complex, hierarchical organizations of behavior centered on major drive systems (fight-flight, hunger, sex), determined not by a simple chain of physiological and behavioral changes triggered by specific external stimuli, but rather, in their very organization, by the integration of experience. In contrast to the older formulation as givens changed by the environment, instincts are now being conceived as organizations which, through learning, integrate various inborn patterns ("building blocks") into flexible overall plans. In what follows, I will apply this thinking to the generalization of observations included in Chapter 2 (dealing with stage 1 and 2 of early intrapsychic development). In human beings, the instinctive "building blocks" are inborn perceptive and behavior patterns which determine early attachment, inborn affect dispositions (represented by the combined activation of hypothalamic and other "reward" or "punishment" centers), the nonspecific reticular activating system, neurovegetative discharge patterns, and structured memory traces of increased extroceptive and introceptive perceptions. Erotogenic zones in this formulation represent specialized extroceptive functions linked to the activation of inborn behavior patterns.

Affect dispositions constitute the primary motivational systems which integrate the perception of (1) central (pleasurable or unpleasurable) states, (2) physiological discharge phenomena, (3) inborn perceptive and behavior patterns, and (4) environmental responses as they impinge on specialized and general extroceptive and introceptive perceptions. The earliest "self-object-affect" units are, I suggest, constellations of affectively integrated and cognitively stored perceptions of affective, physiological, behavioral, and environmental changes—perceptions within which the "self" and "nonself" components are as yet undifferentiated.

MacLean's model of three concentric brains (MacLean, 1967, 1972) is relevant to this conceptualization. He describes, first, a lowest or "reptilian" brain, which includes the primitive, mainly hypothalamic centers of "pleasure" and "unpleasure," together with the nonspecific reticular activating system and the control of inborn behavior patterns in the striatal complex. Second, he describes an intermediate or "limbic" brain, which includes the major "affective memory" structures (Arnold, 1970a, 1970b); I would suggest that this includes, at least functionally, those basic intrapsychic structures which incorporate internalized object relations in the context of primitive affect dispositions and the memory traces of reciprocal interpersonal behavior activated in the context of such affective states. Third, he describes the highest, neocortical brain, which relates to the higher level cognitive functions that, by implication, are less involved in early, affect-laden learning.

A general implication is that instincts in the human being develop gradually out of the assembly of these "building blocks," so that the series of pleasurable affect-determined units and the series of unpleasurable affect-determined units gradually evolve into the libidinally invested and aggressively invested constellations of psychic drive systems—that is, into libido and aggression, respectively, as the two major psychological drives. In other words, affects are at first primary organizers of instinctive components such as specialized extroceptive perception and innate behavior patterns and, later on, constitute the "signal" activator of the organized hierarchy of "instinctually" determined behavior.

How does this formulation relate to Freud's concepts of instinct and drive? Holder's analysis of "instinct and drive" (1970, pp. 19-22) highlights Freud's clear differentiation of biological *Instinkte* (reflecting an "inherited recognition of external situations") from the psychological "frontier concept" of *Trieb* (reflecting an "excitation occurring in an organ which subsequently may find a conscious or unconscious representation"). *Instinkte* are related more to self-preservation and are discontinuous, while *Triebe* represent a more continuous or cyclical stimulation. Comparing this formulation with the contemporary concepts of instincts derived from the work of Tinbergen (1951) and Lorenz (1963) (which implies that instincts constitute an integrated hierarchy of component systems or building blocks which, under specific environmental circumstances, release innate response mechanisms), one might conclude that the overall organization of *Instinkte* is the result of the ongoing influence of psychosocial learning on the activation of such component systems.

In other words, Freud's *Triebe* (which I prefer to translate "drives") may reflect the eventual hierarchy of the basic (mostly unconscious) psychological states which derive from partial, discontinuous, "instinctive" components (such as early specialized perceptions, affect states and innate behavior patterns) "released" in the fundamental "environment" of the infant-mother relationship. In this formulation, primitive affect dispositions embedded in a matrix of internalized object relations (primitive self- and object-representations, originally undifferentiated from each other and linked behavior perceived as reciprocal in the context of such affect dispositions) are the major organizers of the overall drives as general intrapsychic motivational systems: love and hatred and their predecessors and earliest expressions are represented by such primitive affect dispositions. The economic factor reflected in the intensity of instincts and their vicissitudes originally depends on the constitutionally determined intensity of affect activation and/or threshold of various inborn components of the original intrapsychic units, as well as on the pathological excess or absence of external stimulation (the extent to which there is or is not an average, expectable environment, a sufficient primary maternal function).

I will now examine some supportive formulations in the field of instinct theory and affect theory coming from both psychoanalytic authors and researchers in related fields. In reviewing this literature, I will attempt to clarify and develop further my thinking about the relationships among drives, affects, object relations, and overall structures of the mind.

Bowlby (1969, p. 38) characterizes behavior "that traditionally has been termed instinctive" as presenting the following four main characteristics: (a) a recognizably similar and predictable pattern in almost all members of a species; (b) a usually predictable sequence rather than a simple response; (c) a result usually contributing to the preservation of the individual or the species; and (d) a development often independent of the opportunities for learning it.

Tinbergen (1951, p. 112) defines an instinct as "a hierarchically organized nervous mechanism which is susceptible to certain priming, releasing and directing impulses of internal as well as of external origin, and which responds to these impulses by coordinated movements that contribute to the maintenance of the individual and the species." In the hierarchical organization of instinctive behavior, he suggests, higher level centers determine broad, "appetitive," exploratory behavior, which (depending upon the development of further external and/or internal stimuli) is followed by lower levels of hierarchical organization ending up in a level of the "consummatory act" characterized by rather fixed, rigid, behavior patterns of a relatively simple type. The consummatory act, Tinbergen suggests, is dependent on the centers of the lowest level of instinctive behavior, but appetitive behavior may be activated by centers of all the levels above that of the consummatory act and is highly dependent upon both "inborn releasing mechanisms" and learning. In other words, the higher instinctive patterns are purposive and adaptive; internal factors such as internal sensory stimuli, hormones, and complex stimuli stemming from the highest level central nervous system (that is, "motivation") either determine overt response or control the threshold of the response to external stimuli; external stimuli may, in turn, activate all these internal factors.

Lorenz (1963) considers the relatively fixed, functionally uniform behavior patterns constituting hereditary coordinations or "instinct movements" "independent building blocks" which can be integrated in various combinations according to the total internal and external environment within which the individual exists at a given moment. These fixed motor patterns, he suggests, have their own spontaneity and "inherently spontaneous function," which is usually increased or decreased by "the impulse of an exogenous stimulus or by another, independent endogenous drive" (p. 86).

Bowlby (1969), in contrast to the causal hierarchy system of Tinbergen, suggests another mode of hierarchical organization that gives a much greater flexibility, namely, a "planned hierarchy," as had been proposed in the work of Miller, Gallanter and Pribram (1960). Bowlby states (p. 78):

> In a hierarchical system of this sort, each plan and sub-plan is to be regarded as a set of instructions for action. As in the case of a military operation, the master plan gives only main objectives and general strategy; each commander down the hierarchy is then expected to make more detailed plans and to issue more detailed instructions for the execution of his part in the master plan. By leaving detail to subordinates not only does the master plan remain simple and intelligible, but the more detailed plans can be developed and executed by those with knowledge of current local conditions. With planned hierarchy there can more easily be flexibility. The overwhelming advantage of an organization of this sort is, of course, that the same set goal can be achieved even though circumstances vary over a wide range.

These formulations of Tinbergen, Lorenz, and Bowlby provide, in my opinion, an important frame of reference for reformulating psychoanalytic instinct theory in the context of object relations theory. Freud's formulation that the sexual instinct is made up of a number of component instincts which derive from erotogenic zones (Freud, 1910, 1912, and 1917-1918) implies a theory of instinct closely related to that of the ethologists' consideration of instinct as a hierarchy of integrated "building blocks," namely, inborn behavior patterns which eventually are subordinated to higher levels, purposive structures representing the broader "plans" of a certain overall drive. In Freud's formulation, genital libido occupies such a higher level hierarchical position, and the other (pregenital) sexual component instincts eventually are subordinated to and integrated with genital sexuality. I will suggest in Chapter 7 that pregenital erotic drives (related to oral and body surface erotogenic zones), genital drive derivatives, and aggressive drive derivatives all are organized within an evolving sequence of internalized object relations.

Let us examine once more the earliest levels of intrapsychic developments. As I proposed in Chapter 2, the affect dispositions of the units of internalized object relations carry out the major organizing function which originally separates "all good" from "all bad" internalized object relations and colors the specific interactions between self and object represented in these internalized self- and object-representations. When a baby gets hungry, he cries. When feeding starts, the crying response stops, and a general expression of relaxation and well-being replaces the earlier one of distress. After some time, when the baby is able to discriminate sensorial input and memories fixating feeding sensations have presumably become established, the baby may stop crying even before he is fed—for example, when the light goes on in his previously dark room. When the nipple touches his mouth, the hungry baby initiates sucking and swallowing behavior. Sucking is a final, "consummatory" behavior pattern. Crying, however, is not linked to feeding only but represents a behavior pattern which may shift into various subpatterns and be integrated with other instinctual series of behavior patterns related to fight and flight. Sucking, although less variable than the crying pattern, later may relate to other instinctual behavior patterns, particularly sexual ones. Thus we observe that inborn, relatively flexible behavior patterns serving instinctive needs appear originally to be activated by physiological imbalance. Later on, however, these same behavior patterns may appear in different (emotionally determined) contexts, in combination with different "instinctual series" of behavior patterns, and motivated by intrapsychic factors quite different from the original physiological disequilibrium which first triggered them.

From the viewpoint of the origin of the organization of intrapsychic structures, the physiological equilibrium upset by hunger (lowering of the blood sugar level→activation of hypothalamic centers involved in blood sugar regulation→persistence of the low blood sugar→activation of other hormonal and autonomic nervous system responses) cannot, on a purely physiological level, be reestablished. Presumably, at this point there occurs the activation of (1) hypothalamic hunger centers, (2) a general alerting response mediated by the reticular activating system, and (3) inborn behavior patterns involving general exploratory behavior and the crying response in particular. At the same time, a generally unpleasant, painful affective quality is presumably activated in "pain" or "punishment" centers of the hypothalamus and related limbic and mid-brain structures. A general amplification of multiple perceptions of the hungry baby (involving painful visceral sensations as well as the perception of his own activated behavior [crying]) is registered in limbic ("affective memory") structures. Thus, attempts at behavior regulation replace or expand the purely physiological mechanisms, and the components of this new, behavioral regulatory constellation are integrated into intrapsychic structures. Over a period of weeks, repeated experiences of this kind are integrated gradually into the memory of this situation. For example, when mother (by now expected) does not appear, the perceptions of darkness and cold, of increasing frustration and pain, and of increasing intensity and scope of crying and associated motor behavior are integrated into one experience under the affect "rage." In this context, rage anticipates the later, cognitively elaborated significance of this total experience in which intense, unpleasurable affect is linked with the perception of generalized motor and physiological discharge phenomena. As the baby cannot yet differentiate self from nonself, painful affect, painful visceral contractions, and the perception of a dark room belong to one, undifferentiated self-object representation—part of the prototype of the "all bad" self-object representation.

In contrast, the gratifying experience during the feeding situation builds up an affectively opposite "all good" self-object image. Under these circumstances, the baby experiences the activation of a "pleasure" or "reward" center within the hypothalamus or related structures, which provides a pleasurable coloring to the perception of the motor patterns of sucking and related attachment behavior, of touch, smell, and the intraceptive and proprioceptive sensations representing the nonspecific "coenesthetic" constellations of stimulus modalities activated during sucking and the swallowing of milk. Again, the child cannot yet differentiate between elements such as pleasurable bodily sensations, the perception of light, and the perception of mother's breast. This "all good" undifferentiated self-object representation is built up separately from the "all bad" one, and successive experiences of gratifying types elaborate this experience, leading gradually to differentiation of self, object, and affects within the perception. As the central nervous system matures, perception of the environment permits the infant to gradually differentiate mother's reciprocal behavior from his own and to arrive at more and more complex perceptions of the self and the object in each affectively colored situation. The baby's response to mother's behavior comes gradually under conscious control, thus modifying, elaborating, and enriching inborn behavior patterns. Pleasurable affects differentiate themselves further, from satiation pleasure to highly sophisticated specific enjoyment linked with gratification of particular erotogenic zones, of exploratory behavior, and eventually of new interpersonal needs; the infant's interpretation of the interpersonal relationship with mother determines new concepts of the self and of the object, including fantasy formation and symbolic interpretation.

The implication of all these formulations for the theory of affect is that affects constitute developmental series of subjective experiences, which start out from the primary undifferentiated states of unpleasure and pleasure, are continuously integrated with corresponding levels of perceptive integration (of neurovegetative and motor discharge phenomena) and cognitive interpretation, and are stored as "affective memory." As affects evolve, their discharge patterns decrease in importance, and the cognitive elements become more elaborated and subtle. Higher level cognitive structures are in a sense emancipated from the original matrix of early experience in which primitive affects and primitive cognitive structures are integrated as primary intrapsychic units. This definition implies (1) the conception of affects as both central states and discharge phenomena, (2) a rejection, on clinical grounds, of the existence of "pure" affects without any cognitive implications (although the cognitive implications of conscious affects may be repressed), and (3) the conception of affects as primary, inborn dispositions to qualitatively specific subjective experiences along the line of pleasure and unpleasure, "located" in the undifferentiated ego-id matrix out of which the early ego—and eventually the organized id, organized ego, and superego—evolve.

This conception, I think, is related to Engel's (1963, pp. 269-270) formulation:

> The earliest affect experiences are relatively undifferentiated and reflect basic biological tendencies which are more likely to be identifiable by their impact on the observer than by any data obtainable from the infant organism. Accordingly, we speak of these as the primal and undifferentiated affects. The primal undifferentiated affects indicate only satiety or need, pleasure or unpleasure, as communicated to the environment and within the organism. With the development of the mental apparatus, the progressive internalization of the environment, and the delineation of self and object representations, distinctive affect qualities evolve, differently experienced and variably reportable. These we refer to as the differentiated affects. While agreeing with Freud (1926) that the ego is the seat of all affects, it is worth noting that these distinctive qualities of the differentiated affects reflect differing aspects of drive, ego, and self-object activities, as Schmale (1958) first emphasized.

Neurophysiologists and psychologists, as well as psychoanalysts, continue to struggle within their respective fields with the implications of the controversy between the James-Lange theory of affect—namely, that affect is the perception of the bodily changes occurring during the activation of affective behavior patterns (in psychoanalytic terminology, affects are primarily discharge phenomena)—and Cannon's theory—namely, that the bodily changes are the expression of affects but neither their cause nor identical with them (in psychoanalytic terminology, affects are psychic tension states, although they may reach a level or intensity leading to discharge).

Brierley's (1937) review of the problem of affects in psychoanalytic theory and practice is, in my opinion, still eminently relevant. She pointed out that there has been a tendency to postpone the psychoanalytic exploration of affect theory because of unresolved problems in our instinct theory and suggested that "so far from waiting on the theory of instinct, we might reasonably expect that a closer study of affect would contribute to the solution of some of the problems of instinct" (p. 45). She criticized Freud's suggestion (1915b) that ideas are cathexes, while affects and emotions correspond to processes of discharge, the final expression of which is perceived as feeling. Brierley believed instead that affects are tension-phenomena reflecting a certain intensity of instincts, and she agreed with McDougall (1928) that various instincts give rise to qualitatively different primary affects. In this connection, it is of interest that McDougall stressed the importance of cognitive factors in differentiating "primary" feelings from "complex" feelings and the need for subjective exploration of this entire field.

Brierley also suggested that ego nuclei tend to coalesce in terms of similar emotional experience, and stated: "It is positively toned 'good' objects with their correlated 'good' body-systems which provide a stable core for the slowly growing me-system, the coordinated personal ego which seems to emerge about the second year" (pp. 51-52). She also pointed out (p. 54) regarding the dilemma created by the apparent existence of repressed affects:

> A certain paradox exists here in theory. By definition, the id is an unorganized reservoir of instinctual drives and yet the repressed unconscious, which always exhibits some degree of organization, is also attributed to it. It would seem that we should transfer the repressed unconscious to the primitive ego system. In dealing with affect we are dealing not only with impulse-object tensions but also with inter- and intra-ego tensions.

Rapaport's (1953) review of Freud's evolving theories of affect provides a fundamental clarification of the problems of psychoanalytic affect theory. He has discerned three phases. In the first phase (1894-1900) Freud "equates affect with the quantity of psychic energy, which was later conceptualized as drive cathexis" (p. 480).

Affect and libido were used interchangeably, and the affect of anxiety was explained as libido transformed by being repressed. The second phase of Freud's thinking (1900-1923) is characterized by the conception of affect as a motor or secretory function, that is, as a discharge phenomenon. Rapaport (p. 483) quotes Freud's paper on repression (1915a) where Freud states, "Affectivity manifests itself essentially in motor (i.e., secretory and circulatory) discharge resulting in an (internal) alteration of the subject's own body without reference to the outer world: motility, in actions designed to effect changes in the outer world." Within this theoretical formulation, drives are represented by ideas and affect charge: "We have adopted the term charge of affect for this other element in the mental presentation; it represents that part of the instinct which has become detached from the idea, and finds proportionate expression, according to its quantity, in processes which become observable to perception as affects" (p. 484). The third phase of Freud's theory of affects (after 1923) is related to the structural theory; affects now appear as ego functions, used as signals by the ego, and thus become structures. Rapaport points out that this third theory implies the recognition of innate "affect-discharge channels" (p. 498) and quotes Fenichel's summary of Freud's final theory regarding anxiety; namely, that anxiety is first experienced as a trauma by the ego, then becomes a danger signal, and, eventually, may again become an overwhelming trauma in the form of panic when the signal function fails. Rapaport reaches the conclusion that affects use inborn channels and thresholds of discharge and that they "arise as safety-valve functions when drive discharge by drive action is not possible because of the absence of the drive object in reality" (p. 505). He considers both affect charge and idea as drive representations and concludes that delays of discharge, enforced by reality conditions and achieved by defenses, bring about a damming up of drives which "makes for more intensive and more varied use of the affect-discharge channels and of the corresponding 'affect charges' " (p. 505).

Jacobson (1953) emphasizes that psychoanalysis has so far failed to develop a consistent affect theory and comments: "In fact, the development of the psychoanalytic drive theory appears to have halted our efforts to form equally clear theoretical concepts of the affects and their relations to the psychic drives" (p. 3). She points to the problems in the terminology in this field and suggests that the term "affect" might be reserved for the more violent states, such as rage or fear, and the term "feelings" to the milder and more enduring inner experiences, such as sympathy and pity, happiness, love and resentment. In analyzing the controversy between the tension concept and the discharge concept of affect, she points out that theories that consider affects to be tension phenomena or caused by a damming up of psychic energy seem to ignore the pleasurable nature of certain affects. She quotes Freud's observation (1924) that there are pleasurable tensions and unpleasurable relaxation of tensions, and that pleasure and unpleasure therefore cannot be referred to an increase or decrease of a quantity. Jacobson suggests that "tension pleasure may induce the urge for more intense excitement; climactic pleasure, the urge for relief; and relief pleasure, the longing for again experiencing pleasurable tension. . . . Wishing would always be wishing for pleasure, but it would represent a striving for cycles of pleasure having different qualities, alternating between excitement and relief; cycles corresponding to our biological existence and rooted in our instinctual life" (pp. 26-27). She concludes that "The pleasure and unpleasure principles would thus be subordinate to the superior, general constancy principle" (p. 29).

It seems to me that Jacobson's criticism of affects as "tension states" is correct, and, as she mentioned, it would be absurd to regard feelings of relief as tension phenomena. However, this argument does not invalidate the position of affects as central (or primary subjective) states, in contrast to the peripheral theories, which consider affects as primarily discharge phenomena. Jacobson's stress on the influence of internalized object relations on the vicissitudes of affects seems to me of particular importance (pp. 32-33):

> Thus, the development of self and object representations and object relations, of ego functions and sublimations, and of adult sexual behavior leads to the development of affect components with new qualities, which are then integrated with earlier infantile affect components into new units. These developments contribute at least as much as the taming power of the ego and superego to the constructive remodeling of the affects and affective qualities, to the molding of complex affect patterns, emotional dispositions

> and attitudes, and enduring feeling states; in short, to the enrichment as well as to the hierarchic and structural organization of emotional life.

Jacobson developed these considerations later on (1957b). In studying normal and pathological moods, she linked the vicissitudes of affect closely with those of the representation of the self and the object world. She considered moods "temporary fixations of generalized discharge modifications," that is, feeling states and discharge reactions which spread out and dominate the whole field of the ego for a certain period and are reflected in qualitative modifications of the concept of the self- and object-representations. Her formulations imply a conception of the ego and superego structures as derived from self- and object-representations, which, in turn, constitute major anchoring points of instinctual drive derivatives. Affects and moods are interpreted by Jacobson in terms of the instinctual conflicts among these structures that have been determined by object relations.

Peto (1967) suggests that affect mobilization under relatively nontraumatic circumstances is an intrasystemic event within the ego, an event which represents the signal function of affects. Beyond a certain intensity of the affect, or when the ego's affect control breaks down, affect expression becomes an intersystemic event; and the affect is reinforced by superego-induced affects and by affect components which are relatively direct drive representations. He suggests that, at this point, "a different shade of the same affect appears which is attached to a new group of images, thoughts, or self- and object-representations."

According to Sandler (1972), the mental apparatus functions to maintain a "feeling homeostasis," and the prime motivators are changes in feeling states. Drives, needs, emotional forces, and other influences arising from the body all exert their effects through changes in feelings.

It seems to me that while all these contributions clarify important clinical and metapsychological aspects of affect theory, they do not resolve satisfactorily the relationship between drives and affects, particularly in regard to questions about the nature of cathexes, the storage of affects as part of the repressed unconscious, and the relationships among biological instincts, psychological drives, and affect patterns. Brierley's and Jacobson's work, however, definitely point in the direction of the conception of affects as primarily subjective, "central" states rather than "peripheral" discharge phenomena. Also, while there seems to be general agreement with Freud's third theory of affect (particularly regarding anxiety), which conceives of affects as arising in the primary undifferentiated matrix of the psychic apparatus and evolving from primitive, violent, diffuse qualities into tamed signal structures with strong cognitive integration, the psychoanalytic literature on affects seems to convey a puzzled struggling with Freud's decision, at the beginning of the second phase of his affect theory, to separate the concept of drive cathexis from that of affect cathexis. Because he realized that efforts to relate biological findings directly to the new psychoanalytic discoveries would be premature, Freud was, at that time, also separating the concept of psychic drives from biological instincts. This led, it seems to me, to artificially separating biological instincts, psychological drives, and affects, so that affects now were two steps removed from their biological foundations. In clinical practice, however, affects have always been at the center of our interest, and, when dealing with patients, as Brierley (1937) pointed out, "whatever the object with which the analyst may be identified at any given moment, and whatever mechanism or combination of mechanisms may be responsible for the creation of the immediate transference situation, the transference relation is always and throughout an affective relation" (p. 55). Therefore, the task of again relating affects to the psychological correlates of biological instincts is a difficult but crucial one within psychoanalytic theory. Before pursuing this subject further, let us examine some recent contributions from general psychology.

Within general psychological and psychophysiological studies of affect, the modern tendency has been, like that of the psychoanalytic literature mentioned, away from the James-Lange theory and, following the work of Cannon (1927) and McDougall (1928), to considering affects as primarily central phenomena, that is, primarily subjective states, and as crucially involved in psychic motivational systems.

Young (1961) concluded from his experimental work that stimulation has affective as well as sensory consequences and that an affective arousal orients the organism toward or against the stimulus object. Affective processes lead to the development of motives, and the strength of the recently acquired motives is related to the intensity, duration, frequency, and proximity of previous affective arousals. The growth of motives is dependent upon learning, as well as upon affective arousals. Young suggests that affective processes can be represented along a bipolar continuum extending from negative, through indifferent, to positive values. He concludes that there are two dimensions of arousal—activating and hedonic—and points out that physiological studies are supporting these experimentally observed dimensions.

Tomkins (1970) proposes that affect systems constitute the primary motivational system and that drive systems are related to affect systems insofar as the latter simplify instinctive needs; biological instincts, the primary sources of psychological drives, operate through "signals" with their respective affective responses as "amplifiers." He suggests that just as the reticular activating system represents a nonspecific amplifier for sensorial input, affects represent specific amplification for drive signal input. For example, sexual excitement reflects affective dispositions rather than the direct intensity of sexual drives.

Pribram and his co-workers (Miller, Gallanter and Pribram, 1960; Pribram, 1970, 1971) suggest that emotions are "plans," "neural programs" which are activated when the organism is disequilibrated. Pribram states that, when for any reason the execution of cognitive plans implying action upon the environment is hampered, mechanisms of internal adaptation and control represented by emotional states, are activated. He goes on to say that this does not mean that all emotion is built into the organism and stresses that emotions are shaped by the experience of the organism. He classifies emotions into positive feelings (of "appetite" related to neurophysiological "go" mechanisms) and into affects proper (related to neurophysiological "stop" mechanisms). In general, he considers feelings to be monitors conveying the motivational urge of various drives toward planned action, and affects to be monitors conveying subjective motivation related to disruption of or escape from certain interactions. Of particular interest is Pribram's review (1971) of the relationship between neurophysiological mechanisms and emotional experience.

Fundamental contributions to the issue of the central versus peripheral nature of affects stem from Schachter's work (1970).

Speaking of the findings of his research on sympathetic activation and hunger, he concludes (p. 119):

> In sum, precisely the same physiological state—an epinephrine-induced state of sympathetic arousal—can be manifested as anger, euphoria, amusement, fear, or as in the informed subjects, as no mood or emotion at all. Such results are virtually incomprehensible if we persist in the assumption of an identity between physiological and psychological states, but they fall neatly into place if we specify the fashion in which cognitive and physiological factors interact. With the addition of cognitive propositions, we are able to specify and manipulate the conditions under which an injection of epinephrine will or will not lead to an emotional state and to predict what emotion will result.

Schachter also suggests that "a purely central theory of emotion or motivation seems as inadequate at coping with all of the facts as a purely peripheral theory." He points out that experimentally produced lesions in the ventramedial area of the hypothalamus (one of the feeding control centers) leads to hyperphagia and to extreme obesity in animals only when the available food is palatable. When the food is unpleasant, the experimental animals eat considerably less and grow thinner than control animals. "It would appear that this feeding control center operates in intimate interaction with environmental stimuli." Schachter suggests that the external circumstances of the stimulated animal play an extraordinary role in determining whether or not electric brain stimulation leads to emotional display. He concludes, "If we are eventually to make sense of this area, I believe we will be forced to adopt a set of concepts with which most physiologically inclined scientists feel somewhat uncomfortable and ill at ease, for they are concepts which are difficult to reify, and about which it is, at present, difficult to physiologize. We will be forced to examine a subject's perception of his bodily state and his interpretation of it in terms of his immediate situation and his past experience" (p. 120). It needs to be stressed that Schachter's questioning of a "purely central" theory refers to a neurophysiological centrality and not to the subjective centrality of affect I referred to in a broader sense before.

Leeper (1970), drawing upon his many years of work, rejects the traditional separation of emotions and perceptions: "Emotional processes are a more authentic paradigm of perceptual processes than are those simpler examples that usually are cited in chapters and textbooks on perception. I am proposing that emotions are basically perceptions of situations and that, commonly, they are long-sustained perceptions of the more enduring and significant aspects of such situations" (p. 156). He quotes recent neurophysiological evidence showing the interdependence of cortical and subcortical functioning both in cognitive activities and in emotional processes. He refers to work indicating that gustatory and olfactory perceptions usually have a significant affective quality and consequently tend to be important in the behavior of animals and humans. Ethological research indicates that animals have inborn emotional mechanisms that are touched off merely by signals indicating more favorable or less favorable circumstances. Leeper proposes, in summary, a motivational-perceptual theory of emotion, which, it seems to me, implies that emotions organize functional units of perception and are "perceptions of life situations."

Magda Arnold (1970a, 1970b; Arnold & Gasson, 1954) has contributed extensively to the psychological study of affects. In consonance with most recent workers in this field, she uses the term emotions as a general designation of this field. She summarizes (1970b, p. 176):

> We have now isolated two components of emotion: one static, the appraisal, which is a mere acceptance or refusal of the expected effect of the situation on us; another dynamic, the impulse toward what is appraised as good, and away from anything appraised as bad. Accordingly, the emotion becomes a felt tendency toward anything appraised as good, and away from anything appraised as bad. This definition allows us to specify how emotion is related to action: if nothing interferes, the felt tendency will lead to action. It also allows us to state how emotion is aroused: whatever is perceived, remembered, imagined, will be appraised; if it is appraised as desirable or harmful, action tendency is aroused. And as we appraise the situation as more desirable or more harmful, we become aware not only

> that we tend toward or away from it, but also that this is an emotional tendency.

In referring to the central-peripheral controversy, she states: "If emotion is a felt action tendency based on appraisal, it seems reasonable to assume that the physiological changes so impressive in emotion are ancillary to this tendency" (p. 178). In exploring the neurophysiological basis of emotion thus defined, she suggests that the "recall circuit" of the brain includes, together with modality-specific memory, an affective memory circuit and an imagination circuit. She suggests that appraisal via the limbic system initiates modality-specific and affective recall, as well as anticipation, via separate circuits. An action circuit (including the frontal lobe) which utilizes motor memory and motor imagination completes the constellation of circuits mediating emotion and action.

Arnold suggests that appraisal initiates the physiological changes as well as the emotion and that, therefore, every emotion is characterized by an integrated pattern of emotional expression, hormonal and physiological changes, and overt movement. But this integrated pattern may be activated not only by the cognitive appraisal of the environment but also by instinctive behavior reflecting a particular physiological disequilibrium (that also induces appraisal and desire and, therefore, emotion). The physiological state seems to be initiated by hormonal action; and, because emotions are always involved in instinctive behavior, they manifest the same physiological changes as instinctive patterns. This does not mean, however, that physiological patterns are the basis of emotion. Arnold concludes: "In summary, it is possible to account for the physiological changes in various emotions, and even to work out the neural circuits that trigger them. But only on the basis of a phenomenological analysis of the psychological activities from perception to emotion and action will it be possible to work out a theory of brain function that provides a neural correlate for psychological experience" (p. 184).

We have now come full circle: neurophysiological and experimental psychological research have reinforced the central theory of affects and stressed the importance of exploring subjective states, which, of course, constitute the primary field of psychoanalytic research. At the same time, ethological, neurophysiological, and experimental psychological research all point in the direction of the intimate connection between instinct, as presently conceived, and affects. This strengthens the need for reexamining the relationship of instinct and affect in psychoanalytic theory. The general conceptualization I suggested at the beginning of this chapter represents such an effort.

To summarize, my general proposal is that affects represent inborn dispositions to a subjective experience in the dimension of pleasure and unpleasure; that they are activated simultaneously with inborn behavior patterns, which elicit reciprocal environmental (mothering) reactions, and with general arousal, which increases the perception of external and internal stimuli occurring during this interaction; and that all of this leads to the fixation of memory traces in a primitive, "affective memory" constellation or unit incorporating self components, object components, and the affect state itself. Differentiation of affect occurs in the context of the differentiation of internalized object relations; these original units integrate affective and cognitive functions, and affect and cognition at first evolve jointly, only to differentiate much later into specific, higher levels of cognitive functions with relatively little affective participation and higher level affective functions with complex cognitive implications. Pleasurable and painful affects are the major organizers of the series of "good" and "bad" internalized object relations and constitute the major motivational or drive systems which organizes intrapsychic experience. Libido and aggression are not external givens in this development but represent the overall organization of drive systems in the general polarity of "good" and "bad." Affect states first determine the integration of both internalized object relations and the overall drive systems; later, affect states signal the activation of the drive and represent it in the context of the activation of specific internalized object relations. Libido and aggression represent the two overall psychic drives which integrate instinctive components and the other building blocks first consolidated in units of internalized object relations.

REFERENCES

Arnold, M. B. (1970a). Brain function in emotion: a phenomenological analysis. In: *Physiological Correlates of Emotion,* ed. P. Black. New York: Academic Press, pp. 261-285.

———(1970b). Perennial problems in the field of emotion. In: *Feelings and Emotions,* ed. M. B. Arnold. New York: Academic Press, pp. 169-185.

Arnold, M. B., and Gasson, J. A. (1954). Feelings and emotions as dynamic factors in personality integration. In: *The Nature of Emotion,* ed. M. B. Arnold. Baltimore: Penguin Books, 1969, pp. 203-221.

Bowlby, J. (1969). *Attachment and Loss, Vol. 1: Attachment.* New York: Basic Books, Inc.

Brierley, M. (1937). Affects in theory and practice. In: *Trends in Psychoanalysis.* London: Hogarth Press, 1951, pp. 43-56.

Cannon, W. B. (1927). The James-Lange theory of emotion. In: *The Nature of Emotion,* ed. M. B. Arnold. Baltimore: Penguin Books, 1969, pp. 43-52.

Engel, G. L. (1963). Toward a classification of affects. In: *Expression of the Emotions in Man,* ed. P. H. Knapp. New York: International Universities Press, pp. 266-299.

Freud, S. (1910). A special type of choice of objects made by men. *Standard Edition* 11: 163-175.

———(1912). On the universal tendency to debasement in the sphere of love (contributions to the Psychology of Love II). *Standard Edition* 11: 178-190.

———(1915a). Repression. *Standard Edition* 14: 141-158.

———(1915b). The unconscious. *Standard Edition* 14: 159-215.

———(1917-1918). The taboo of virginity (contributions to the Psychology of Love III). *Standard Edition* 11: 192-208.

———(1926). Inhibitions, symptoms and anxiety. *Standard Edition* 20: 87-156.

Holder, A. (1970). Instinct and drives. In: *Basic Psychoanalytic Concepts of the Theory of Instincts, Vol. III,* ed. H. Nagera. New York: Basic Books, pp. 19-22.

Jacobson, E. (1953). On the psychoanalytic theory of affects. In: *Depression.* New York: International Universities Press, 1971, pp. 3-47.

Leeper, R. W. (1970). The motivational and perceptual properties of emotions as indicating their fundamental character and role. In: *Feelings and Emotions*, ed. M. B. Arnold. New York: Academic Press, pp. 151-185.

Lorenz, K. (1963). *On Aggression*. New York: Bantam Books.

MacLean P. D. (1967). The brain in relation to empathy and medical education. *Journal of Nervous and Mental Disease* 144: 374-382.

———(1972). Cerebral evolution and emotional processes: new findings on the striatal complex. *Annals of the New York Academy of Sciences* 193: 137-149.

McDougall, W. (1928). Emotion and feeling distinguished. In: *The Nature of Emotion*, ed. M. B. Arnold. Baltimore: Penguin Books, 1969, pp. 61-66.

Miller, G. A., Gallanter, E., and Pribram, K. H. (1960). *Plans and the Structure of Behavior*. New York: Holt, Rinehart & Winston.

Miller, J. G. (1969). Living systems: basic concepts. In: *General Systems Theory and Psychiatry*, ed. W. Gray, F. J. Duhl, and N. D. Rizzo. Boston: Little, Brown, pp. 51-133.

Peto, A. (1967). On affect control. In: *The Psychoanalytic Study of the Child*. New York: International Universities Press, 1971, 22: 36-51.

Pribram, K. H. (1970). Feelings as monitors. In: *Feelings and Emotions*, ed. M. B. Arnold. New York: Academic Press, pp. 41-53.

———(1971). *Languages of the Brain*. New Jersey: Prentice-Hall.

Rapaport, D. (1953). On the psychoanalytic theory of affects. In: *The Collected Papers of David Rapaport*, ed. M. M. Gill. New York: Basic Books, 1967, pp. 476-512.

Sandler, J. (1972). The role of affects in psychoanalytic theory, physiology, emotion and psychosomatic illness. *A Ciba Foundation Symposium*, London, April.

Schachter, S. (1970). The assumption of identity and peripheralist-centralist controversies in motivation and emotion. In: *Feelings and Emotions*, ed. M. B. Arnold. New York: Academic Press, pp. 111-121.

Schmale, Jr., A. H. (1958). Relationship of separation and depression to disease. *Psychosomatic Medicine* 20: 259-277.

Tinbergen, N. (1951). An attempt at synthesis. In: *The Study of Instinct*. New York: Oxford University Press, pp. 101-127.

———(1957b). Normal and pathological moods: their nature and functions. In: *Depression*. New York: International Universities Press, 1971, pp. 66-106.

Kernberg, O. (1972). Early ego integration and object relations. *Annals of the New York Academy of Sciences* 193: 233-247.

Tomkins, S. S. (1970). Affect as the primary motivational system. In: *Feelings and Emotions*, ed. M. B. Arnold. New York: Academic Press, pp. 101-110.

Young, P. T. (1961). Affective processes: In: *The Nature of Emotion*, ed. M. B. Arnold. Baltimore: Penguin Books, 1969, pp. 222-237.

four

A Historical Overview

SOME IMPLICATIONS FOR PSYCHOANALYTIC METAPSYCHOLOGY

The general proposals I have formulated in Chapter 3 (regarding instinctual or drive development, the relationship between instincts and affects, and internalized object relations as major organizers of instinctive development and structure formation) seem to me to be in harmony with Freud's dual instinct theory, namely, the theory of libido and aggression as the two major instincts. The stress here is on "libido" and "aggression," in contrast to what Heimann and Valenstein (1972) have called "Freud's most speculative venture into global theory, i.e., his speculative superordinal proposition of two classes of primal drives, namely the life and death instincts, later called by Freud the primary forces of life and death" (p. 33). I am not aware of any evidence from psychoanalysis or any related science which would justify calling libido and aggression "life" and "death" instincts.

Libido and aggression arise out of the undifferentiated matrix common to the ego and the id. These two intrapsychic drives are organized under the influence of the developing internalized object relations, which, in turn, are integrated (starting from the original units described) under the organizing influence of affects. This formulation may clarify various psychoanalytic notions, such as the fusion of instincts. It seems to me that the mechanism of fusion of instincts and of the related processes of "neutralization," which were studied so extensively by Hartmann, may be considered fusion and integration of opposite affect dispositions (which, in essence, reflect aspects of libido and aggression) as part of the integration of opposite self-images and their respective object representations at the various stages of development outlined in Chapter 2. In short, it is the integration of internalized object relations (or rather, of polar opposite units of such internalized object relations) which brings about fusion of affect dispositions and a broadening and deepening of the affect dispositions available to the ego. In this way, the overall organizations of libido and aggression are intimately related. I shall illustrate one aspect of these developments in my analysis of how skin eroticism is transmuted into tenderness (Chapter 7).

My formulations are also in agreement with the general definitions of the metapsychological viewpoints offered by Rapaport and Gill (1959). Their concept of structure, detailed under the heading "The Structural Point of View" (pp. 802-804), seems relevant here. They stress the structural implications of inborn channels and thresholds of affect discharge and, more generally, follow Hartmann in including early intrapsychic structures as component elements of ego, id, and superego (the definite overall structures of intrapsychic reality). I think the structuralization of internalized object relations constitutes a major determinant of the overall structures of the mind.

My analysis also implies that primary process functioning, a general characteristic of earliest development, precedes the establishment of the id as an integrated structure, a viewpoint compatible with Hartmann's conception of the primary undifferentiated matrix out of which ego and id evolve. Also, Arlow and Brenner's analysis of the primary and secondary processes (1964, Chapter 7) arrives at conclusions regarding the characteristics of the primary process which seem to me in agreement with my general formulation. I refer here to their stress on the fact that no sharp line of demarcation can be drawn between primary and secondary process phenomena, that primary and secondary processes are not identical with thinking, and that the concept of time appears only gradually in the course of ego maturation. However, I am in disagreement with their general definition of the primary process as "mobility of instinctual cathexes and their tendency to rapid discharge" (p. 90). In this connection, "timelessness" as a characteristic of primary process functioning needs to be reexamined from the viewpoint of internalization of object relations. Hartocollis (1972) has recently proposed that the development of psychological time depends on the integration of internal representations of self and object, on the one hand, and of elementary ego apparatuses and functions, on the other.

Primary process, in my conception, corresponds to the characteristics of mental functioning during the early phases of integration of object relations, particularly stages 2 and 3. Primary process includes the characteristics of earliest cognitive functions, of earliest affective functions, and the rapid shifts and displacements of primitive affects over various self- and object-representations, which derive from the primitive units of self- and object-representation under the predominance of primitive affect dispositions. In other words, it is characterized by certain traits of primitive cognition and primitive affect and certain self and object "linkages" which reflect a primitive intrapsychic relation between self- and object-representations rather than the realistic relation of the self to external objects of later phases of development.

I have stressed that the earliest intrapsychic experience integrates affect and cognition in the context of the earliest units of internalized object relations. We cannot, therefore, speak of "pure affect" or "pure primary process thinking" as independent aspects of primary process functioning. This viewpoint is supported by the recent work of Ross (1975) and Spitz (1972). Spitz states: "(1) I believe that no memory trace can be stored in the psychic system without involving affect at some point; (2) that perception in the sense of the possibility of the perceived becoming conscious cannot take place without the intervention of affect." And later: "For the newborn to cross the river at all, affect must quicken the percept. The percept can only acquire existence after affect has endowed it with duration, with biological time. Only then can cohesion develop as a bond between percept and percept, as well as between percept and affect" (pp. 731, 733-734).

Moore (1968) has further contributed to the understanding of affect development along these lines, particularly by exploring the relationships between affects and neurophysiological functions, on the one hand, and between affects and the development of early object relations and drives, on the other. He stresses the importance of the limbic system, with its connections to the hypothalamus and the cortex, in dealing with the physiological and, later, affective tension and discharge that precede the differentiation of ego and id from their undifferentiated matrix. He suggests that in the initial stages just after birth, Freud's original formulation in which affects are equated with drive cathexes "might well apply" and concludes, "In this early period, therefore, drive representation can only take the form of physiological discharge, and motor behavior and ideation lag considerably behind the development of affective expression." Moore also points out that object relations contribute crucially to the ontogenesis of emotional expression, proposing that "with structural differentiation, we might speak of an affective system or apparatus, which has both an afferent and efferent function, having to do with affect perception, on the one hand, and with the utilization of the affect charge, on the other." These formulations and his elaborations of them in his presentation to the 1973 Panel on Affects (Moore, 1973) are quite close to the general theoretical model I proposed in Chapter 3.

Brenner (1974a, 1974b) suggests that the entire range of subjective emotional experiences of later life derives from feelings of pleasure or unpleasure, or from mixtures of the two, and that "what has been referred to by many writers as taming of the affects, or their modulation, by the progress of ego development in later childhood and adult life, is just this process of increasingly complex and varied ideational content associated with experiences of pleasure or unpleasure as the result of ego maturation and development. . . . Pleasure and unpleasure are, as it were, biological givens in an infant's psychological development, . . . the undifferentiated matrix from which the entire gamut of the affects of later life develop" (1974b, p. 7). Brenner also stresses the ongoing importance of ego development, particularly the development of structural aspects of the ego, in the differentiation of affects and implies that affects and ideas cannot be separate in their origin: ideas are essential aspects of affect.

Knapp (1963) has also stressed the intimate relationship between emotional and cognitive (especially symbolic) functions. After pointing out that emotions are also related to objects in the environment, he examines the relationship between the concepts of emotion and drive. He states:

> The concept of emotion and the concept of drive embrace a continuum, an observation which Novey (1959) has also made. The notion of "psychic energy," stemming from instincts so remote as to be almost mystical, is being re-

> placed in the minds of many by the ethological conception of instinctual drives as inherent, neurologically organized patterns of behavior. Even so, the scope of the term "drive" is wide. It may refer to processes of long-term mobilization or readiness for action. One thus speaks of a person as having strong sexual or aggressive drives. The concept can also connote emergent manifestations, the immediate accumulation of "tension" preceding overt expression. It becomes a matter of precise language for a speaker to indicate what phenomenon of drive or affect he means, whether something in the hierarchy of broad motivational tendencies, or some actual process of arousal, with or without conflict, or some progressively more rarified cognitive impression of one of the preceding. Such a view would fit emotional responses along a scale running from the more to the less differentiated, not necessarily paralleling a similar, continuum of "ideas."

My formulations imply that cathexes are, first of all, affective cathexes, that is, the quantitative element or economic factor involved in the intensity of primitive affect dispositions, which are activated in the context of primitive units of internalized object relations and constitute the organizers of such primitive units. Gradually, as these units become more complex structures within the ego, and, eventually, differentiate into ego, id and superego (the overall psychic structures), affects also differentiate; their quantitative or economic aspects become intimately linked with the overall organization of motivational systems or drives into the libido series and the aggression series. However, it needs to be kept in mind that the overall psychic manifestations of instincts or drives represent the organization of internalized object relations while incorporating affective and cognitive elements in them, so that the intensity of the drive depends upon the state of activation of an entire intrapsychic system rather than simply upon "instinct," or even a "pure" affect (without cognitive or object relation elements).

Affects have a crucial function in signaling the predominant quality of libidinal, aggressive, or combined libidinal-aggressive motivational systems, but their quantitative elements or cathexes depend more and more on a person's total interpretation of the immediate affective arousal in terms of its meaning for self and object, in terms of ego values and superego pressures, etc. Therefore, it seems to me most practical to use the term *cathexis* when referring to the function of affects as indicators of predominant motivational systems, with the understanding that, originally, cathexes were almost "pure" affective cathexes. Eventually, the affect has more of a signal function, indicating the intensity of the overall motivational system rather than the intensity of an instinct not related to internalized object relations or higher cognitive functions.

In short, one might say that cathexes are at first affect cathexis and have a crucial function in organizing overall instincts as psychic drive systems; eventually, cathexes become instinctual or drive cathexes, indicating by means of a predominant affective state the intensity and type of overall motivational system that prevails in a certain situation. From a different viewpoint, one may say that affects organize internalized object relations into the overall structures of the mind and, simultaneously, organize aggression and libido as the major drives. Affects are the element of psychic experience which remains closest to the biological sources of psychic functioning. Biologically determined intensities of affects can be channeled into ever more complex intrapsychic motivational systems, but there is no direct relationship between biological pressure and psychic functioning. Like the environment, the information stemming from the physiological sub-strata of the mind is interpreted in terms of intrapsychic structures.

The conceptualization I have proposed may help clarify our understanding of the stages of development of both aggression and libido. In general terms, I have suggested that internalized object relations (organized around primitive affect) serve as the earliest guiding principles or general organizers channeling inborn behavior patterns into drive systems centering on self- and object-representations. This viewpoint, it seems to me, is compatible with Hartmann's (1948) suggestion that, for the human being, sex and aggression do not serve self-preservation or species-preservation directly but enter into structures, especially the ego, to serve the functions of self-preservation and adaptation. He has noted that the prolonged helplessness of the young human being leads to the ego's taking on many of these functions, which in other species are carried out by instincts. I would add that the condensation of aggression and libido into internalized object relations constitutes the intrapsychic structuring of instinctual needs in terms of man's social nature. Thus, the channeling of aggression into the matrix of the psychic apparatus from which the ego and the self develop serves a biologically protective function; prolonged infantile dependency determines the need to channel aggression predominantly into internalized self- and object-representations rather than to discharge it externally onto the mothering figure. This inward direction of aggression is normally elaborated in stable internalized object relations, particularly within the ego and the superego, thereby guaranteeing the successful neutralization of aggression. The failure of this adaptive intrapsychic channeling of aggression may be considered, in broad terms, one reason for self-destructiveness in man.

This conceptualization may also clarify the nature of narcissism as a major motivational system. Since this issue has been explored in earlier work (Kernberg, 1970, 1974), I will limit myself here to a summary statement of my position. In agreement with Hartmann (1950), I think the term *narcissism* should be reserved to the normal and pathological vicissitudes of the libidinal investment of the self. Therefore, one cannot analyze narcissism as if it were a drive existing separately from internalized object relations or affect dispositions. I disagree with Kohut (1971), who thinks that narcissism is defined "not by the target of the instinctual investment (i.e., whether it is the subject himself or other people) but by the nature or quality of the instinctual charge" (p. 26). I do not think there exists such a thing as the nature or quality of instinctual (in this case, libidinal) charges unrelated to the respective development of affects and internalized object relations. The normal or pathological nature of narcissism depends upon the normal or pathological nature of the self and its component elements, which, in turn, are intimately related to the normal or pathological nature of internalized objects and their component object-representations.

The developmental model proposed in Chapter 2 is based upon the work of Jacobson (1964), Mahler (1968), and van der Waals (1965), which indicates the intimate connection between investment in the self and investment in objects. This connection derives from their conclusions that self- and object-representations stem from a common, undifferentiated self-object representation out of which narcissistic and object investment develop simultaneously. Also, insofar as pathological narcissism is characterized by a pathological self structure which has defensive functions against underlying conflicts involving both love and aggression (and related internalized object relations reflecting such conflicts), one cannot divorce the study of normal and pathological narcissism from the vicissitudes of both libidinal and aggressive drives (Kernberg, 1974).

In short, in contrast to the traditional psychoanalytic view in which a narcissistic investment of libido comes first and an object investment of libido only later, and in contrast to Kohut's view that narcissistic investment and object investment start out together but then evolve independently, I think that the development of normal and pathological narcissism always involves the relationship of the self to object-representations and external objects, as well as the struggle between love and aggression. There is an ever-present dyadic, polar quality of human experience (which may be played out temporarily in purely intrapsychic terms): a polarity which involves simultaneously self and object, love and aggression.

REVIEW OF LITERATURE ON OBJECT-RELATIONS THEORY

I will limit the comparison of my formulations on object-relations theory to those whose authors subscribe to the restricted definition proposed in Chapter 2.

Psychoanalytic object-relations theory stems from Freud's work, specifically from his structural theory as presented in "The Ego and the Id" (Freud, 1923). In a much-quoted statement, Freud said, "The character of the ego is a precipitate of abandoned object cathexis and . . . contains a record of past object choices. . . . The effects of the first identifications in early childhood will be profound and lasting." In the same paper, in analyzing the origin of the superego, he again stressed the importance of internalized object relations in determining psychic structure: "This leads us back to the origin of the ego ideal; for behind [it] there lies hidden the first and most important identification of all, the identification with the father. . . . The superego is, however, now merely a deposit left by the earliest object choices of the id; it also represents an energetic reaction formation against those choices." Thus, the origins of both the ego and the superego are linked with the precipitates of past object relations. I would add that the origin of the id as an integrated structure is also linked with these precipitates. In some of his last writings, Freud (1927, 1938, and 1940) pointed to the phenomenon of ego splitting as a puzzling division of the ego which can be observed in perversions and other psychopathological conditions; this phenomenon later became a nodal point in the development of object-relations theory.

Melanie Klein's contributions to object-relations theory are intimately linked with her general theoretical and technical approach. From the late 1920s to 1946, when she wrote "Notes on Some Schizoid Mechanisms" (which represents the consolidation of her theoretical position), she stressed the importance of very early internalized object relations in determining the vicissitudes of intrapsychic conflict and psychic structures (Segal, 1964). In the late 1920s and early 1930s, she stressed the importance of pregenital aggression, especially oral sadism, in determining fantastic primitive internal objects and the basic structure of the superego. Her theories gradually evolved toward the description of the vicissitudes of aggression and libido as being intimately linked with, respectively, "bad" and "good" internal objects. She described (1934, 1940, 1946) a series of defensive mechanisms by which the early ego tries to deal with bad internal objects and bad external objects, especially splitting and projective identification. Thus, Melanie Klein linked psychoanalytic instinct theory with early object relations and early constellations of defensive operations. These constellations were the paranoid-schizoid and the depressive positions.

I have already reviewed (1969) the Kleinian school from an ego psychological viewpoint and will stress here only the following issues. (1) Melanie Klein fully accepted the problematic concept of the death instinct. She saw the death instinct as the basic content of anxiety and as the force determining early projective mechanisms to protect the ego from its effects. I consider this an unwarranted extension of Freud's speculative hypothesis regarding a death instinct and a dogmatic statement not backed by any convincing evidence. (2) A second, related problem is that of the violent nature of primitive, especially oral, aggression: Is this aggression inborn, or is it a consequence of early frustration and deprivation? Kleinian authors stress the inborn, biological predisposition. While I agree that the inborn determinants of economic factors (that is, the intensity of the affective, behavioral, and other neurophysiological components which enter into aggressively determined internalized object relations, and general affective and cognitive thresholds) together with environmental influences crucially contribute to the organization of the aggressive drive, this is a far cry from positing an inborn death instinct. Also, Kleinians seriously underestimate the importance of environmental factors, specifically the vicissitudes of normal and pathological mothering. (3) A third issue is Melanie Klein's assumptions regarding highly complex psychic structures which are in operation at very early stages of development. In contrast to this view, I have stressed the gradual development of the various structures determined by object relations throughout the first few years of life.

Fairbairn (1952, 1963), after working during the late 1930s and in the 1940s with patients presenting serious schizoid features, contributed to the understanding of primitive object relations predating those which Melanie Klein had described under the heading of the "depressive position" in her papers on manic-depressive illness and mourning. He described in detail schizoid defensive operations, particularly splitting. In deference to his contributions, Melanie Klein changed the "paranoid" period of development (which predated the depressive one in her original theory) to "paranoid-schizoid position." Fairbairn considered the basic structures of the mind—a "central," a "libidinal," and an "antilibidinal" ego (roughly corresponding to the ego, id, and superego)—as deriving from the splitting of an original ego. He conceived these structures as split-off, internalized object relations. The central ego and its corresponding "ideal object," the libidinal ego and its corresponding "exciting object," and the antilibidinal ego with its corresponding antilibidinal or "rejecting object" represent a modification of Melanie Klein's conception of good and bad internal objects in terms of a structural theory. However, Fairbairn departed in radical ways from the Kleinian orientation which had influenced him. He objected to the predominance Melanie Klein gave to the death instinct and to instincts in general as determining object relations. He felt that the primary objective of the developing psychic apparatus is the establishment of relations with other human beings, originally with the mothering person. The ego, in his opinion, is primarily object-seeking and does not primarily seek instinctual gratification (Wisdom, 1963).

For example, Fairbairn saw the nature of sexual interest in objects as derived from the basic need of establishing loving relationships with others. In cases in which sexual excitement appears to replace an authentic interest in others, Fairbairn saw a particular deterioration of object relations rather than a regression to a more primitive, "purely instinctual" search for sexual gratification. He implied that the transformation of other human beings into purely sexually exciting objects is a pathological development, which may stem from severe early frustration of dependent needs and subsequent pathological schizoid developments in the ego. This analysis illustrates the stress in Fairbairn's theory on the ego's primary object-seeking qualities in contrast to traditional instinct theory. From a clinical viewpoint, he opened a new perspective: the need to examine conditions such as sexual promiscuity and, particularly, sexual deviations from the viewpoint of "part object" relations. In other words, the personality structure of patients who avidly search for sexual gratification from the bodies or parts of bodies of other people (while showing a remarkable incapacity to become engaged with other human beings in any consistent way) may reflect early structural distortions of the ego related to very early mother-infant conflicts rather than regressive defenses from predominantly oedipal conflicts and unconscious guilt about sexuality. The splitting of the ego that Freud observed in patients presenting perversions would, from Fairbairn's viewpoint, reflect early schizoid ego distortion.

Fairbairn rejected Freud's dual instinct theory and replaced it with a radical object-relations theory. Regarding the violent nature of primitive aggression, Fairbairn (1952, 1963), Guntrip (1961, 1968), and Winnicott (1960) stress the fundamental etiological importance of the presence or failure of what Winnicott has called "good enough mothering." Guntrip (1971) has recently extended Fairbairn's thinking into a total opposition to psychoanalytic instinct theory, denying in the process the importance of instincts in determining personality in general. I disagree with this view and certainly do not consider object-relations theory to be opposed in any way to the modern conception of instincts or to psychoanalytic instinct theory. It seems to me that Fairbairn himself leaves this question open when he says (1952, p. 167):

> Whilst 'impulses' necessarily involve object-relationships, they cannot be considered apart from ego-structures, since it is only ego-structures that can seek relationships with objects. "Impulses" must accordingly be regarded as representing simply the dynamic aspect of ego-structures; and there consequently arises a necessity for the replacement of the old impulse-psychology by a new psychology of dynamic structure. . . .

I also disagree with Fairbairn's basic model of the three major intrapsychic structures, that is, the exciting object-infantile libidinal ego, the rejecting object-infantile antilibidinal ego, and the ideal object-central ego. It seems to be that this model oversimplifies the structural development of internalized object relations, such as the successive structural levels determined by object relations (which constitute superego forerunners and are eventually integrated into the definite superego). This same criticism applies even more strongly to Kleinian formulations regarding the structures derived from internalized object relations. I would, however, stress the importance of Fairbairn's clinical analyses mentioned before, indicating that the pathology of sexual development is intimately linked with the evolving patterns of intrapsychic and interpersonal object relations (Chapters 7, 8).

Bowlby (1969), in his detailed analysis of early infant development, concludes that the infant's clinging, smiling, crying, etc., are instinctive components, which become integrated into a general instinct pattern of attachment. His hypothesis of attachment to mother as a primary drive contrasts with traditional psychoanalytic theory's consideration of the development of love as a secondary drive stemming from the need for nourishment and oral gratification. In this regard, Bowlby's theory might be considered a kind of object-relations theory, but, in contrast to Fairbairn's theory of primary object drive, Bowlby stresses the behavioral, actual interpersonal patterns, almost completely neglecting the intrapsychic buildup of structures reflecting interpersonal problems.

It is striking that in his book (1969) there are almost no references to the "internal world" and that only toward the end, after acknowledging the importance of this issue, does he state: "They are matters, however, that raise too many giant problems (and giant controversies) for it to be sensible to attempt to deal with them here. In any case, systematic research has only just begun and little that is firm is yet known" (p. 354). I do not find this neglect of instincts as intrapsychic developments and of internalized object relations as major structuring organizers of psychic reality justifiable.

At this point it may be helpful to examine briefly the concepts of "true self" and "false self" within the context of psychoanalytic object-relations theory. Winnicott (1954) and Guntrip (1968) have emphasized the existence of a false self—a superficial, socially oriented, basically inauthentic self (as opposed to the true self implying the integration of a person's conscious and unconscious internal world). From the viewpoint of the model proposed here, the existence of mutually dissociated or split-off ego states (related to nonintegrated self-object units) represents one basic precondition for the establishment of the false self. The chameleon-like adaptability of some infantile characters, the overdependency on immediate interactions (regardless of the discontinuity between such interactions and other present or past experience) seen in the "as if" character, and the malignant identification of the narcissistic character with a pathologically condensed ideal self-ideal object formation all represent different formations of such a "false self."

An authentic self can come about only when diverse self-images have been organized into an integrated self-concept, which relates, in turn, to integrated object-representations. Therefore, clinically speaking, the road to authenticity is the road to integration of mutually dissociated aspects of the self. There are many patients whose "true self" does not lie hidden under repressive barriers, but exists only as a potential, fragmented structure. This potential structure may become actual only after efforts at integration in the course of a psychotherapeutic relationship.

So far I have discussed the contributions to object-relations theory made by the British school. Members of the American culturalist school have also made contributions to object-relations theory. Harry Stack Sullivan, whose theory of the organization of personality centered on interpersonal relations (Sullivan, 1953; Mullahy, 1952, 1953, 1955), saw the person functioning in situations rather than in the expression of instinctual impulses. Situations, for Sullivan, were defined by people, real or imaginary. Thus, he proposed that in every concrete interpersonal situation each participant interacts with another in terms of his own past relations with others, real or imaginary. Sullivan pointed out the crucial importance of the early mother-child relationship in determining the central dynamism of the self or self-system. He described three types of early "personifications" which determine the structure of the self-system: (1) the "good me," the self developing in the context of good relationships with mother in the course of which mother is able (by means of her need-relieving behavior or tenderness) to bring about a feeling in the child that his self is a good one; (2) the "bad me," which comes about, Sullivan suggests, when the infant experiences his needs as rebuffed, or when a need for tenderness is not gratified by mother, and (3) the "not me," a dissociated, extremely painful and frightening aspect of the self-experience induced by extreme frustration or trauma.

Sullivanian psychotherapy stresses the need to solve negative distortions of the interpersonal field and relies on the natural growth tendencies of the patient to develop his personality under the influence of presently favorable interpersonal relationships. Psychotherapeutic cure is related to expansion of the self and to the decrease of parataxic distortions, anxiety, and dissociation.

My major criticism of Sullivan centers on his neglect of instinctive determinants of human behavior and his failure to elaborate a structural theory. Guntrip (1961) criticized (rightly, I think) Sullivan's neglect of the intrapsychic, unconscious conflicts related to internalized object relations; his stress on actual present and past interpersonal relations misses an important dimension of psychoanalytic object-relations theory. Sullivan did not clarify sufficiently the origin of "personifications." He lacked an elaborated structural theory, and numerous questions might be raised regarding functions and structures of the personality within Sullivan's system. However, his stress on the fundamental nature of interpersonal relationships as determinants of intrapsychic and interpersonal structures represents an important contribution to object-relations theory. His emphasis on cultural factors has found later support in Erikson's ego psychological analysis. Above all, his emphasis on internalized object relations as basic motivational systems, together with the direct application of this theory to the psychotherapeutic treatment of psychotic patients, has provided important clinical evidence for psychoanalytic object-relations theory. Frieda Fromm-Reichmann (1959), Otto Will, (1961, 1967), and Harold Searles (1965) have broadened Sullivan's theoretical and clinical approaches and carried them into the mainstream of psychoanalytic theory and practice.

Turning now to contemporary ego psychological approaches to psychoanalytic object-relations theory, the work of Erikson, Hartmann, Sandler, Mahler, and especially Jacobson have influenced my formulations. Various authors have pointed to the mutual relationships of the formulations of these theoreticians. Recently, Blanck and Blanck (1972) have highlighted some of the basic issues involved in these theories regarding early development, the origin of the ego, and processes of internalization and object relations.

Erikson (1950, 1956), in his formulations regarding ego identity, developed the subjective aspects of the ego as an important psychic structure. He defined ego identity as including a sense of sameness or continuity both in one's self and one's meanings for others. He described ego identity as developing out of yet transcending the integration of introjections and identifications. He stressed the importance of social roles as part of ego identity and the unconscious striving for the continuity of the individual's character and the inner solidarity with group ideals and group identity that it incorporates. Erikson describes ego identity as a configuration evolving in consonance with and under the influence of critical stages of development. What I wish to stress is the intimate relationship between three related structures: introjections, identifications, and ego identity. The clinical and metapsychological usefulness of an integrated conceptualization of these mechanisms instrumental in the development of the self and one's relation with others has influenced me in adopting Erikson's definitions of them as a starting point in my own work. After Erikson, it has become generally accepted that there are self-components in the ego and that the integration of different aspects of one's self is a special and important function and structure of the ego.

Erikson's (1963) thinking about drives, is, I believe, in harmony with my general position. He states (p. 95):

> The drives man is born with are not instincts; nor are his mother's complementary drives entirely instinctive in nature. Neither carry in themselves the patterns of completion,

> of self-preservation, of interaction with any segment of nature; tradition and conscience must organize them.
>
> Man's inborn instincts are drive fragments to be assembled, given meaning, and organized during a prolonged childhood by methods of child training and schooling which vary from culture to culture and are determined by tradition.
>
> To accomplish this, child training utilizes the vague instinctual (sexual and aggressive) forces which energize instinctive patterns and which in man, just because of his minimal instinctive equipment, are highly mobile and extraordinarily plastic.

Hartmann (Hartmann et al., 1946; Hartmann, 1950) clarified the relationship between the ego as an overall psychic structure and the self as a particular structure within the ego. He defined self-representation as the structure of the ego which expresses the self and contrasted libidinal cathexis of the self with libidinal cathexis of objects (object cathexis). Narcissism, Hartmann proposed, represents not the libidinal cathexis of the ego but the libidinal cathexis of the self. (This has been the starting point of my own analysis of pathological narcissism.) Hartmann and Loewenstein (1962) have reexamined the conceptual problems related to internalization, identification, introjection, and incorporation. It is of special interest that they described identifications as both the process and the result of fashioning one's self after other persons and that they considered the existence of identifications which are forerunners of the superego. This illustrates once again the growing agreement on the gradual development of the superego on the basis of internalization of particular object relations, which stem in part from a period much earlier than the classical oedipal one traditionally linked to the integration of the superego.

It is difficult to do justice in a brief review to the many crucial contributions of Edith Jacobson to the metapsychological and clinical aspects of psychoanalytic object-relations theory. She first presented a synthesis of her viewpoints in her 1954 paper, "The Self and the Object World," and later expanded and partially modified it in her book carrying the same title (Jacobson, 1964).

One of her crucial concepts is that out of an originally fused self-object representation gradually develop the separate representations of self and objects. The implication is that the investment of libido of this fused self-object representation represents simultaneously the origin of self love or narcissism and of object love, so that narcissism and object investment develop simultaneously. After the original differentiation of self- and object-representations, Jacobson suggests, excessive refusion of self- and object-representations creates a condition in which self- and object-representations cannot again be differentiated and in which, therefore, ego boundaries continue to be blurred and fluid.

Jacobson points out that such a regressive refusion as a defense against excessive frustration and rage, if prolonged beyond the early infantile stages of development, constitutes the prototype of a psychotic identification. A schizophrenic patient in intensive psychotherapeutic treatment, after an initial stage of noninvolvement, may oscillate between blissful states of merging with the therapist in an ideal, symbiotic relationship and of frightening states in which he sees himself and the therapist merged in murderous rage toward each other. The entire world of the patient appears contaminated by these polar affect states, which have in common an absence of boundaries between self and nonself.

The definition of ego boundaries, therefore, depends on the differentiation of self- and object-images and on an environment sufficiently gratifying to prevent excessive refusion of self- and object-representations. One type of fused self-object representation is at first invested only with libido, another type with aggression. Only at a later stage of development, Jacobson suggests, do "good" and "bad" self-representations merge and eventually bring about a more realistic, integrated representation of the self. Jacobson suggests that when more integrated self- and object-representations are developed, discrepancies between magical, ideal conceptions of the self and of objects and their realistic evaluations foster the development of ideal self-representations (in contrast to real self-representations) and ideal object-representations (in contrast to real object-representations). Ideal self- and ideal object-representations become forerunners of the superego; primitive "bad" (feared or hated) object-representations also are part of early superego forerunners, and only the synthesis of "bad" superego forerunners and idealized superego forerunners permits a more realistic evaluation of the parents' prohibitions and demands. These, in turn, become the more realistic superego introjections of the oedipal period. In more general terms, Jacobson analyzed the development of the superego from its earliest precursors to the superego consolidation at the end of adolescence. She described not only different types of self- and object-representations as they enter into the superego but also the relationship between such superego introjections and ego identifications, on the one hand, and the developmental stages and psychosocial experiences of the child, on the other. Jacobson's analysis of the superego is probably the most comprehensive study of the structure and functions of that psychic entity. The fundamental nature of Jacobson's influence on my own formulations must be evident to the reader.

Sandler and Rosenblatt, in "The Concept of the Representational World" (1962), further develop the relationships among the ego, self-representations, and object-representations. They suggest that one of the functions of the ego is the establishment of what they call the "representational world." The representational world may be described as a stage, in the center of which is the self-representation (stemming from the integration of self-images), surrounded by object-representations (differentiated out of the integration of object-images).

Sandler, Holder, and Meers (1963) clarify the relationship between the ego ideal and the representational world, contributing in the process to the analysis of various object-relations determined structures within the ego and the superego. Although I disagree with the definitions of introjection and identification formulated in that paper, their overall developmental outline clarifies crucial issues in what I have called (Chapter 2) stages 4 and 5 of development. In a later paper, Joffe and Sandler (1965) come close to the conceptualization which underlies my restricted definition of object-relations theory in stating: "One might say that for the representation of every love object there is a part of the self representation which is complementary to it, i.e., the part which reflects the relation to the *object* and which constitutes the link between self and object. We can refer to this as the object-complementary aspect of the self representation" (p. 399).

Mahler (1968) has made crucial contributions to the earliest stages of development of internalized object relations. In describing normal autism and autistic psychosis, and normal and pathological symbiosis, she highlights the consequences of normal and pathological development (in what I have called stages 1 and 2). The direct observational material about normal and seriously ill children presented in Mahler's work has contributed to bringing together clinical practice and theory of early development. From the late 1950s on, Mahler and her co-workers have described the so-called separation-individuation process of child development. From the 1960s on, Mahler described subphases of that process (1971, 1972, 1973), clarifying the mutual relationship between the mother-child interaction during separation-individuation, and the respective intrapsychic vicissitudes of self and object differentiation and integration. She sees the development of excessive aggression and pathological splitting of the representations of mother into "good" and "bad" as a consequence of pathological resolution of the rapprochement subphase of separation individuation, and as the core etiological factor in borderline pathology in children and adults. This corresponds quite closely to what I have described as the pathology of stage 3 of development: the borderline conditions. Recently, Lichtenberg and Slap (1973) have related my thinking regarding splitting mechanisms to Mahler's work. In the process, they have made an original contribution to the understanding of "splitting representations" as a factor in pathological intersystemic suborganization.

SOME FURTHER APPLICATIONS OF PSYCHOANALYTIC OBJECT-RELATIONS THEORY

Areas in which object-relations theory has provided important contributions are the recent psychoanalytic theory of depressive psychoses (Jacobson, 1971) and the theory of intensive, psychoanalytically derived treatment of schizophrenia. These psychoanalytic theories of schizophrenia have been applied in the psychotherapeutic approaches of Rosenfeld (1965), Searles (1965), and Bion (1967). It is interesting to observe that the Sullivanian approach of Searles, coming, as it does, from a theoretical background completely different from that of Rosenfeld and Bion, has evolved into technical formulations quite similar to those of these Kleinian authors. All three of them stress the importance of the analyst as a real person who has to tolerate uncertainty, lack of contact, and confusion for a long time before the psychotic patient is able to activate fully an infantile-dependent relationship in the therapeutic interaction. The first, "out of contact" phase, in Searles' terms, then gives rise to a highly shifting, symbiotic relationship in which primitive affect states are activated while the patient cannot differentiate himself from the therapist. The slow building up of tolerance of the therapeutic interaction, as the patient loses his fear over the destructive nature of his primitive rage, gradually permits a better delimitation of boundaries in the interaction between patient and therapist. Finally, a phase of integration may occur in the patient in which he can accept himself as an individual different from the therapist and integrate his loving and hateful feelings toward him.

My work with patients presenting borderline personality organization heavily depends upon object-relations theory. I have mentioned earlier how borderline conditions are characterized by pathological fixation at the stage of ego development after self- and object-images have been differentiated but before integration of libidinally and aggressively determined self- and object-images has taken place. From a therapeutic viewpoint, borderline personality organization requires special modifications of technique (Chapter 6). The interpretation of the predominant defensive operations in borderline patients actually strengthens ego functions, permitting repression and its related defenses to take over defensive functions previously held by splitting and its related defenses. The characteristic transference resistances of borderline patients can also be clarified on the basis of object-relations theory (Kernberg, 1968). On the same theoretical basis, I have proposed a psychoanalytic classification of character pathology which permits the discrimination of degrees of severity (Chapter 5).

In more general terms, the diagnostic understandings reached on the basis of object-relations theory may help clarify many complex and controversial clinical areas. For example, the differentiation of the normal emotional turmoil of adolescence from more serious disturbances related to an underlying syndrome of identity diffusion may be better understood from the vantage point of object-relations theory (Kernberg, 1975c, Chapter 8).

Dicks (1967) applied psychoanalytic object-relations theory to the diagnosis and treatment of marital conflicts. He proposes that chronic marital conflict involves mutual contradictions at several levels of interaction into which marital relationships can be broken down. He describes, as a first level, the social and cultural background and common interests which keep marriage partners together; as a second level, he describes the conscious personal expectations of their own and their partner's roles within the marital relationship; and, as the third level, he points to the unconscious activation of self- and object-images in both partners, reaching an equilibrium where the unconscious reciprocal roles which best fit their activated unconscious internal object relations are stabilized.

Dicks proposes that, if there is conflict within one of these levels but harmony at the other two, the couple will stay together, although in chronic conflict. If there is basic disagreement at two or all three of these levels, the marriage will usually end in divorce. Thus, for example, a marriage may last in spite of great discrepancies in the social and cultural background of the partners, if their conscious expectations of each other and the predominant unconscious self-object dispositions in their reciprocally activated roles are in harmony. Or, a couple in serious, chronic neurotic marital conflict may stay together because of their harmonious social, cultural, and conscious mutual role expectations and in spite of severe, unconsciously determined role conflicts. The treatment of marital conflicts can then proceed on the basis of direct diagnosis of conflicts at these three levels. What interests us especially is the diagnosis of the unconscious relationship reenacted in the reciprocal confirmation of unconscious self and object roles in the interaction and the diagnosis of the intrapsychic pathology on the basis of the unconscious interpersonal one.

Another application of object-relations theory has been to the diagnosis and psychotherapeutic management of small groups. Bion (1959) describes the curious development in nonstructured small groups when the group as a unit activates primitive defensive mechanisms in the members, especially in the context of predominance of conflicts around pregenital aggression. In other words, intensive regression may occur in nonstructured small groups and, by reciprocal activation of all its members, may bring about a total emotional situation remarkably similar to that of early stages of ego development. The theoretical implications of these findings have probably not yet been fully understood. It may well be that normal defensive operations sufficient for dyadic relationships break down in the face of multiple uncertainties within a group, or that group situations activate primitive instinctual urges and fears, the disposition to which is not resolved in the usual ways of individual character formation (Chapter 9). In any case, object-relations theory has allowed us to utilize these regressive group phenomena diagnostically and therapeutically (Rioch, 1970) and may prove an important tool in further exploration of group phenomena—for example, the potential for surprisingly rapid regression in unstructured groups and the outbreak of violence.

Kenneth Rice and co-workers (Rice, 1963, 1965, 1969; Miller and Rice, 1967) have applied Bion's findings regarding the regressive phenomena in small groups to the study of group processes within social organizations. They conclude that regression (toward what Bion calls "basic assumptions," implying the loss of rationality and a paralyzing ineffectiveness of the small group) occurs when certain administrative requirements linking the internal life of the group with its external environment are not met. They define the qualities for leadership of small groups, large groups, and social organizations which may protect the task of the group from the disorganizing, regressive features of such group phenomena. Rice broadened this analysis into a systems theory approach to human organizations, within which the intrapsychic conflicts and object-relations-determined structures of the individual, the unconscious and conscious conflicts of groups, and the functions and conflicts of the entire organization may be comprehensively studied. Object-relations theory, in this regard, may have important practical implications for the social sciences (Sutherland, 1963, 1969; Sutherland and Gill, 1970). Talcott Parsons' work (1964a, 1964b) provides an important link between psychoanalytic object-relations theory and general sociological theory. His theory of action—which implies that the basic unit of the personality system, the social system, and the cultural system is an interaction between two persons which becomes internalized and part of the personality—corresponds quite closely to the definition of object-relations theory in Chapter 2.

In conclusion, I have attempted to integrate object-relations theory with psychoanalytic instinct theory and a contemporary ego psychological approach. Object-relations theory stresses the uniqueness of the individual. It studies the development of a highly individualized self, a person aware of himself and of other human beings, and the development of interpersonal relationships in depth as a major precondition for the fulfillment of personal psychic needs. Object-relations theory, I think, represents a synthesis of a more impersonal psychoanalytic metapsychology, of individual psychology and psychopathology, and of man's transcendence of his biological and psychological development. In this regard, psychoanalytic object-relations theory links psychoanalysis as a science with a humanistic philosophy of man (Wisdom, 1971). Yankelovich and Barrett (1970) stress the need for psychoanalytic science to develop in the direction implied in a psychoanalytic personology. I think that psychoanalytic object-relations theory is moving in that direction. It seems to me that within the recent trends in the development of personality theories, psychoanalysis stands between the mechanistic behavior theories at the one extreme, and the ahistorical, nongenetic existential approaches, at the other. Psychoanalytic object-relations theory reaches out in both directions and attempts to extend the objective, scientific study of the personality without losing sight of the subjective uniqueness of the individual.

REFERENCES

Arlow, J. A., and Brenner, C. (1964). *Psychoanalytic Concepts and the Structural Theory.* New York: International Universities Press.

Bion, W. R. (1959). *Experiences in Groups.* New York: Basic Books.

———(1967). *Second Thoughts: Selected Papers on Psychoanalysis.* London: Heinemann.

Blanck, G., and Blanck, R. (1972). Toward a psychoanalytic developmental psychology. *Journal of the American Psychoanalytic Association* 20: 668-710.

Bowlby, J. (1969). *Attachment and Loss. Vol. I: Attachment.* New York: Basic Books.

Brenner, C. (1974a). On the nature and development of affects—a unified theory. *Psychoanalytic Quarterly* 43: 532-556.

———(1974b). Depression, anxiety, and affect theory. *International Journal of Psycho-Analysis* 55: 25-32.
Dicks, H. V. (1967). *Marital Tensions*. New York: Basic Books.
Erikson, E. H. (1950). Growth and crises of the healthy personality. In: *Identity and the Life Cycle*. New York: International Universities Press 1959, 1: 50-100.
———(1956). The problem of ego identity. *Journal of the American Psychoanalytic Association* 4: 56-121.
———(1963). *Childhood and Society*. Second Edition. New York: Norton.
Fairbairn, W. D. (1952). *An Object-Relations Theory of the Personality*. New York: Basic Books.
———(1963). Synopsis of an object-relations theory of the personality. *International Journal of Psycho-Analysis* 4: 224-225.
Freud, S. (1923). The ego and the id. *Standard Edition*. London: Hogarth Press, 1961, 19: 13-66.
———(1927). Fetishism. *Standard Edition* 21: 235-239.
———(1938). Splitting of the ego in the process of defense. *Standard Edition* 23: 273-278.
———(1940). An outline of psycho-analysis. *Standard Edition* 23: 139-171.
Guntrip, H. (1961). *Personality Structure and Human Interaction*. London: Hogarth Press.
———(1968). *Schizoid Phenomena, Object Relations and the Self*. New York: International Universities Press.
———(1971). *Psychoanalytic Theory, Therapy, and the Self*. New York; Basic Books.
Hartmann, H. (1948). Comments on the psychoanalytic theory of instinctual drives. *Psychoanalytic Quarterly* 17: 368-388.
———(1950). Comments on the psychoanalytic theory of the ego. In: *Essays on Ego Psychology*. London: Hogarth; New York: International Universities Press, 1964, pp. 113-141.
———, Kris, E., and Loewenstein, R. (1946). Comments on the formation of psychic structure. *Psychoanalytic Study of the Child* 2: 11-38.
———, and Loewenstein, R. (1962). Notes on the superego. *Psychoanalytic Study of the Child* 17: 42-81.
Hartocollis, P. (1974). Origins of time: a reconstruction of the ontogenetic development of the sense of time based on object-relations theory. *Psychoanalytic Quarterly* 43: 243-261.
Heimann, P., and Valenstein, A. (1972). The psychoanalytic concept of aggression: an integrated summary. *International Journal of*

Psycho-Analysis 53: 31-35.

Jacobson, E. (1964). *The Self and the Object World.* New York: International Universities Press.

———(1971). *Depression.* New York: International Universities Press.

Joffe, W. G., and Sandler, J. (1965). Notes on pain, depression, and individuation. *Psychoanalytic Study of the Child* 20: 394-424.

Kernberg, O. (1968). The treatment of patients with borderline personality organization. In: *Borderline Conditions and Pathological Narcissism.* New York: Jason Aronson, 1975, pp. 69-109.

———(1969). A contribution to the ego-psychological critique of the Kleinian school. *International Journal of Psycho-Analysis* 50: 317-333.

———(1970). Factors in the psychoanalytic treatment of narcissistic personalities. In: *Borderline Conditions and Pathological Narcissism.* New York: Jason Aronson, 1975, pp. 227-262.

———(1972). Early ego integration and object relations. *Annals of the New York Academy of Sciences* 193: 233-247.

———(1974). Further contributions to the treatment of narcissistic personalities. In: *Borderline Conditions and Pathological Narcissism.* New York: Jason Aronson, 1975, pp. 263-314.

———(1975c). Cultural impact and intrapsychic change. In: *Adolescent Psychiatry,* Vol. 4, eds. C. Feinstein and P. Giovacchini. New York: Jason Aronson, 1975, pp. 37-45.

Klein, M. (1934). A contribution to the psychogenesis of manic-depressive states. In: *Contributions to Psycho-Analysis, 1921-1945.* London: Hogarth Press, 1948, pp. 282-310.

———(1940). Mourning and its relation to manic-depressive states. In: *Contributions to Psycho-Analysis, 1921-1945.* London: Hogarth Press, 1948, pp. 311-338.

———(1946). Notes on some schizoid mechanisms. In: *Developments in Psychoanalysis,* eds. M. Klein, P. Heimann, S. Isaacs, and J. Riviere. London: Hogarth Press, 1952, pp. 292-320.

Knapp, P. H. (1963). Introduction: emotional expression—past and present. In: *Expression of the Emotions in Man,* ed. P. H. Knapp. New York: International Universities Press, pp. 3-15.

Kohut, H. (1971). *The Analysis of the Self.* New York: International Universities Press.

Lichtenberg, J. D., and Slap, J. W. (1973). Notes on the concept of splitting and the defense mechanism of the splitting of representations. *Journal of the American Psychoanalytic Association 21:* 722-787.

Mahler, M. S. (1968). *On Human Symbiosis and the Vicissitudes of Individuation. Vol. I: Infantile Psychosis*. New York: International Universities Press.

———(1971). A study of the separation-individuation process and its possible application to borderline phenomena in the psychoanalytic situation. *Psychoanalytic Study of the Child* 26: 403-424.

———(1972). On the first subphases of the separation-individuation process. *International Journal of Psycho-Analysis* 53: 333-338.

———(1973). Personal communication.

Miller, G. A., and Rice, A. K. (1967). *Systems of Organization*. London: Tavistock Publications.

Moore, B. E. (1968). Some genetic and developmental considerations in regard to affects. Reported by L. B. Lofgren. *Journal of the American Psychoanalytic Association* 16: 638-650.

———(1973). Toward a theory of affects: the affect in search of an idea. Reported by P. Castelnuovo-Tedesco. *Journal of the American Psychoanalytic Association* 22: 612-625.

Mullahy, P. (1952). *The Contributions of Harry Stack Sullivan*. New York: Hermitage House.

———(1953). A theory of interpersonal relations and the evolution of personality. In: *Conceptions of Modern Psychiatry*, ed. H. S. Sullivan. New York: Norton, pp. 239-294.

———(1955). *Oedipus, Myth and Complex*. New York: Grove Press.

Novey, S. (1959). A clinical view of the affect theory in psychoanalysis. *International Journal of Psycho-Analysis* 40: 94-104.

Parsons, T. (1964a). Social structure and the development of personality: Freud's contribution to the integration of psychology and sociology. In: *Social Structure and Personality*. London: The Free Press, pp. 78-111. Also in: *Psychiatry*, 1958, 21: 321-340.

———(1964b). The superego and the theory of social systems. In: *Social Structure and Personality*. London: The Free Press, pp. 17-33. Also in: *Psychiatry*, 1952, Vol. 15, No. 1.

Rapaport, D., and Gill, M. (1959). The points of view and assumptions of metapsychology. In: *The Collected Papers of David Rapaport*, ed. M. Gill. New York: Basic Books, 1967, pp. 795-811.

Rice, A. K. (1963). *The Enterprise and its Environment*. London: Tavistock.

———(1965). *Learning for Leadership*. London: Tavistock.

———(1969). Individual, group and intergroup processes. *Human Relations* 22: 565-584.

Rioch, M. J. (1970). The work of Wilfred Bion on groups. *Psychiatry* 33: 56-66.

Rosenfeld, H. A. (1965). *Psychotic States: A Psychoanalytic Approach*. New York: International Universities Press, pp. 13-127; 155-168.

Ross, N. (1975), Affect as cognition: with observations on the meanings of mystical states. *International Review of Psycho-Analysis*, 2:79-93.

Sandler, J. (1972). The role of affects in psychoanalytic theory, physiology, emotion and psychosomatic illness. *A Ciba Foundation Symposium*, London, April.

———, and Rosenblatt, B. (1962). The concept of the representational world. *Psychoanalytic Study of the Child* 17: 128-145.

———, Holder, A., and Meers, D. (1963). The ego ideal and the ideal self. *Psychoanalytic Study of the Child* 18: 139-158.

Searles, H. F. (1965). *Collected Papers on Schizophrenia and Related Subjects*. New York: International Universities Press.

Segal, H. (1964). *Introduction to the Work of Melanie Klein*. London: Heinemann; New York: Basic Books.

Spitz, R. A. (1972). Bridges: on anticipation, duration, and meaning. *Journal of the American Psychoanalytic Association* 20: 721-735.

Sullivan, H. S. (1953). *The Interpersonal Theory of Psychiatry*. New York: Norton.

Sutherland, J. D. (1963). Object relations theory and the conceptual model of psychoanalysis. *British Journal of Medical Psychology* 36: 109-124.

———(1969). Psychoanalysis in the post-industrial society. *International Journal of Psycho-Analysis* 50: 673-682.

———, and Gill, H. S. (1970). The object relations theory of personality. In: *Language and Psychodynamic Appraisal*. The Tavistock Institute of Human Relations, pp. 8-18.

van der Waals, H. G. (1965). Problems of narcissism. *Bulletin of the Menninger Clinic* 29: 293-311.

Will, O. (1961). Psychotherapy in reference to the schizophrenic reaction. In: *Contemporary Psychotherapies*, ed. M. I. Stein. New York: Free Press, pp. 128-156.

———(1967). Schizophrenia: the problem of origins. In: *The Origins of Schizophrenia*, ed. J. Romano. Proceedings of the First Rochester International Conference on Schizophrenia, pp. 214-227.

Winnicott, D. W. (1954). Metapsychological and clinical aspects of regression within the psycho-analytical set-up. In: *Collected Papers*. New York: Basic Books, 1958, pp. 278-294.

———(1960). Ego distortion in terms of true and false self. In: *The Maturational Processes and the Facilitating Environment.* New York: International Universities Press, 1965, pp. 140-152.

Wisdom, J. O. (1963). Fairbairn's contribution on object-relationship, splitting and ego structure. *British Journal of Medical Psychology* 36: 145-159.

———(1971). Freud and Melanie Klein: psychology, ontology, and Weltanschauung. In: *Psychoanalysis and Philosophy,* ed. C. Hanley and M. Lazerowitz. New York: International Universities Press, pp. 327-362.

Yankelovich, D., and Barrett, W. (1970). *Ego and Instinct.* New York: Random House.

PART II

APPLICATIONS

five

A Psychoanalytic Classification of Character Pathology

This chapter is a proposal for a classification of character pathology which integrates recent developments in our understanding of severe forms of character pathology, especially the so-called borderline conditions, with recent developments in psychoanalytic metapsychology. This classification attempts (1) to establish psychoanalytic criteria for differential diagnoses among different types and degrees of severity of character pathology; (2) to clarify the relationship between a descriptive characterological diagnosis and a metapsychological, especially structural, analysis; and (3) to arrange subgroups of character pathology according to their degree of severity. It should help in the diagnosis of character pathology by providing the clinician with more systematic information about its descriptive, structural, and genetic-dynamic characteristics and by singling out the predominant constellations of character and other defenses peculiar to each form of character pathology. Finally, this proposed classification should help in determining the prognosis for psychological treatment in these conditions by correlating types of character pathology with degrees of indication for psychoanalytic treatment and for psychoanalytically oriented psychotherapy.

Freud (1908, 1931) and Abraham (1921-1925) described character pathology in psychoanalytic terms and suggested the first classifications of character pathology. These early classifications were based on their understanding of instinctual, especially libidinal, motivations. Fenichel (1945), after criticizing these and other attempts to develop a psychoanalytic typology of character pathology and after incorporating W. Reich's findings (1933), suggested a classification combining dynamic and structural explanations.

From a dynamic viewpoint, Fenichel classified character traits into "sublimation" and "reactive" types, depending on whether the instinctual energy was discharged freely as part of the character trait or was checked by some countercathectic measure forming part of that character trait. The sublimatory type of character trait, Fenichel stated, was mostly normal and did not lend itself easily to further typing. In contrast, the reactive type of character traits reflected pathological developments of the personality. Fenichel suggested the subdivision of reactive character traits into attitudes of avoidance (phobic attitudes) and of opposition (reaction formation).

From the structural viewpoint, Fenichel (1945) defined character as "the ego's habitual modes of adjustment to the external world, the id, and the superego, and the characteristic types of combining these modes with one another." Accordingly, character disturbances were "limitations or pathological forms of treating the external world, internal drives, and demands of the superego, or disturbances of the ways in which these various tasks are combined."

Combining the dynamic and structural viewpoints, he proceeded to classify the reactive character traits into pathological behavior toward the id (including here among others the classical oral, anal, and phallic character traits); pathological behavior toward the superego (including here moral masochism, apparent lack of guilt feelings, criminality, and "acting-out" characters); and pathological behavior toward external objects (including pathological jealousy, social inhibitions, and pseudosexuality). Fenichel, however, appeared not to be fully satisfied by his proposed classification. He acknowledged that every person shows traits of both sublimatory and reactive types, and he suggested that the reactive characters may be "most satisfactorily subdivided by analogy to the neuroses, for the simple reason that mechanisms similar to the various forms of symptom formation are likewise operative in the formation of character traits." Following this lead, he described phobic and hysterical characters as the characterological equivalents of their respective symptomatic neuroses.

Prelinger et al. (1964), in their comprehensive review of psychoanalytic concepts of character, comment that Fenichel's attempt to classify character types "is generally accepted in psychoanalytic theory today."

I believe that a reexamination of Fenichel's classification is in order because of the development of psychoanalytic understanding of the pathology and treatment of character disorders since the publication of his classic work (Eissler, 1953; Erikson, 1956; Friedlander, 1947; Greenson, 1958; Johnson and Szurek, 1952; Rosenfeld, 1964; Stone, 1954), as well as the broadening of psychoanalytic understanding of borderline character pathology (Boyer and Giovacchini, 1967; Deutsch, 1942; Frosch, 1964, 1970; Knight, 1953; Zetzel, 1968). I shall attempt to incorporate recent findings regarding the degree of severity and the prognosis of character disorders into a psychoanalytic classification of character pathology. In so doing, I shall emphasize recent findings regarding the structural consequences to the ego and superego of pathological object relations (Fairbairn, 1952; Giovacchini, 1963; Jacobson, 1964; Sutherland, 1963; van der Waals, 1952), and I shall expand my earlier analyses of the structural disturbances in patients with borderline conditions (Chapter 1; Kernberg, 1967, 1968).

My proposed classification will incorporate three major pathological developments: (1) pathology in the ego and superego structures; (2) pathology in the internalized object relations; and (3) pathology in the development of libidinal and aggressive drive derivatives.

THE ASSUMPTIONS UNDERLYING THE PROPOSED CLASSIFICATION

1. *Regarding Instinctual Development.* In contrast to earlier attempts at psychoanalytic classification of character pathology on the basis of the stages of libidinal development, the proposed classification assumes that, clinically, three main levels of instinctual fixation can be encountered: a higher level, at which genital primacy has been reached; an intermediate level, at which pregenital, especially oral, regression and fixation points predominate; and a lower level, at which a pathological condensation of genital and pregenital instinctual strivings takes place, with a predominance of pregenital aggression. This proposed classification incorporates the findings regarding instinctual developments in patients with borderline personality organization reported in earlier work (Kernberg, 1967).

2. *Regarding Superego Development.* The proposed classification assumes that a relatively well integrated although excessively severe superego characterizes the higher level of organization of character pathology only, and that the intermediate and lower levels of organization of character pathology reflect varying degrees of lack of superego integration as well as the predominance of sadistic superego forerunners over other superego components. Jacobson's comprehensive analysis of normal and pathological stages of superego development (1964) constitutes the basis for these propositions.

3. *Regarding Defensive Operations of the Ego and, in Particular, the Nature of Pathological Character Traits.* Following the structural model elaborated in Chapter 1, two overall levels of defensive organization of the ego are assumed: (1) a basic level at which primitive dissociation or splitting is the crucial mechanism, and (2) a more advanced level at which repression becomes the central mechanism, replacing splitting. In the proposed classification, the higher level of organization of character pathology presents the repression characteristic of the advanced level of defensive organization, together with related mechanisms such as intellectualization, rationalization, undoing, and higher levels of projection. The same is true for the intermediate level of organization of character pathology, except that, in addition, the patient shows some of the defense mechanisms which, in stronger form, characterize the lower level. At that lower level, primitive dissociation or splitting predominates, with a concomitant impairment of the synthetic function of the ego and the presence of the related mechanisms of denial, primitive forms of projection, and omnipotence. The proposed classification assumes a continuum of pathological character traits, ranging from the sublimatory traits at the one extreme, through inhibitory or phobic traits, reaction formation traits, to instinctually infiltrated traits at the other extreme. The implication is that the lower the level of defensive organization of the ego, the more predominant the pathological character traits in which defense and direct impulse expression are linked, so that the primal impulse expression shows through the defense. The normal character shows a predominance of sublimatory character traits. In the higher level of organization of character pathology, inhibitory and reactive character traits predominate; in the intermediate level of organization, character defenses combining

reaction formations against instincts with yet a partial expression of the rejected instinctual impulses make their appearance; and at the lower level, instinctually infiltrated character defenses predominate.

4. *Regarding the Vicissitudes of Internalized Object Relations.* No particular pathology of internalized object relations is present at the higher level, at which ego identity and its related components, a stable self concept and a stable representational world, are well established; the same is true at the intermediate level, with the exception of more conflictual object relations than at the higher level. At the lower level, severe pathology of the internalization of object relations is present. Object relations have a "partial" rather than "total" character. In other words, object constancy, the child's capacity to retain his attachment to a loved person and to the internal representation of that person in spite of frustration and hostility in that relationship (Arlow et al., 1968) is not firmly established. This incapacity for a relationship in which good and bad aspects of the object and of the self (and of their respective representations) can be tolerated and integrated is reflected in the syndrome of identity diffusion (Erikson, 1956; Kernberg, 1967).

What follows is an outline of the structural characteristics of the higher, intermediate, and lower levels of organization of character pathology and the type of pathological character formation that belongs to each level. Bibliographic references will indicate sources describing these characterological types and their differential diagnosis.

HIGHER LEVEL OF ORGANIZATION OF CHARACTER PATHOLOGY

At the higher level, the patient has a relatively well integrated, but severe and punitive superego. The forerunners of his superego are determined by sadistic impulses, bringing about a harsh, perfectionistic superego. His ego, too, is well integrated, ego identity (Erikson, 1956) and its related components, a stable self concept (Jacobson, 1964), and a stable representational world (Sandler and Rosenblatt, 1962) being well established. Excessive defensive operations against unconscious conflicts center on repression. The character defenses are largely of an inhibitory or phobic nature, or they are reaction formations against repressed instinctual needs. There is very little or no instinctual infiltration into the defensive character traits. The patient's ego at this level is somewhat constricted by its excessive use of neurotic defense mechanisms, but the patient's overall social adaptation is not seriously impaired. He has fairly deep, stable object relations and is capable of experiencing guilt, mourning, and a wide variety of affective responses (Winnicott, 1955). His sexual and/or aggressive drive derivatives are partially inhibited, but these instinctual conflicts have reached the stage where the infantile genital phase and oedipal conflicts are clearly predominant and there is no pathological condensation of genital sexual strivings with pregenital, aggressively determined strivings in which the latter predominate.

Most hysterical characters (Abraham, 1920; Easser and Lesser, 1965; Shapiro, 1965), obsessive-compulsive characters (Fenichel, 1945), and depressive-masochistic characters (Laughlin, 1956) are organized at this level.

INTERMEDIATE LEVEL OF ORGANIZATION OF CHARACTER PATHOLOGY

At the intermediate level, the superego is more excessively punitive than that of the higher level disorders, but it is less integrated. It tolerates the contradictory demands of sadistic, prohibitive superego nuclei, on the one hand, and rather primitive (magical, overidealized) forms of the ego ideal, on the other hand (Jacobson, 1964). These latter demands to be great, powerful, and physically attractive coexist with strict demands for moral perfection, and they can be observed in the patient's partially blurred superego-ego delimitations. Deficient superego integration can also be observed in the partial projections of superego nuclei (as expressed in the patient's decreased capacity for experiencing guilt and in paranoid trends), contradictions in the ego's value systems, and severe mood swings. These mood swings are caused by the primitive nature of the superego's regulation of the ego (Jacobson, 1964). The poor integration of the superego, which is reflected in contradictory unconscious demands on the ego, also explains the appearance of pathological character defenses combining reaction formations against instincts with a partial expression of instinctual impulses. At this level, the patient has fewer inhibitory character defenses than the person at the higher level; reaction formations are more prominent; and his character traits are infiltrated by instinctual strivings, as seen in dissociated expressions of unacceptable sexual and/or aggressive needs and a "structured impulsivity" in certain areas. Repression is still the main defensive operation of the ego, together with related defenses such as intellectualization, rationalization, and undoing. At the same time, the patient shows some dissociative trends, some defensive splitting of the ego in limited areas (that is, mutual dissociation of contradictory ego states) (Chapter 1; Freud, 1938), and projection and denial. Pregenital, especially oral, conflicts come to the fore, although the genital level of libidinal development has been reached. While pregenital, especially oral, features predominate in the clinical picture, such features reflect, to a major extent, regression from oedipal conflicts; further, the aggressive components of pregenital conflicts are toned down, in contrast to the primitivization of aggression at the lower level of organization of character pathology.

Object relations at this level are still stable in the sense of a capacity for lasting, deep involvements with others, and of tolerating the markedly ambivalent and conflictual nature of such relationships.

Most oral types of character pathology (Abraham, 1921-1925) are organized at this level, especially what is now designated the "passive-aggressive" (Brody and Lindbergh, 1967) personality type. Sadomasochistic personalities (Frank et al., 1952), some of the better functioning infantile (or "hysteroid") personalities (Easser and Lesser, 1965; Zetzel, 1968), and many narcissistic personalities (Kernberg, 1970; Rosenfeld, 1964) are at this intermediate level. Many patients with a stable, crystallized sexual deviation (Fenichel, 1945) and with the capacity to establish, within such a deviation, relatively stable object relations are also at this level.

LOWER LEVEL OF ORGANIZATION OF CHARACTER PATHOLOGY

At the lower level, the patient's superego integration is minimal and his propensity for projection of primitive, sadistic superego nuclei is maximal. His capacity for experiencing concern and guilt is seriously impaired (Winnicott, 1955), and his basis for self-criticism constantly fluctuates. The individual at this level commonly exhibits paranoid traits, stemming both from projection of superego nuclei and from the excessive use of rather primitive forms of projection, especially projective identification (Klein, 1946) as one major defensive mechanism of the ego. The delimitation between ego and superego is completely blurred: primitive, narcissistically determined forms of the ego ideal are practically indistinguishable from primitive forms of narcissistic ego strivings for power, wealth, and admiration (A. Reich, 1953). The synthetic function of the patient's ego is seriously impaired, and he uses primitive dissociation or splitting (Fairbairn, 1952; Jacobson, 1957a; Kernberg, 1967) as the central defensive operation of the ego instead of repression. The mechanism of splitting is expressed as contradictory ego states alternating with each other, and this dissociation is reinforced by the patient's use of denial, projective identification, primitive idealization, devaluation and omnipotence. This omnipotence reflects a defensive identification of the patient's self concept with forerunners of his ego ideal, namely, idealized, condensed primitive self- and object-images. His pathological character defenses are predominantly of an impulsive, instinctually infiltrated kind; contradictory, repetitive patterns of behavior are dissociated from each other, permitting direct release of drive derivatives as well as of reaction formations against these drives. Lacking an integrated ego and the capacity to tolerate guilt feelings, such patients have little need for secondary rationalizations of pathological character traits.

These patients' capacity for encompassing contradictory ("good" and "bad") self- and object-images is impaired, mainly because of the predominance of pregenital aggression as part of both ego and superego identifications. Excessive pregenital aggression also causes a pathological condensation of pregenital and genital conflicts with predominance of pregenital aggression (Kernberg, 1967) and is evidenced by sadistically infiltrated, polymorphous perverse infantile drive derivatives which contaminate all the internalized and external object relations of these patients. Thus, their oedipal strivings appear intimately condensed with pregenital sadistic and masochistic needs, and there may be direct expression of oedipal impulses such as in masturbatory fantasies involving the original parental objects.

Their inability to integrate libidinally determined and aggressively determined self- and object-images is reflected in their maintaining object relations of either a need-gratifying or a threatening nature. They are unable to have empathy for objects in their totality; object relations are of a part-object type, and object constancy has not been reached. Their lack of integration of self-representations is reflected in the absence of an integrated self concept. Their inner world is peopled by caricatures of either the good or the horrible aspects of persons who have been important to them; and these exaggerated representations are not integrated to the extent that the person could feel that one of his inner objects had a "good side" and a "bad side." By the same token, his inner view of himself is a chaotic mixture of shameful, threatened, and exalted images. The absence of both an integrated world of total, internalized object representations and of a stable self concept produces the syndrome of identity diffusion (Erikson, 1956). In fact, identity diffusion is an outstanding characteristic of this lower level of character pathology. The lack of integration of libidinal and aggressive strivings contributes to a general lack of neutralization of instinctual energy (Hartmann, 1950, 1955) and to a severe restriction of the conflict-free ego.

All these factors, in addition to the disintegrating effects of the predominant mechanisms of splitting and related defenses and the lack of crucial ego organizers such as an integrated self concept and an integrated superego, contribute to severe ego weakness. Ego weakness is reflected especially in the patient's lack of anxiety tolerance, of impulse control, and of developed sublimatory channels as evidenced by chronic failure in work or creative areas (Kernberg, 1967). Primary process thinking infiltrates cognitive functioning, and, although not always evident on clinical contacts, it is especially manifest on projective psychological testing (Rapaport et al., 1945-1946).

Most infantile personalities (Easser and Lesser, 1965; Greenson, 1958; Kernberg, 1967; Zetzel, 1968) and many narcissistic personalities (Kernberg, 1970; Rosenfeld, 1964) exhibit this level of organization of character pathology. All patients with antisocial personality structure are at this level (Cleckley, 1964; Friedlander, 1947; Johnson and Szurek, 1952). The so-called chaotic, impulse-ridden character disorders (Fenichel, 1945; W. Reich, 1933), the "as-if"

(Deutsch, 1942) characters, the "inadequate personalities" (Brody and Lindbergh, 1967), and most "self-mutilators" (Kernberg, 1967) belong to this group. Patients with multiple sexual deviations (or a combination of sexual deviation and drug addiction or alcoholism) and with severe pathology of object relations (reflected in their bizarre sexual needs) are organized at this level (Frosch, 1964; Kernberg, 1967). The same is also true for the so-called prepsychotic personality structures, that is, the hypomanic, schizoid, and paranoid personalities (Brody and Lindbergh, 1967; Shapiro, 1965).

The next step down along this continuum would carry us to the field of the psychoses. The lower level of organization of character pathology I have been describing consists, in effect, of the group of patients who are generally included in the field of borderline disorders or "psychotic characters" (Frosch, 1964), or present "borderline personality organization" (Kernberg, 1967). The differential diagnosis between patients with borderline personalities and those with psychoses centers on the persistence of reality testing (Frosch, 1964; Weisman, 1958) in the former and its loss in the latter. This difference depends, in turn, on the differentiation between self- and object-representations (Jacobson, 1954, 1964) and its derived delimitation of ego boundaries; these are present in the lower level of organization of character pathology, lost or absent in the psychoses.

The above-mentioned assumptions underlying the proposed classification are related to one another in a model of development of the psychic apparatus centered on the development of internalized object relations, which has been spelled out in Chapter 1 and earlier work (Kernberg, 1967, 1968, 1970). What follows is a brief summary of these propositions.

THE MUTUAL RELATIONSHIPS OF THE STATED ASSUMPTIONS: AN OBJECT-RELATIONS-CENTERED MODEL OF DEVELOPMENT

The internalization of object relations represents a crucial organizing factor for both ego and superego development. Introjections, identifications, and ego identity formation form a progressive sequence in the process of internalization of object relations. The essential components of internalized object relations are self-images, object-images, and specific affect states or dispositions linking each self-image with a corresponding object-image. Two essential tasks that the early ego has to accomplish in rapid succession are: (1) the differentiation of self-images from object-images; and (2) the integration of self- and object-images built up under the influence of libidinal drive derivatives and their related affects with their corresponding self- and object-images built up under the influence of aggressive drive derivatives and their related affects.

The first task is accomplished in part under the influence of the development of the apparatuses of primary autonomy: perception and memory traces help to sort out the origin of stimuli and gradually differentiate self- and object-images. This first task fails to a major extent in the psychoses, in which a pathological fusion between self- and object-images determines a failure in the differentiation of ego boundaries and, therefore, in the differentiation of self from nonself. In the lower level of organization of character pathology, that is, borderline personality organization, differentiation of self- from object-images is sufficient to permit the establishment of integrated ego boundaries and a concomitant differentiation between self and others.

The second task, however (of integration of libidinally determined and aggressively determined self- and object-images), fails to a great extent in borderline patients, mainly because of the pathological predominance of pregenital aggression. The resulting lack of synthesis of contradictory self- and object-images interferes with the integration of the self concept and with the establishment of "total" object relations and object constancy. The need to preserve the "good" self- and "good" object-images and good external objects in the presence of dangerous "all bad" self- and object-images leads to a defensive division of the ego, in which what was at first a simple defect in integration is used actively to keep "good" and "bad" self- and object-images apart. This is, in essence, the mechanism of splitting, an essential defensive operation of the borderline personality organization. It is reinforced by subsidiary defensive operations (especially projective mechanisms) and thus determines an overall ego organization different from the intermediate and higher levels of organization of character and ego development, where repression and related mechanisms replace splitting and its subsidiary mechanisms.

All good" and "all bad" self- and object-images seriously interfere with superego integration because they create fantastic ideals of power, greatness, and perfection rather than the more realistic demands and goals of an ego ideal constructed under the influence of more integrated, toned down ideal self- and object-images. Projection of "bad" self- and object-images determines, through reintrojection of distorted experiences of the frustrating and punishing aspects of the parents, a pathological predominance of sadistic superego forerunners and a subsequent incapacity to integrate the idealized superego components with the sadistically threatening ones. All of this leads to a lack of superego integration and a concomitant tendency to reproject superego nuclei. Thus, dissociative or splitting processes in the ego are reinforced by the absence of the normal integrative contribution of the superego, and contradictory internalized demands, together with the insufficiency of the ego's repressive mechanisms, contribute to the establishment of contradictory, instinctually infiltrated, pathological character traits. This development is maximal at the lower level of organization of character pathology but to some extent also is present at the intermediate level of organization.

In contrast, when "good" and "bad" internalized object relations (involving self-images, object-images, ideal self-images, ideal object-images) are so integrated that an integrated self concept and a related integrated "representational world" develops, a stable ego identity is achieved. At this point, a central ego core is protected from unacceptable drive derivatives by a stable repressive barrier, and the defensive character traits that develop have the characteristics of reaction formations or inhibitory traits. The development of this level of integration within the ego also creates the precondition for the integration of the sadistically determined superego forerunners with the ego ideal and the subsequent capacity to internalize the realistic, demanding, and prohibitive aspects of the parents. All of this fosters further superego integration and, eventually, depersonification and abstraction within the superego. The superego may now act as a higher level organizer of the ego, providing further pressures for a harmonious integration of any remaining contradictory trends within the ego. The toning down of such an integrated, more realistically determined superego permits a more flexible management of instinctual drive derivatives on the ego's part, with the appearance of sublimatory character traits. At the higher level of organization of character pathology, the integration of the superego is still excessively under the influence of sadistic forerunners, to the extent that the superego, although well integrated, remains harsh and excessively demanding. Repressive and sublimatory handling of pregenital drive derivatives, especially of pregenital aggression, is effective to the extent that there is less infiltration of genital drive derivatives by pregenital, especially aggressive trends, and the oedipal-genital level of development clearly predominates. At this, the higher level of organization of character pathology, excessive severity of the superego centers on excessive prohibition and/or conflicts around infantile sexuality. Object constancy, a capacity for stable and deep object relations, and a stable ego identity have been reached at this level.

Normality represents a further (and final) progression along this continuum, with a well-integrated, less severe and punitive superego, realistic superego demands, an ego ideal and ego goals which permit an overall harmony in dealing with the external world, as well as with instinctual needs. The predominance of sublimatory character traits reflects such an optimum expression of instinctual needs, of adaptive and sublimatory integration of pregenital trends under the primacy of genitality, in the context of mature, adult object relations. A firm repressive barrier against a residuum of unacceptable, infantile instinctual needs is complemented by a large sector of a conflict-free, flexibly functioning ego and the capacity to suppress some realistically ungratifiable needs without excessive stress.

DIAGNOSTIC, PROGNOSTIC, AND THERAPEUTIC IMPLICATIONS

From a diagnostic point of view, the proposed classification of character pathology may help to differentiate types of character pathology which, at first, may present diagnostic difficulties in individual cases. Thus, for example, the differential diagnosis between hysterical and infantile character pathology is greatly helped by utilizing structural as well as descriptive considerations. The presenting pathological character traits may at first seem hysterical.

However, a thorough examination of those traits in terms of what they reveal regarding the superego structure, the predominant defensive operations of the ego, and the kind of conflicts the patient is struggling with may point to the fact that the predominant pathological character constellation is of an infantile rather than a hysterical type. Also, while certain types of character pathology typically coincide with a certain degree of severity, this may not be true in every case. Thus, for example, a patient with infantile personality may, on the basis of a structural analysis, appear to be functioning at the intermediate rather than the lower level of organization of character pathology, with consequences for the prognosis and treatment recommendations. One additional diagnostic advantage of the proposed classification of character pathology is the possibility it offers, on the basis of the structural characteristics of the patient, of predicting the kind of defensive operations that will predominate in the treatment, especially as transference resistances.

From the viewpoint of overall prognosis, the proposed classification reflects three degrees of severity of characterological illness. The prognosis for psychoanalytic treatment of patients in the higher level of organization of character pathology is very good; these patients respond very well to psychoanalysis. The prognosis is less favorable at the intermediate level; these patients usually require lengthier psychoanalytic treatment, and the goals of analysis must at times be less ambitious. The prognosis for the lower level of organization of character pathology is always serious; at this level, standard, nonmodified psychoanalytic treatment is usually contraindicated, or a preparatory period of expressive psychotherapy is required (Eissler, 1953; Stone, 1954; Zetzel, 1968).

Some therapeutic implications of the proposed model have already been mentioned as part of the prognostic considerations. For patients at the higher level of organization of character pathology, psychoanalysis is the treatment of choice. These patients may seek treatment for symptoms of a rather recent, minor, or situationally determined type, which may improve with brief psychotherapy. Ideally, however, they should be treated with psychoanalysis rather than one of the modified psychotherapeutic procedures because at this level the maximum improvement in personality functioning can be expected from analytic treatment. For patients functioning at the intermediate level of organization of character pathology, psychoanalysis is still the treatment of choice unless there is some special contraindication. These patients, however, will usually require lengthy psychoanalysis, and it may be that in some selected cases a modified treatment is preferable, either simply at the start or over the entire course of treatment. For patients with the lower level of organization of character pathology, psychoanalysis is usually contraindicated. A special, modified psychoanalytic procedure, with the introduction of parameters of technique (Eissler, 1953), is the treatment of choice at this level (Chapter 6). A few patients at this level may still require or may be able to benefit from nonmodified, classical psychoanalysis. However, even in the case of these patients, the proposed classification may be useful in that it highlights, in addition to the prognostic "warning," the typical defensive operations predominant in their transference reactions and the particular, severe pathology of their superego, which may present extremely difficult treatment problems.

LIMITATIONS AND EXCEPTIONS

Several questions may be raised regarding the proposed classification of character pathology.

1. *How consistent is the relationship between the level of organization of character pathology and the actual, overall functioning of the individual?*

The actual functioning of the individual in adapting to his interpersonal environment and his intrapsychic needs depends largely on the level of his structural, intrapsychic organization. The higher the level of ego organization, the higher is the type of character defenses and the more predominant are the general manifestations of ego strength (inpulse control, anxiety tolerance, sublimatory capacities).

Actual psychological functioning, however, also depends on the particular quality of the pathological character traits and on the interpersonal environment within which such character traits express themselves. Thus, for example, a patient with a masochistic character structure and the higher level of character organization may appear much more disturbed in his interpersonal relationships than his character organization would otherwise warrant, because his unconscious emphasis on self-defeat may bring about interpersonal situations that are potentially disruptive or highly inappropriate for him. In contrast to this example, a patient with a narcissistic personality and a lower level character organization may function in a much better way than the ordinary patient with borderline personality organization because of the protective and socially isolating nature of narcissistic character traits (Kernberg, 1970). In this case, the nonspecific manifestations of ego weakness (lack of anxiety tolerance, impulse control, and sublimatory channels) may be absent, in spite of a typical defensive ego organization of the lower level character pathology and of severe superego pathology.

The actual functioning of the individual also depends on the degree of pathological superego pressures his ego is subjected to. Thus, for example, a patient with a depressive-masochistic personality structure and a particularly strict, sadistic but well integrated superego may experience severe depressions of such a disorganizing nature that nonspecific manifestations of ego weakness make their appearance. Again, actual functioning may be much worse than what one would expect from the underlying level of organization of character pathology. Finally, the particular quality of a neurotic symptom also may influence the general functioning of the individual. Particular symptoms may have such a crippling effect on a person's life situation that his overall functioning may be much more disturbed than his level of organization of character pathology would suggest.

A comparative study of a patient's actual functioning and of his underlying level of organization of character pathology may be of great help in determining the analyzability of the patient. For example, in narcissistic personalities with overt borderline functioning (such as indicated by nonspecific manifestations of ego weakness and clinical manifestations of primary process thinking), psychoanalysis is usually contraindicated. (In spite of their underlying borderline structure, we expect a better surface functioning in narcissistic personalities.) Other patients with nonspecific manifestations of ego weakness and severe disturbances of their interpersonal life may, however, have a good indication for psychoanalysis if, structurally, they belong to the intermediate or higher level of organization of character pathology and their ego functioning is disturbed because of massive pressures from a sadistic but well-integrated superego.

2. *How consistently is a descriptive characterological diagnosis related to the corresponding level of organization of character pathology?*

While actual functioning does not reflect directly the underlying level of organization of character pathology, the relationship between a descriptive characterological diagnosis and the underlying level of character organization is much closer. The closeness of the relationship is marked at the higher and lower levels of character organization, but it is less clear at the intermediate level.

In general terms, the intermediate level of organization of character pathology is broader and more complex than either the higher or the lower one. Subclassifications may be warranted at this intermediate level, and I have observed at least two subgroups. One is represented by a mixture of defensive operations stemming from both repression and splitting. This type of intermediate-level character organization usually shows a combination of reactive character traits and instinctually infiltrated ones. For example, there are some hysterical personalities with infantile trends who present dissociative tendencies and episodic acting out in which repressed sexual or aggressive impulses become conscious (although dissociated from the usual self experience of the patient). The other subgroup of ego organization at the intermediate level is expressed by a layer of higher level ego organization centering on repression, underneath which is a layer of the lower level ego organization centering on splitting. This form of structural organization is rather infrequent but of great theoretical interest because it illustrates the mutual relationship of certain defensive operations of the ego and the nature of pathological character traits. Some patients with hysterical personality, generalized repression of some instinctual needs, and rather solid reaction formations experience occasional regressions or breakdowns; at such times, they may experience depersonalization, affect storms, strong paranoid trends, and present complex behavior patterns involving both defenses against and direct expression of primitive instinctual needs. What is so striking in these patients is that at the regressed level they still operate with complex ego patterns and defenses and that reality testing is preserved in the middle of serious malfunctioning. These cases present a failure of the repressive barrier and the activation of a more primitive ego structure when the higher level repressive structure fails.

3. *How stable are the three levels of organization of character pathology?*

Patients of the kind mentioned, who may abruptly shift in their level of structural organization as a consequence of a double layer of ego organization, are one example of structural instability. In more general terms, there exists a minority of patients whose character organization is unstable. In these patients a higher level of organization of character pathology (and particularly of ego organization centering on repression) represents a defensive orgaization against a lower level of character and ego organization. The grouping of these patients with the intermediate level of organization of character pathology is not quite satisfactory.

In contrast to these cases, most other patients present a remarkable stability in their level of structural organization. Whatever changes occur are slow, gradual developments within a psychoanalytic treatment or a psychoanalytically oriented psychotherapy. The transitory psychotic regressions that borderline patients present as an expression of a transference psychosis are not true structural changes but only a product of temporary loss of reality testing related to the pathological activation of projective and other primitive defensive operations. Such psychotic regressions are usually quite reversible (Frosch, 1970).

4. *How consistently are the structural organization of the ego and the superego related to each other?*

In the section The Mutual Relationships of the Stated Assumptions: An Object-Relations-Centered Model of Development, I proposed that there exists, indeed, a close correspondence between the level of structural organization of ego and superego and that the vicissitudes of internalized object relations are a crucial organizing factor determining that correspondence. Thus, for example, a certain level of ego organization is a prerequisite for the development of higher level superego structures, on the one hand, and for the eventual integration and abstraction of the superego, on the other.

There are exceptions, however, reflecting irregularities in the development of some psychic structures, especially at the lower level of organization of character pathology. For example, there are patients with rather typical borderline organization of the ego who do have a better integration of superego functions than one would expect. Such patients have a better capacity to tolerate guilt and concern for themselves and others and, while projection of superego pressures does occur, there is still a remnant of relatively integrated, abstracted superego functions which remains undisturbed. These patients have a better prognosis for treatment, and for some of them a nonmodified psychoanalysis may even be the treatment of choice.

SUMMARY

I have proposed a classification of character pathology in an attempt (1) to establish psychoanalytic criteria for differential diagnoses among different types and degrees of severity of character pathology; (2) to clarify the relationship between a descriptive characterological diagnosis and a metapsychological—especially structural—analysis; and (3) to arrange subgroups of character pathology according to their degree of severity.

This classification reflects a conviction as to the usefulness of a diagnostic study of patients involving structural and genetic-dynamic considerations in addition to purely descriptive ones. The developments in psychoanalytic technique and in modified, psychoanalytically oriented procedures have provided us with an armamentarium of psychotherapeutic tools. The establishment of diagnostic criteria derived from psychoanalytic theory could improve our capacity for optimal individualization of psychological treatment.

REFERENCES

Abraham, K. (1920). Manifestations of the female castration complex. In: *Selected Papers on Psycho-Analysis*. London: Hogarth Press, 1927, pp. 338-369.

———(1921-1925). Psycho-analytical studies on character-formation. In: *Selected Papers on Psycho-Analysis*. London: Hogarth Press, 1927, pp. 370-417.

Arlow, J. A., Freud, A., Lampl-de Groot, J., and Beres, D. (1968). Panel discussion. *International Journal of Psycho-Analysis* 49: 506-512.

Boyer, L. B., and Giovacchini, P. L. (1967). *Psychoanalytic Treatment of Schizophrenic and Characterological Disorders*. New York: Jason Aronson, pp. 208-335.

Brody, E. B., and Lindbergh, S. S. (1967). Trait and pattern disturbances. In: *Comprehensive Textbook of Psychiatry*, ed. A. R. Freedman and H. I. Kaplan. Baltimore: Williams & Wilkins, pp. 937-950.

Cleckley, H. (1964). *The Mask of Sanity*, 4th ed. Saint Louis: Mosby, pp. 326-401.

Deutsch, H. (1942). Some forms of emotional disturbance and their relationship to schizophrenia. *Psychoanalytic Quarterly* 11: 301-321.

Easser, B. R., and Lesser, S. R. (1965). Hysterical personality: a reevaluation. *Psychoanalytic Quarterly* 34: 390-405.

Eissler, K. R. (1953). The effect of the structure of the ego on psychoanalytic technique. *Journal of the American Psychoanalytic Association* 1: 104-143.

Erikson, E. H. (1956). The problem of ego identity. *Journal of the American Psychoanalytic Association* 4: 56-121.

Fairbairn, W. D. (1952). *An Object-Relations Theory of the Personality*. New York: Basic Books.

Fenichel, O. (1945). *The Psychoanalytic Theory of Neurosis*. New York: Norton, pp. 268-310, 324-386, 463-540.

Frank, J. D., et al. (1952). Two behavior patterns in therapeutic groups and their apparent motivation. *Human Relations* 5: 289-317.

Freud, S. (1908). Character and anal erotism. *Standard Edition* 9: 167-175.

———(1931). Libidinal types. *Standard Edition* 21: 215-220.

———(1938). Splitting of the ego in the process of defence. *Standard Edition* 23: 273-278.

Friedlander, K. (1947). *The Psycho Analytical Approach to Juvenile Delinquency*. New York: International Universities Press, pp. 183-187.

Frosch, J. (1964). The psychotic character: clinical psychiatric considerations. *Psychiatric Quarterly* 38: 81-96.

———(1970). Psychoanalytic considerations of the psychotic character. *Journal of the American Psychoanalytic Association*, 18: 24-50.

Giovacchini, P. L. (1963). Integrative aspects of object relationships. *Psychoanalytic Quarterly* 32: 393-407.

Greenson, R. R. (1958). On screen defenses, screen hunger, and screen identity. *Journal of the American Psychoanalytic Association* 6: 242-262.

Hartmann, H. (1950). Comments on the psychoanalytic theory of the ego. In: *Essays on Ego Psychology*. London: Hogarth Press; New York: International Universities Press, 1964, pp. 113-141.

———(1955). Notes on the theory of sublimation. In: *Essays on Ego Psychology*. New York: International Universities Press, 1964, pp. 215-240.

Jacobson, E. (1954). Contribution to the metapsychology of psychotic identifications. *Journal of the American Psychoanalytic Association* 2: 239-262.

———(1957a). Denial and repression. *Journal of the American Psychoanalytic Association* 5: 61-92.

———(1964). *The Self and the Object World*. New York: International Universities Press.

Johnson, A. M., and Szurek, S. A. (1952). The genesis of antisocial acting out in children and adults. *Psychoanalytic Quarterly* 21: 323-343.

Kernberg, O. (1967). Borderline personality organization. In: *Borderline Conditions and Pathological Narcissism*. New York: Jason Aronson, 1975, pp. 3-47.

———(1968). The treatment of patients with borderline personality organization. In: *Borderline Conditions and Pathological Narcissism*. New York: Jason Aronson, 1975, pp. 69-109.

———(1970). Factors in the psychoanalytic treatment of narcissistic personalities. In: *Borderline Conditions and Pathological Narcissism*. New York: Jason Aronson, 1975, pp. 227-262.

Klein, M. (1946). Notes on some schizoid mechanisms. In: *Developments in Psychoanalysis*, eds. M. Klein, P. Heimann, S. Issacs, and J. Riviere. London: Hogarth Press, 1952, pp. 292-320.

Knight, R. P. (1953). Borderline states. In: *Psychoanalytic Psychiatry and Psychology*, eds. R. P. Knight and C. R. Friedman. New York: International Universities Press, pp. 3-15.

Laughlin, H. P. (1956). *The Neuroses in Clinical Practice*. Philadelphia: Saunders, pp. 394-406.

Prelinger, E., Zimet, C. N., Schafer, R., and Levin, M. (1964). *An Ego-Psychological Approach to Character Assessment*. Glencoe: Free Press.

Rapaport, D., Gill, M. M., and Schafer, R. (1945-1946). *Diagnostic Psychological Testing*, 2 Vols. Chicago: Year Book Publishers.

Reich, A. (1953). Narcissistic object choice in women. *Journal of the American Psychoanalytic Association* 1: 22-44.

Reich, W. (1933). *Character Analysis*. 3rd ed. 1949. New York: Noonday Press.

Rosenfeld, H. (1964). On the psychopathology of narcissism: a clinical approach. *International Journal of Psycho-Analysis* 45: 332-337.

Sandler, J., and Rosenblatt, B. (1962). The concept of the representational world. *Psychoanalytic Study of the Child* 17: 128-145.

Shapiro, D. (1965). *Neurotic Styles*. New York: Basic Books.

Stone, L. (1954). The widening scope of indications for psychoanalysis. *Journal of the American Psychoanalytic Association* 2: 567-594.

Sutherland, J. D. (1963). Object relations theory and the conceptual model of psychoanalysis. *British Journal of Medical Psychology* 36: 109-124.

van der Waals, H. G. (1952). Discussion of the mutual influences in the development of ego and id. *Psychoanalytic Study of the Child* 7: 66-68.

Weisman, A. D. (1958). Reality sense and reality testing. *Behavioral Science* 3: 228-261.

Winnicott, D. W. (1955). The depressive position in normal emotional development. *British Journal of Medical Psychology* 28: 89-100.

Zetzel, R. (1968). The so-called good hysteric. *International Journal of Psycho-Analysis* 49: 256-260.

six

Transference and Countertransference in the Treatment of Borderline Patients

AN OVERVIEW

An outline of my approach to the treatment of borderline patients (1975b), together with clinical material, should illustrate the differences between the technique used with borderline patients and that used with other types of patients. I will have two points of emphasis. First is the difference between the particular psychotherapeutic approach proposed for borderline patients and that used in a standard psychoanalysis. The second is the common principles underlying standard psychoanalytic technique and technical interventions made in the course of any session with borderline patients. My therapeutic approach may be subsumed under two headings: (A) transference interpretation limited by the deployment of special parameters of technique (Eissler, 1953) and (B) systematic resolution of the constellations of primitive object relations activated in the transference.

A. *Transference interpretation limited by the deployment of special parameters of technique.* (1) The predominantly negative transference of borderline patients should be systematically elaborated only in the "here and now," without attempting to achieve full genetic reconstructions. The reason is that lack of differentiation of the self concept and lack of differentiation and individualization of objects interfere with the ability of these patients to differentiate present and past object relations, resulting in their confusing transference and reality and failing to differentiate the analyst from the transference object. Full genetic reconstructions, therefore, have to await advanced stages of the treatment. (2) The typical defensive constellations of these patients should be interpreted as they enter the transference; the implication is that the interpretation of the predominant, primitive defensive operations characteristic of borderline personality organization strengthens the patient's ego and brings about structural intrapsychic change which contributes to resolving this organization. (3) Limits should be set in order to block acting out of the transference, with as much structuring of the patient's life outside the hours as necessary to protect the neutrality of the therapist. The implications are that, although interventions in the patient's external life may sometimes be needed, the technical neutrality of the therapist is essential for the treatment; moreover, it is important to avoid allowing the therapeutic relationship, with its gratifying and sheltered nature, to replace ordinary life, lest primitive pathological needs be gratified in the acting out of the transference during and outside the hours. (4) The less primitively determined, modulated aspects of the positive transference should not be interpreted. This fosters the gradual development of the therapeutic alliance; however, the primitive idealizations that reflect the splitting of "all good" from "all bad" object relations need to be interpreted systematically as part of the effort to work through these primitive defenses. (5) Interpretations should be formulated so that the patient's distortions of the therapist's interventions and of present reality (especially of the patient's perceptions in the hour) can be systematically clarified. One implication is that the patient's magical utilization of the therapist's interpretations needs to be interpreted. (6) The highly distorted transferences (at times, of an almost psychotic nature), reflecting fantastic internal object relations related to early ego disturbances, should be worked through *first* in order to reach *later* the transferences related to actual childhood experiences. All transferences, of course, recapitulate childhood fantasies, actual experiences, and defensive formations against them, and it is often difficult to sort out fantasies from reality. However, the extreme nature of the fantasied relationships reflecting very early object relations gives the transference of borderline patients special characteristics—our next point.

B. *Systematic resolution of the constellations of primitive object relations activated in the transference.* A predominant characteristic of the transference of borderline patients, particularly in early stages of treatment, is the presence of overwhelming chaos, meaninglessness or emptiness, or conscious suppression or distortion. The most general reason for this state of affairs is the predominance of "primitive transferences," that is, the activation in the transference of part-object relations—units of early self- and object-images and the primitive affects linking them—which do not represent the characteristic developments of internal object relations of neurotic patients and of normal people. The ordinary transference neurosis is characterized by the activation of the patient's infantile self or aspects of that infantile self linked to or integrated with his infantile self in general, while the patient reenacts emotional conflicts of this infantile self with parental objects that are, in turn, integrated and reflect the parental figures as experienced in infancy and childhood. In contrast, the nonintegrated self- and object-representations of borderline patients are activated in the transference in ways that do not permit the reconstruction of infantile conflicts with the parental objects as perceived in reality. Rather, the transference reflects a multitude of internal object relations of dissociated or split-off self aspects with dissociated or split-off object-representations of a highly fantastic and distorted nature.

The basic cause of these developments in borderline patients is their failure to integrate the libidinally and aggressively determined self- and object-images (Chapters 1, 2 and 5). Such a lack of integration derives from the pathological predominance of aggressively determined self- and object-images and a related failure to establish a sufficiently strong ego core around the (originally nondifferentiated) good self- and object-images. The problem with borderline patients is that the intensity of aggressively determined self- and object-images and of defensively idealized, "all good" self- and object-images makes integration impossible. Because of the implicit threat to the good object relations, bringing together extreme loving and hateful images of the self and of significant others would trigger unbearable anxiety and guilt; therefore, there is an active defensive separation of such contradictory self- and object-images. In other words, primitive dissociation or splitting becomes a major defensive operation.

The overall strategical aim in working through the transference developments of borderline patients is to resolve these primitive dissociations of the self- and object-representations and thus to transform primitive transferences—that is, the primitive level of internalized object relations activated in the transference—into the transference reactions of the higher level or integrated, more realistic type of internalized object relations related to real childhood experiences. Obviously, this requires intensive, long-term treatment along the lines I have suggested (1975b)—usually not less than three sessions a week over a number of years. The strategy of interpretation of the transference may be divided into three steps.

These three steps represent, in essence, the sequence involved in the working through of primitive transference developments in patients with borderline personality organization. In this process, the dissociated or generally fragmented aspects of the patient's intrapsychic conflicts are gradually integrated into significant units of primitive internalized object relations. Each unit is constituted by a certain self-image, a certain object-image, and a major affect disposition linking them. The units of internalized object relations become activated in the transference; and, when they can be interpreted and integrated with other related or contradictory units (particularly when libidinally and aggressively invested units can be integrated), the process of working through the transference and of the resolution of primitive constellations of defensive operations characteristic of borderline conditions has begun.

The first step consists in the psychotherapist's efforts to reconstruct, on the basis of his gradual understanding of what is emotionally predominant in the chaotic, meaningless, empty, distorted, or suppressed material, the nature of the primitive or part-object relation that has become activated in the transference. He needs to evaluate what, at any point in the contradictory bits of verbal and behavioral communication, in the confused and confusing thoughts and feelings and expressions of the patient, is of predominant emotional relevance in the patient's present relation with him and how this predominant material can be understood in the context of the patient's total communications. In other words, the therapist by his interpretative efforts transforms the prevalent meaningless or futility in the transference (which dehumanizes the therapeutic relationship) into an emotionally significant, although highly distorted, fantastic transference relationship.

In the second step, the therapist must evaluate this crystallizing, predominant object relation in the transference in terms of the self-image and the object-image involved and clarify the affect of the corresponding interaction of self and object. The therapist may represent one aspect of the patient's dissociated self and/or one aspect of the primitive object-representation; and patient and therapist may interchange their enactment of self- and object-images. These aspects of the self- and object-representations need to be interpreted and the respective internal object relations clarified in the transference.

In the third step, this particular part-object relation activated in the transference has to be integrated with other, related and opposite, defensively dissociated part-object relations until the patient's real self and his internal conception of objects can be integrated and consolidated.

Integration of self and objects, and thus of the entire world of internalized object relations, is a major strategic aim in the treatment of patients with borderline personality organization. Integration of affects with their related fantasied or real human relations involving the patient and the significant object is another aspect of this work. The patient's affect dispositions reflect the libidinal or aggressive investment of certain internalized object relations, and the integration of split-off, fragmented affect states is a corollary of the integration of split-off, fragmented internalized object relations.

SOME CLINICAL ILLUSTRATIONS

Case 1: The patient, a businessman in his middle thirties, was in psychoanalytic treatment with the diagnosis of narcissistic personality. For months, his associations were characterized by a lack of emotional depth or relevance and an apparently aimless shift from subject to subject without any emergence of intrapsychic conflict or a deepening description of his internal or external reality. People and situations, as he described them, had a bizarre, almost lifeless quality. Although the patient was able to function well socially, there were many indications that this was only a surface adaptation and that other people were aware of his inability to establish meaningful, individualized relationships. The patient was very puzzled by what he sensed as other people's subtle rejection of him. In the hours with him, I frequently had to struggle with my own boredom and distractability.

In this particular hour, the patient wore a special attire, which impressed me as a mixture of a particular adolescent vogue and the regional dress of the patient's family. His first associations were to what he perceived as my critical way of looking at him because of the way he was dressed. He went on to comment on what he regarded as my rather conventional and slightly neglectful way of dressing and wondered to what extent I might be critical of people who were up to date with their clothes because I did not dare to be as free in my own ways and therefore envied him his naturalness and freedom of taste.

His associations then moved to various aspects of his activities in the last two days. He mentioned a person he had met who knew someone from his home town, and then, with an ironic smile, he suddenly said that while he was lying down on the couch he had had the fleeting impression—a disgusting impression—that a spider was crawling across it. He corrected himself, saying that it was a special kind of spider, rather like a scorpion, which reminded him of certain dangerous spiders of the countryside near his home town; he added that he had not mentioned this earlier because it seemed at once irrelevant and disagreeable. But perhaps, he added, this was the kind of subject matter I, as an analyst, would be particularly eager for. He then adopted his usual relaxed and serious expression and described various insects of the countryside he came from and his expertise in distinguishing various species. He said, with pride in his voice, that the people where he came from were forced to be strong and tough and independent. When his associations reverted to his business affairs, I interrupted at one point to ask about his smile while he talked about the spider. He said with some irritation that he had already mentioned that this was "analyst's stuff," and he was slightly amused by that.

I remarked that most of what he had said so far had been expressed in a rather monotonous and indifferent tone and that his smile seemed a significant change. I also said that his smile, which apparently reflected some ironical thoughts about the outlandish things analysts were interested in, was in contradiction to the feeling of disgust he apparently had associated with the image of that spider crawling across the couch. The patient said he understood what I was saying but that he couldn't do anything further with it. After a short silence, which seemed to convey his expectation that I might add to my comments, he resumed his associations, now talking about other aspects of his business ventures and about a social program for the following evening, which he was looking forward to.

At this point, I was struggling with a variety of impressions and feelings. First, as in many earlier sessions, I felt that my effort to highlight one of the patient's fleeting emotions had come to nothing; it was as if he had once more demonstrated my lack of understanding, my picking on some secondary or trivial detail while missing the main subject matter of his associations. The quiet sense of security of the patient himself, his relatively subtle but definite depreciation of me and of psychoanalysis seemed to me, at the moment, so obvious and overwhelming that it would defy my efforts at confrontation. And yet I was struck by the flagrant contradiction between what I sensed as the patient's artificial relaxation and his—to him—disgusting fantasy of a dangerous spider crawling on the couch at the moment he was lying down on it. I also remembered, now, that I actually thought, for a fleeting moment, that the patient looked strangely insecure, almost pathetic, in an attire that, given his official business functions at that time of the day, was not fully appropriate.

I finally said that I wondered whether he had difficulties in further exploring the spider theme because it was so much in contradiction to his general perception of himself as relaxed, cool, elegant, and secure. I wondered whether it could be that this image or fantasy of the spider reflected his fear that disgusting thoughts or feelings or aspects of himself might come out in the hour; could it be that he had seen me as critical of his attire because he thought I (rather than he) suspected that behind his cool facade there might be such painful, disgusting things to explore.

After a short silence, the patient said that he had not mentioned a fantasy he had had after wondering whether there was indeed a spider on the couch. The fantasy was that there were spiders coming out of his body and crawling all over the couch and the room. He then suddenly remembered that a few weeks ago he had had a dream in which he woke up in the night to find spiders crawling all over himself, his bed, and his room. He looked anxious now, and he said

—with more fear than conviction—that although there were, indeed, disgusting things coming out of him now, they had nothing to do with him as a person. He then speculated at length about the symbolic meanings of spiders in psychoanalytic theory. I interrupted to say how one part of him was trying to protect him from exploring the source of his fear and disgust by using psychoanalytic labels and seeing his problems in terms of frightening animals from his past rather than frightening feelings or experiences of the present. He replied that the only other thought in his mind was, if indeed spiders did come out from him, it would be like an invasion of my office, my books, and my furniture, and I would lose the sense of security, self-satisfaction, and stability that he associated with me (and that, as we had explored in the past, he had felt very envious about). And then, with an expression which seemed to combine sadness and disgust, he said that now he did not know any more whether it was my office or he that was disgusting.

This example illustrates the task of the therapist in transforming "meaninglessness" in the hour into a significant human interaction and the great difficulties in achieving this when ordinary free association seems to lead nowhere and when the patient's dissociated behavior and affect, together with the emotional reactions he induces in the therapist, have to be integrated as part of this effort.

Case 2: A high school graduate in his early twenties had come for treatment because of severe chronic social isolation, inability to pursue advanced studies in spite of high intelligence, and a chronic spasm of both hands, which had been diagnosed by many neurologists as a conversion symptom. The diagnosis was paranoid personality, with borderline personality organization and conversion symptoms; the treatment was psychoanalytic psychotherapy, three sessions a week. The son of a man in the West whose business interests required many trips throughout the country, the patient had been brought up in various cities and was now living with a foster-care family in town. His parents and brothers and sisters visited him for various days every few months. The patient was pursuing some studies at a local college in a rather disorganized fashion and had a part-time job at a local store, where his knowledge of several parts of the country was useful. He had a distant relationship with a girl friend and spent many hours alone roaming through the city or watching TV in his room. Information about his past relevant to the session to be described includes the following:

His father was a warm but domineering, irascible, and occasionally physically violent person, whom the patient feared throughout most of his life. The mother was rather quiet and kept in the background but exerted great influence on the father, of which the patient was vaguely aware. From early childhood, the patient's terror of his father had become obvious to all the family, and conscious efforts on the father's part to establish a better relationship with his son led nowhere. During his adolescence, the patient had become involved in a political group of the extreme right which had as one of its targets the revival of admiration for Nazi Germany and the persecution of Jews. Another enemy was American capitalism and imperialism, pictured by the patient as a conspiracy of international Jewry. Between the ages of 18 and 20, the patient had become disillusioned with this political group and from then on had not engaged in further political activity.

Throughout his adolescence, because of serious emotional difficulties at home and at school, he had seen various psychiatrists, one of whom had engaged him in intensive long-term psychotherapy. During the early sessions of the patient's treatment with me, he said he thought this psychiatrist was a homosexual and that he was subtly trying to induce the patient to become a homosexual as well. The patient described to me, over a period of several weeks, how, on one occasion, the psychiatrist had touched his arm and he had felt that this was a direct homosexual approach. The psychiatrist had initially stimulated the patient to bring his own drawings to the hours or to draw during them and, on one occasion, had smilingly asked the patient whether what he had drawn was a boy or a girl. When the psychiatrist touched the patient's arm, they had been talking about a confusion of whether another person mentioned by the patient was a man or woman, and the patient had felt that this was a clear indication that the psychiatrist was telling him that he (the patient) was a woman and not a man, and that he (the psychiatrist) would seduce him. The patient's spasm of his left hand started shortly after this experience and later developed in the right hand as well.

When I attempted to clarify whether the patient was convinced that his psychiatrist had tried to seduce him or whether he now thought this was a fantasy, he became rather tense. He said he realized it was a fantasy, but his emotional tone, I felt, betrayed a strong sence of conviction. When I confronted the patient with his behavioral expression—his reacting as if he were really convinced of this, he said that he had struggled for many years to clarify whether this was a reality or a fantasy and that his reason told him it was a fantasy but that his feelings made him wonder.

The patient had also attempted to find out whether I was Jewish or German; he thought my features were Jewish but my name was German, and he thought he had heard that I had had my training in a German-speaking country. On various occasions he attempted to speak German with me. Over a period of six months, the patient became more and more anxious in the hours. He would come late, often remain silent for up to twenty minutes, or occasionally not appear at all. It was obvious that he was extremely frightened of me and that his severely paranoid character constellation predominated as a major transference resistance in the treatment.

On the particular day to be described, he came dressed in a black leather jacket and sat in a chair as far away from me as possible. He talked about his studies, an outing with his girl friend, a forthcoming visit from his father, and then fell silent. I first tried to stimulate him to speak, which did not lead anywhere. I then mentioned that he had looked rather anxious and fearful on coming into the office and that I wondered to what extent his silence was an expression of fear of me, the fear being so intense that he did not even dare talk about it. The patient stared at me seriously with an expression I finally interpreted in my mind as a blend of suspiciousness and admiration.

After some further silence, I told the patient that I saw him looking at me with suspiciousness, but perhaps also with awe and admiration, and that, in trying to put this together with his prolonged silence, I was thinking that what frightened him must be something so uncanny and strange he saw in me that he wouldn't dare to express it. The patient now smiled slightly, and I asked him what this smile meant. He did not respond. I said I could not tell whether the smile was one of appreciation because I had correctly understood his expression or one of amusement because I was so far off the mark. In any case, I said, I sensed that he was less afraid of me now. Perhaps, I added, what I said had helped to reassure him that whatever it was he was seeing in me might be part of his fantasy rather than reality.

At this moment, the patient asked me whether I was aware that I looked like Eichmann. I thought about this for awhile and then said that his comment reminded me of the many times he had felt that I was a German Nazi and that this concern might have a double effect on him. On the one hand, my being a Nazi meant that I was associated with that part of him which felt like a Nazi attacking the Jews, and at that level it might be reassuring to him that we, therefore, were allies. On the other hand, insofar as he thought that his having been a Nazi was something ill advised and problematic and that if I were a Nazi I would be too cruel, cold, and contemptuous to provide him the understanding he needed for his serious psychological problems, my looking like Eichmann must be terrifying to him. I also said that, since he had come in wearing a black leather jacket, he might experience himself today as being under the control of that part of him that wanted to be a Nazi, and perhaps he had been fearful, on coming into the office, that I might not be a true Nazi, and seeing me as a Nazi was reassuring because I was not in danger from him. But his silence might reflect his feeling that, although I was not in danger from the Nazi part of him, it was also useless to expect any help from me as a Nazi.

A long silence followed, in which the patient looked increasingly sad and dejected. I stimulated him to talk, without effect, and, after some further silence, pointed out to him that he looked sad to me. I told him that he looked to me as though he felt alone in the room. He then said he knew perfectly well that I was not Eichmann and that he did not believe I was a Nazi. He also showed me his arms, saying that he had felt a strong spasm of his hands at the beginning of the hour but that now he could move them rather freely. I asked him how he understood that he was less nervous, and he said that he was no longer afraid of me. I encouraged him to explain further what he had understood had gone on in the hour; but he fell silent again, although he continued to look quite relaxed.

After some time, I commented that I had the feeling he was trying to make me explain what was going on inside of him, as if he were giving the responsibility for understanding what was going on in the hour completely to me. I said I understood that initially he might have been too frightened to think but did not feel this was true any longer, and so there had to be another explanation for his attempt to make me do the work. The patient replied that he felt relaxed, felt I understood him, that he was not fearful of me, as he was of his father. Another long silence followed, during the course of which I had the following thoughts: The patient wanted to establish a dependent relation with me as a motherly father image, but he was frightened by the homosexual implications of such a longing. Therefore, he had attempted to perceive me as a dangerous Nazi, which reassured him against the sexual temptations intimately linked in his mind with any warm relationship between him and a fatherly figure. The spasm of his hands indicated the heightened homosexual fear in the early part of the hour, their later relaxation the capacity to accept to some extent his dependent longings without feeling homosexually threatened.

I was about to communicate these thoughts to the patient, but I was concerned lest my formulating this understanding bypass our probing of his capacity to contribute to the clarification of these issues and my doing this work for him gratify his acting out of his dependency wishes on me rather than help him to become aware of them and accept them. Actually, confirmatory evidence of the use of the "Nazi relationship" as a defense against dependent longings (which were feared because of their homosexual implications) became apparent in the next few sessions, and the patient himself was able to verbalize these homosexual fears in this context later on.

I must stress the length of the silences and the difficulties I had to struggle with in attempting to understand what was going on in that hour. This example illustrates the focusing on the immediate reality of the patient-therapist relation, combined with a gradual deepening of the interpretation of this relation to include all the elements present in the hour, as part of the effort to interpret and work through the silence.

The case also illustrates another technical principle in the treatment of borderline conditions: the relatively rapid deepening of the level of interpretation required when comments on a surface level prove insufficient to modify and resolve transference acting out in the session, namely, the patient's silence. The general implication is that transference acting out, whether expressed directly in the hours or in the patient's behavior outside the hours, requires an acceleration of the interpretive process, so that, in order to resolve acting out by essentially interpretive means, a rapid evaluation of the full potential meaning in depth of a certain behavior becomes desirable. While this principle also applies to all kinds of patients in a standard psychoanalytic situation and in psychoanalytic psychotherapy, it is particularly relevent in the case of borderline patients, where acting out is prevalent and at times seriously threatens the treatment or the patient's life situation. We have to recognize, of course, that the urgency of the problems posed by certain acting out can be missed, particularly in the early stages of treatment, and that at times we cannot understand what the acting out is all about and may have to wait, trying to work with such ego resources as the patient still has available at such junctures.

Case 3: A 20-year-old young man was in treatment because of serious school failure, chronic rebelliousness at school and at home, minor difficulties with the law, and a generally chaotic lifestyle, which seemed beyond the understanding and control of the parents and school authorities. The diagnosis was a narcissistic personality functioning on a borderline level, with antisocial features, and the treatment was psychoanalytic psychotherapy (three sessions a week), with some degree of external structure provided by a psychiatric social worker.

In psychotherapy, his principal characteristics were a combination of grandiosity and bravado, punctured by occasional moments of panic and despair when one of his "plans" fell through, or when his fantasies of being able to control the world crashed against an unpleasant and undeniable aspect of reality. During such moments, he would attempt to use me as a counselor or lawyer to advise him how to deal with other, dangerous, "unmanageable" authorities. As soon as the crisis was over, his grandiose, derogatory, man-of-the-world facade would take over. Rather than sit in any other chair in the office, he usually sat in my analytic chair, stretched himself to full length, and started the hour by condescendingly asking me how I was doing. (As this was a face-to-face psychotherapy, formally there was nothing wrong with his sitting in my chair—as the patient correctly remarked.) After some time, he established jovial contacts with various receptionists in the building, and several of my other patients had commented in their associations that they could not understand why such a healthy and well-looking young man was coming to see me.

The hours were largely filled with his complaints about the stupidity, ignorance, and unfairness of various authorities, relatives, and friends; efforts of mine to confront him with the fact that he attributed blame to everybody else while he always appeared impeccably innocent and righteous were met with an incredulous smile or —when I became insistent—with outright indignation. I had asked myself on various occasions why this patient continued coming regularly to the hours and suspected him of using his going to a psychiatrist as an insurance against disciplinary measures in the school, as well as justification for frequent absences from school. On many occasions I had pointed out to the patient that I found myself in the curious position either of listening to him silently—with the implication that I was agreeing with him—or, if I "dared" to question any of his statements, of becoming one more example of his world of unfair grownups and, particularly, unfair grownups in a position of authority, with whom he was struggling at all times.

I had also pointed out to him that he must have realized from my various comments that I often questioned what he was saying and that I had opinions or ways of looking at what he said that were different from his own. Therefore, I stressed, he must also have experienced my silence as criticism or even hypocrisy, and so he was in the uncomfortable position of coming to see a hypocrite or an angry authoritarian ally of his parents. I also had wondered with him what he felt he was getting out of our sessions. On various occasions, the patient had responded that he felt I was understanding, honest, and knowledgeable; and, although he was not getting anything at all from the psychotherapy, it was an agreeable experience for a change to meet with a person having these attributes. Frankly, his avowals did not convince me.

What I am trying to convey is not only the almost impenetrable grandiosity this patient revealed in the hours but also the charm with which he could say and defend outrageous things. As long as I did not contradict him openly, he maintained an amused and friendly security in the hour. Open challenge brought about attacks of rage against me, the intensity of which I at first found almost frightening. I gradually realized that the main intent of his rage was to shut off any view of himself or of reality that contradicted his own and that, if I remained silent, his rage diminished. I had rarely experienced a more effective control over my psychotherapeutic efforts in the treatment of a nonpsychotic patient.

The patient was also lying to me; on various occasions he provided me with partial information regarding antisocial behavior he was engaging in, particularly involving drugs; and on some occasions it was only the communication from the police to the parents, which reached the social worker and finally myself, that permitted me to know what was going on in his life. The patient knew that the psychiatric social worker was in contact with me, and our understanding (corresponding to the general strategy I follow in these cases) was that I would receive full communication from the psychiatric social worker but only communicate to her information from him that he had explicitly authorized.

In contrast to his rage upon being contradicted, when I confronted the patient with the fact that he had been lying to me, he did not become particularly indignant and tried to explain away "misunderstandings" that had occurred. Implicitly, he acknowledged that he had been lying to me, and I gradually focused more and more on this aspect of our relationship. I pointed out to him how, in contrast to his image of me as an understanding, knowledgeable, and honest person, he was providing me with false information—which made a caricature of any understanding and knowledge I could acquire about him—and treating me in dishonest ways which belied any interest that my honesty could have for him.

Over a period of time, I told him that I had to question everything he had said to me so far, including his appreciation of me as somebody who was knowledgeable and honest. I really could not be knowledgeable under circumstances in which he was feeding me lies, and what honesty could I have as a psychotherapist of a patient who was lying to me and therefore not providing me with the essential information on the basis of which I might be able to add my realistic understanding to his own?

I told him I wondered what was in it for him, and I speculated to what extent he might feel that he and I were involved in a con game, in which he was providing me with money for phony services, money paid by his parents for his psychotherapy, and I was providing him with an alibi for his difficulties in school, difficulties which were tolerated because he was in psychiatric treatment, and also providing him with hours that constituted a cover for other activities. I told him that I was hesitant to say all this, because it might sound harsh and critical; and yet, if this was true, anything less would, in turn, be dishonest or ignorant and just feed into the con game situation.

I was as careful as I could be not to make this kind of comment when I felt so frustrated or angry at him that I could not say for sure whether I was motivated by his need for clarification or by my need to get rid of my feelings. In other words, I tried to intervene only when I felt concerned for him and yet objective enough to feel that I could present to him this picture of a disastrous relationship—or lack or relationship—between us. From a strategic (in contrast to a tactical) viewpoing, I was attempting to focus upon and interpret the patient's narcissistic character constellation, proceeding as tactfully as I could to highlight and, I hoped, to dissolve the corroding effects on the therapeutic situation of his superego pathology.

My approach might be misunderstood as an exclusive focus on the negative aspects of the transference. When the transference is, indeed, predominantly negative—and particularly malignant in destroying human interaction, as in this kind of patient—it needs to be interpreted. The therapist's focusing on whatever remnant of a capacity for an authentic human relation remains is very important under these circumstances. In this case, I tried to convey by my attitude of respect, by my acknowledging how hard it was for the patient to listen to anything contradictory to his thinking, that I appreciated his effort and courage in nonetheless keeping his appointments with me. I would, however, never attempt to foster, establish, or even tolerate a pseudopositive relationship based on an acceptance of the patient's corrupted and corrupting superego pathology.

In more general terms, what I have been trying to illustrate is the need, even under these rather extreme psychotherapeutic circumstances, to diagnose what causes the development of meaninglessness in terms of the interaction between patient and therapist and to reduce the meaninglessness to the predominant human relationship (and the defenses against it) activated at that point. I again want to stress that the understanding of even very primitive transference paradigms activated in the sessions depends on the reconstruction of significant human interactions and conflicts out of the general dispersal, destruction, suppression, or distortion of them that is characteristic of borderline patients.

FURTHER OBSERVATIONS ON TRANSFERENCE MANAGEMENT

Various technical problems and dangers arise in the transferences of borderline patients. First, the therapist may be tempted by the primitive nature of the transferences to interpret them directly, as if they reflected the actual, earliest, or most primitive human experiences; he might go so far as to interpret the material as a genetic reconstruction of the first few years or even the first few months of life, thus confusing or condensing primitive fantasy and actual earliest development—a failing which characterizes some of the Kleinian work with borderline and other patients.

Second, the confusing and confused intense activation of affects, in which the patient retains little capacity to maintain an observing attitude toward what he is experiencing, may shift the therapist's attention to an exclusive focus on the decreased or defective ego functioning and thus lead him to neglect the object-relations implications of what is activated in the transference. For example, the therapist may focus, in an isolated fashion, on the patient's difficulty in experiencing or expressing his feelings, on his difficulties in overcoming silence, his tendency toward impulsive actions, or his temporary loss of logical clairty, instead of on the total primitive human interaction (or the defenses against it) activated in the transference. This is the danger of a simplistic ego-psychological approach which neglects the full analysis of the total human interaction.

Third, a mistake in the opposite direction would be to interpret the object relation in depth, without sufficient attention to the patient's ego functions—his capacity, for example, to understand and elaborate that interpretation or to become aware of his tendencies to use the interpretation magically rather than as a communication within a shared work relationship with the therapist. When the patient eagerly wants to comply with the therapist's "intentions"—or oppose them at any cost—this relationship to the interpretations needs to be interpreted; and when the patient insists in seeing as real what to the therapist appears as a transference distortion, this discrepancy needs to be worked through fully before interpretation of that transference reaction can proceed.

A fourth danger is that of relying exclusively on the analysis of the primitive object relation in the transference in the here and now, considering the transference a corrective emotional encounter and neglecting the task of gradual integration of self-images and object-images into more realistic internalized object relations and advanced types of transference, which permit more realistic genetic reconstructions. Under these circumstances, the therapist may unwillingly or unwittingly contribute to the stability of primitive transferences (as the treatment replaces life) and interfere with the patient's ego growth.

The technical approach I have proposed for borderline patients implies giving attention simultaeously to the immediate interaction, to the patient's perceptions and their distortions in the hour, and to the underlying, primitive, fantastic internalized object relations activated in the transference, so that what is most superficial and what is deepest are integrated into human experiences of ever-growing complexity. In this process, whatever remnant the patient has of a capacity for self-observation and autonomous work on his problems need to be explored, highlighted, and reinforced, so that attention is given to the patient's ego functioning, particularly its self-observation, hand in hand with the clarification and verbalization of primitive object relations reflected in his conscious and unconscious fantasies.

The general rule of interpretation, to proceed from surface to depth, very much holds in the case of borderline patients (Fenichel, 1941). It is helpful to first share with the patient our observations, stimulate him to integrate them one step beyond what is immediately observable, and only proceed to interpret beyond his own awareness once it is clear that he cannot do it on his own. In addition, whenever we interpret beyond the patient's awareness of the transference situation, the reasons for his incapacities to be aware of it beyond a certain point should become part of that interpretation. Insofar as primitive transference dispositions imply a rapid shift into a very deep level of human experience, the therapist working with borderline patients has to be flexible enough to shift from a sharp focus on the immediate reality to a sharp focus on the nature of the fantasied object relation activated in the transference, a fantasied relation that often includes bizarre and primitive characteristics the therapist has to dare to make verbally explicit as far as his understanding permits. However, as a sequence to such verbalization of the deeper aspects of the immediate interaction, the therapist has to return to the patient's work with this interpretation, to be alert to the danger that he may see the therapist's interpretation as a magical statement, a magical understanding activated by the therapist in the patient, rather than a realistic putting together of all the information in the verbal and nonverbal communications from him.

COUNTERTRANSFERENCE

I have suggested elsewhere (1965, p. 54) that

> one can describe a continuum of countertransference reactions ranging from those related to the symptomatic neuroses at one extreme, to psychotic reactions at the other, a continuum in which the different reality and transference components of both patient and therapist vary in a significant way. When dealing with borderline or severely regressed patients, as contrasted to those presenting symptomatic neuroses and many character disorders, the therapist tends to experience, rather soon in the treatment, intensive emotional reactions having more to do with the patient's premature, intense and chaotic transference and with the therapist's capacity to withstand psychological stress and anxiety, than with any specific problem of the therapist's past. Thus, countertransference becomes an important diagnostic tool, giving information on the degree of regression in the patient, his predominant emotional position vis-a-vis the therapist, and the changes occurring in this position. The more intense and premature the therapist's

> emotional reaction to the patient, the more threatening it becomes to the therapist's neutrality, the more it has a quickly changing, fluctuating, and chaotic nature—the more we can think the therapist is in the presence of severe regression in the patient.

The therapist normally responds to the patient's material with some affective reaction, which, under optimal conditions, is subdued and minor and is a kind of signal rather than an intense emotional activation. At points of heightened transference reactions, or when countertransference reactions complicate the picture, the emotional intensity of the therapist's reaction increases and may interfere with his overall immediate understanding of, or freedom to react to, the patient's material. With borderline patients, not only is the intensity of the therapist's emotional reaction higher after relatively brief periods of treatment, it is also more fluctuating and potentially chaotic. Obviously, rather than respond to the patient under the sway of these affective reactions, the therapist has to be able to tolerate them and utilize them for his own understanding. Insofar as what the patient is activating in the transference and the analyst is perceiving in his affective response to it is not only a primitive affect but a primitive object relation connected with an affect (that is, the therapist perceives a primitive self-image relating to a primitive object-image in the context of the particular activated affect), the therapist's diagnosis of his own emotional reaction implies the diagnosis of the patient's (often dissociated) primitive object relations in the transference.

How are we to understand that the borderline patient is able to induce such a complex reaction in the therapist? The therapist's effort to empathize with the patient leads him, in the case of borderline patients, to draw upon whatever capacity for awareness he has of primitive emotional reactions in himself. This temporary "dipping into" his own depth is reinforced by the patient's nonverbal behavior —particularly by those aspects of it that, in more or less subtle ways, imply an effort to exert control over the therapist, to impose on him the role assigned to the self or to an object-image within the primitive activated transference. We probably still do not know enough about how one person's behavior may induce emotional and behavioral reactions in another person. The relations among direct emotional empathy, the creative use of evenly suspended attention—a function akin to daydreaming in the therapist—and the direct impact of behavioral perception all combine to bring about a temporary regressive reaction in the therapist, which permits him to identify with the patient's primitive levels of functioning.

Nowadays, the term *countertransference* is often used to refer to the therapist's total emotional reaction to the patient. For the most part, however, and particularly for those with an ego-psychological approach, the term is reserved to the therapist's specific unconscious transference reactions to the patient. In other words, this latter, restricted definition of countertransference focuses on its pathological implications, while the former, broader one focuses on the intimate relationship between the general affective responses of the therapist and his specific countertransference potential. From the viewpoint of treatment of borderline patients, it is an advantage to consider the total emotional reaction of the therapist as a continuum of affective responses from mild, realistic signal affects to intense emotional reactions, which may temporarily interfere with the therapist's neutrality and which constitute a compromise formation determined by the transference and specific countertransference reactions. In any case, the therapist needs to be free to utilize this material both for resolving analytically his own excessive reactions to the patient and for diagnosing primitive object relations activated in the transference. This process, which I have attempted to illustrate by the above cases, may sometimes be very painful and induce intense secondary anxiety in the therapist.

For example, one borderline patient with strong masochistic personality features was able to mention, after many months of treatment, that she could feel that a man was really interested in her only if he was willing to kill her. This patient had a great number of fantasies of sexual intercourse with men in which the participants mutilated each others' genitals. It took a long time to bring the patient to express these fantasies fully in the sessions. Several months before this point, the patient had referred vaguely to the disturbing excitement she felt when watching sexual cruelty in a film and, later on, had mentioned how relieving it could be at times when blood flowed from a wound. In that session, she had also commented on how constrained psychotherapists really were and on the paradox that only those who were hostile could be trusted to be really honest in their interactions with patients.

I will not attempt to describe the bizarre, disjointed, chaotic ways in which pieces of this fantasy—which later became a full-fledged transference paradigm—emerged in the sessions. In retrospect, it all fit together, but I had to struggle for a long time to understand something I intuitively felt was going on. Sometime during the session mentioned, several months before full understanding of this predominant transference pattern occurred, I suddenly remembered a film I had seen (*Investigation of a Citizen Beyond Suspicion*) which depicted a police officer who was a sadist and killed a woman during intercourse and who was later charged with investigating the crime. The film, which I had seen many months before and had not thought about since, came back suddenly with full intensity, particularly the moment when the police officer, in the middle of intercourse with his girl friend, slashes her throat and blood spills over both of them while she dies. The memory came to me with a sense of anxiety and disgust, and I tried to dismiss it. Only weeks later, the memory of that film sequence came back, in connection with the patient's associations about the subject of sex and violence and her conviction that only if accompanied by violence could sex reveal authentic love. I could now pursue further my analysis of the activation of that memory in my mind.

It now seemed to me that the patient was perceiving me as two alternative objects and was trying to induce in me reactions corresponding to them. I felt that my countertransference reaction had, indeed, activated in me these two primitive objects. The first, similar to the police officer, was that of a strict, harsh, unforgiving accuser and punisher of criminal activities—in the last resort, a primitive, sadistic superego forerunner related to very distorted early images of a combined father-mother nature; the second, a sexually exciting, seducing, and physically violent and destructive primitive oedipal father image. I interpreted my inability to explore fully my own memory and emotional reaction as due to the activation of whatever potential for sadistic fantasies existed in me; and so, in dealing repressively with my own activated countertransference potential, I temporarily missed the transference information contained in my memory.

This approach is in contrast to alternative ways of dealing with primitive transferences. One is to minimize or even deny the importance of exploring primitive emotional and fantasy material in the transference and in the therapist's total emotional reaction to it in favor of focusing predominantly or exclusively on the contradictory and confused nature of the patient's communication—on his decreased or defective ego functioning, his limited capacity to formulate clearly what is going on in his mind, his difficulty in understanding the exaggerated nature of his emotional response, and his need to control the effects of this response on his behavior. This approach constitutes a type of supportive psychotherapy with borderline patients which I consider not helpful and contraindicated for the vast majority of these cases.

The other approach is to focus so heavily on the transference and countertransference that the patient's capacity or incapacity for working through the understanding he is supposedly gaining is overlooked. The therapist's personality comes so much into the foreground that a focus on the here-and-now encounter obscures the transference elements and brings about the danger of uncontrolled countertransference acting out. In addition, I have already stressed that overenthusiastic, early genetic reconstructions may not only be very misleading but also may increase the confusion between reality and fantasy in the patient's mind and foster transference psychosis.

In conclusion, I have suggested an approach which, I believe, avoids the pitfalls of a traditional supportive one, an exclusively existential-nongenetic one, and a pseudogenetic focus on earliest development.

REFERENCES

Eissler, K. R. (1953). The effect of the structure of the ego on psychoanalytic technique. *Journal of the American Psychoanalytic Association* 1: 104-143.

Fenichel, O. (1941). *Problems of Psychoanalytic Technique.* Albany: Psychoanalytic Quarterly.

Kernberg, O. (1965). Countertransference. In: *Borderline Conditions and Pathological Narcissism.* New York: Jason Aronson, 1975, pp. 49-67.

———(1972). Early ego integration and object relations. *Annals of the New York Academy of Sciences* 193: 233-247.

———(1975b). *Borderline Conditions and Pathological Narcissism.* New York: Jason Aronson, 1975.

seven

Barriers to Falling and Remaining in Love

In this chapter I shall describe a continuum of configurations regarding the capacity for falling in love and remaining in love, illustrating this continuum with case material. Two major developmental stages must be achieved in order to establish the normal capacity for falling—and remaining—in love: a first stage, when the early capacity for sensuous stimulation of erogenous zones (particularly oral and skin erotism) is integrated with the later capacity for establishing a total object relation; and a second stage, when full genital enjoyment incorporates earlier body-surface erotism into the context of a total object relation, including a complementary sexual identification.

The first stage develops gradually and subtly throughout the first five years of life. It is related to the normal integration of internalized object relations, which leads to an integrated self-concept, as well as to an integrated conceptualization of others and the concomitant capacity for relations in depth with significant others. The study of narcissistic character pathology has highlighted the consequences of failure of this first stage. The second stage of development corresponds to the successful overcoming of oedipal conflicts and the related unconscious prohibitions against a full sexual relation. Failure at the second stage is reflected in the neurotic syndromes, sexual inhibitions, and pathology of the love life stemming from unresolved oedipal conflicts.

This sequence of stages in the development of the capacity for falling—and remaining—in love also implies a general hypothesis regarding the vicissitudes of the development of drive derivatives; that is, the developmental stages of libidinal and aggressive drive derivatives depend upon the vicissitudes of the development of internalized object relations rather than upon a sequence of activation of body zones per se. The implication is that internalized object relations are a major organizer of instinctual development in man.

The first configuration along this continuum, represented by an almost total incapacity for establishing genital and tender relations with any other human being, is characteristic of the most severe types of narcissistic personality structure. The second configuration, characterized by sexual promiscuity (usually heterosexual, but at times polymorphous perverse), is typical of moderately ill narcissistic personalities. The third configuration, characterized by primitive idealization of the love object (with clinging infantile dependency upon it) and some capacity for genital gratification, is typical of borderline personality organization. The fourth configuration, characterized by the capacity for establishing stable and deep object relations without the capacity for full sexual gratification, is typical of relatively less severe types of character pathology and neuroses. The fifth and final configuration along this continuum is represented by the normal integration of genitality with the capacity for tenderness and a stable, deep object relation.

THE INCAPACITY TO FALL IN LOVE

Many patients with narcissistic personality structure have never fallen or been in love. Patients who are promiscuous and have intense feelings of frustration and impatience when desired sexual objects do not become immediately available to them may obscure the fact that they have never been in love. Narcissistic patients who present sexual inhibition or sexual deviation, however, or patients who have never been able to engage in any sexual relation other than fleeting sexual encounters clearly show this lack of capacity to fall in love from the beginning of treatment; and I have gradually become aware that this represents a grave prognostic sign for their psychoanalytic treatment. I would even add it to those prognostic elements regarding narcissistic personality structures which I outlined in an earlier study (1970).

Patients with narcissistic personality structure who do have the capacity to fall in love show a type of sexual promiscuity which, in analytic exploration, differs quite markedly from that seen in patients with less severe forms of character pathology. Promiscuous behavior in women with hysterical personality and strong masochistic trends, for example, usually reflects unconscious guilt over establishing a stable, mature, gratifying relation with a man; such a relation would unconsciously represent the forbidden oedipal fulfillment. These hysterical and masochistic patients show a capacity for full and stable object relations in areas other than sexual involvement. Hysterical women with strong unconscious competitive strivings with men may thus develop stable, deep relations with them so long as no sexual component is present; it is only when sexual intimacy develops that unconscious resentment over submission to men or unconscious guilt over forbidden sexuality interferes with the relation and may determine sexual promiscuity.

In contrast, sexual promiscuity of narcissistic personalities is linked with the sexual excitement for a body that "withholds itself" or for a person considered attractive or valuable by other people. Such a body or person stirs up unconscious envy and greed in narcissistic patients, the need to take possession of, and an unconscious tendency to devalue and spoil that which is envied. Insofar as sexual excitement temporarily heightens the illusion of beauty (or food or wealth or power) withheld, a temporary enthusiasm for the desired sexual object may imitate the state of falling in love. Soon, however, sexual fulfillment gratifies the need for conquest, coinciding with the unconscious process of devaluing the desired object and resulting in a speedy disappearance of both excitement and interest. The situation becomes complex, however, because unconscious greed and envy tend to be projected onto the desired sexual object, and, as a consequence, fear of possessive greed coming from this sexual object is a potential threat to the narcissistic patient's need to escape into "freedom." For the narcissistic patient, all relations are between exploiters and exploited, and "freedom" is simply an escape from fantasied devouring possessiveness.

And yet, hidden behind the transitory infatuations and sexual excitements of narcissistic personalities is not just greed and exploitativeness and the desperate need to escape involvement. It is true that there are some narcissistic people who live out lives devoid of meaningful object relations or even of transitory infatuations, spending many adult years alone and lonely; they replace all sexual involvements with masturbation fantasies (usually of a primitive, polymorphous perverse kind) of such relations. But other narcissistic patients, those who do show the driven promiscuity of a narcissistic type, also reveal in analysis a desperate search for human love, as if it were magically bound with body surfaces—breasts or penises or buttocks or vaginas. The endless, repetitive longing for such body surfaces may emerge, upon analysis, as a regressive fixation to split-off erogenous zones caused by the incapacity to establish a total object relation or object constancy (Arlow et al., 1968), a regression caused by the incapacity to tolerate ambivalence, the integration of love and hatred for the same object (in the last resort, mother). In this context, the flight from sexual objects who have been "conquered" may also represent an effort to protect those objects from the narcissistic personality's unconsciously sensed destructiveness. Riviere (1937), discussing the psychology of "Don Juans and Rolling Stones," stressed the oral sources, the envy of the other sex, and the defenses of rejection and contempt as leading dynamic factors in these cases.

What I am trying to stress is that narcissistic patients who from adolescence on have never been involved sexually and emotionally with others of the same or opposite sex are essentially incapable of establishing object relations, while those narcissistic patients who present promiscuous behavior, or even brief infatuations, at least struggle to overcome their basic incapacity for establishing object relations. In this repetition compulsion of the basic conflict lies important potential information regarding early determinants for the incapacity to fall in love. The following examples illustrate the psychopathological continuum within the range of narcissistic personality disturbances.

A man in his middle twenties consulted me because of fear of impotence. Although he had had intercourse occasionally with prostitutes, when he attempted it for the first time with a woman he described as having been a "platonic friend," he failed to achieve a full erection. This failure was a severe blow to his self-esteem and brought about an intensive anxiety reaction. He had never fallen in love and had not been sexually or emotionally involved with either women or men. His masturbation fantasies reflected multiple perverse trends, with homosexual, heterosexual, sadomasochistic, exhibitionistic, and voyeuristic aspects.

Of high intelligence and culture, he worked effectively as an accountant, and several somewhat distant and yet stable relations with both men and women centered on common political and intellectual interests. On the surface, he was not ambitious. He was satisfied with a routine performance at his work and was generally liked because of his friendly, flexible, highly adaptive behavior. His friends were amused with his occasional biting irony and haughty attitude toward other people.

This patient was seen initially as an obsessive personality, but psychoanalytic exploration revealed a typical narcissistic personality structure. He had the deep, mostly unconscious conviction that he was superior to all the petty, competitive struggles in which his colleagues and friends were involved. He was superior also, he felt, to the interests that his friends developed in mediocre, psychologically superficial, but physically attractive women. The fact that he was unable to perform when he graciously consented to have intercourse with his platonic friend was a terrible blow to his self-concept. He thought he should be able to perform sexually with men or women and was above the narrow, conventional morality of his contemporaries.

At one point during the analysis, after many months of examination of his superficially friendly but basically distant and unconsciously depreciatory attitude toward the analyst, this patient became sexually interested in a woman friend of another man (his—relatively—best friend and a colleague at work). The patient was painfully aware that he did not dare approach her because she might respond to him, and he might prove to be impotent again. He developed the fantasy that if he could have a sexual relationship involving this woman and his friend, and hold on to the erect penis of his friend while attempting sexual intercourse with her, he would be successful. The patient, who usually had to arrive at understandings himself rather than depend on the analyst for that purpose (an attitude which I had examined with him consistently over recent months), interpreted his fantasy as follows: He was afraid of approaching a woman because, unconsciously, women were forbidden to him. He needed the authorization of a powerful man—in this case his colleague, who represented a father figure—to assure him that this woman was not mother and that he could be sexually intimate with her.

I was uneasy about his interpretation, not only because of its intellectualizing quality and the transference implications mentioned before but also because of its similarity to a situation in a psychological textbook he had read as part of his "cooperation" with analysis. When I raised these questions, the patient interrupted to tell me he had not read the example I referred to in the textbook. He said I was probably envious of him because he could achieve such an understanding on his own rather than having to read it as I, obviously, had done. He also felt very annoyed because I was so uncertain about everything, in contrast to his colleague, whose inner security he could depend on for help with his own insecurity regarding women. And then, indicating by his attitude that he had now eliminated me from the picture, he continued to describe his fantasies about the triangular sexual relationship. It turned out that in this relationship he saw his friend's girl as admiring the power and physical beauty of the two men who were intimately united in their joint endeavor to gratify and, at the same time, humiliate her sexually.

I pointed out that he had inverted his earlier feelings about the girl —her physical attractiveness, his sexual excitement about her, his admiration for her personality and charm—and was seeing her now as admiring these same qualities in him. I reminded the patient of his eager readings of psychological material and his recent efforts to establish social contacts in the psychoanalytic community in order to obtain what he saw as my privileged knowledge and professional advantage. I also reminded him how he had inverted the situation with me, making me appear envious of his knowledge. I pointed out to him that while he claimed to wish to depend on me in order to be more effective in his external life, really this "dependency" was on an idealized version of me and was similar to his idealized version of his colleague, which basically corresponded to his own conception of himself. He had stressed that the girl would be impressed by the great similarity between his colleague and himself.

I suggested that his sexual fantasy reflected the need to impress upon the girl that he did not really need her; he had his colleague (that is, his own ideal self) as a sexual partner, and under these circumstances to be excited by her and have intercourse with her was acceptable to him. In contrast, if he were feeling sexual excitement and longing for her while under the sway of his intense envy of her, the fear of his own aggression toward her and of her retaliation against him would make sexual intercourse much too dangerous and lead to impotence on his part.

At this point, the patient developed physical symptoms (a feeling of weight on his chest, rapid breathing, and muscular restlessness—usual signs of anxiety). He said he knew this was absurd, but he felt I was trying to convince him of ideas which would make him impotent and even more frightened of women, retaliating in this way for his derogatory attitude toward me earlier in the hour. In other words, the immediate transference development reproduced in the hour what I had interpreted to him as occuring in his fantasy about the girl he wanted to have intercourse with: fear of revenge because of his own depreciatory attacks.

I would stress here, first, the incapacity for a sexual involvement, for falling in love—even in the form of a transitory infatuation—suggesting, as I mentioned earlier, an ominous prognosis for psychoanalytic treatment. (The analysis of this patient ended in failure after more than five years of treatment.) I would also stress the central dynamic feature in this case, namely, intense envy of women and defenses against this envy by devaluation and narcissistically determined homosexual orientation—a frequent development in narcissistic personalities.

The next case illustrates both the presence of some capacity for falling in love and the deterioration of this capacity in a developing series of short-lived infatuations and promiscuity. It also illustrates the hypothesis that progression from the fixation on body surfaces to falling in love with a person is linked to the development of the capacity for experiencing guilt, depression, and concern. In contrast to the first case, this patient, a man in his early thirties, showed some potential for falling in love. In the course of his psychoanalysis, this potential developed dramatically in the context of working through a basic transference paradigm.

The patient originally consulted me because of intense anxiety when speaking in public and an increasingly unsatisfactory sexual promiscuity. He said he had fallen in love on a few occasions in his adolescence but found he soon tired of women he had originally idealized and longed for. After some sexual intimacy with a woman, he would lose all interest and move on to search for another. Shortly before starting his treatment, he had begun a relation with a divorced woman who had three small children. He found her much more satisfactory than most of his previous women. His sexual promiscuity nevertheless continued, and, for the first time, he experienced conflict between his desire to establish a more stable relation with a woman and the numerous affairs he was carrying on at the same time. This patient (whom I also referred to in a different context as an illustration of transference developments in narcissistic patients [1970]) was a successful merchant. He had also studied history. Business friends admired his intellectual capacities and broad knowledge; his friends at the local university were in awe of his capacity to combine intellectual and professional success with business and financial success. He skillfully exploited his expertise in one field whenever he would meet with a group of acquaintances and friends. The patient's simultaneous development of two professions reflected his difficulty in committing himself fully to one field.

His desperate search for sexual experiences with women was the principal subject of the analysis from the beginning. At first, he proudly proclaimed his successes with women and what he thought were his extraordinary capacities for sexual activity and enjoyment. It soon became apparent, however, that his interest in women was geared exclusively to their breasts, buttocks, vaginas, soft skin, and, above all, to gratifying his fantasy that women were teasingly concealing and withholding all their "treasures" (as he used to call them). In conquering women, he felt he would "unwrap" them and "swallow them up." On a deeper level (he became aware of this only after many months of analysis), he had the frightening conviction that there was no way of incorporating women's beauty and that sexual penetration, intercourse, and orgasm were only illusory incorporation of what he admired in women and wanted to make his.

The narcissistic gratification of having "made" a woman was wearing off rapidly, and his awareness of the complete loss of interest he had after a short period of sexual involvement was increasingly spoiling the entire anticipation and development of these ephemeral relations. In recent years he had frequently fantasied having intercourse with other, yet-unconquered women while having intercourse with one who was already his and, therefore, on the road to devaluation. Married women were particularly attractive to him—not, as I first assumed, because of oedipal-triangular conflicts but because other men's finding something attractive in such women bolstered this patient's waning interest in them as possessing a "hidden treasure."

Finally the patient became aware of the intensity of his envy of women, derived from his envy of and rage against his mother. His mother had chronically frustrated him; he felt she had withheld from him, bodily and mentally, all that was lovable and admirable. He still remembered clinging desperately to her warm and soft body while she coldly rejected his expression of love, as well as his angry demands upon her.

Analysis gradually uncovered sadistic masturbation fantasies in this patient's childhood. He would see himself tearing up women, torturing a group of them and then "freeing" the one who seemed innocent, gentle, good, loving, and forgiving—an ideal, ever-giving, ever-forgiving, beautiful, and inexhaustible mother surrogate. Thus, in splitting his internal relations with women into dependency upon an ideal, absolutely good mother and retaliatory destruction of all other bad mothers, he ended up without any capacity to establish a relation in depth in which he could tolerate and integrate his contradictory feelings of love and hate. Instead, the idealization of breasts, female genitals, and other parts of the body permitted him regressively to gratify primitive, frustrated erotism while symbolically robbing women of what was unique of them. By his promiscuity, he also denied the frightening dependency upon a specific woman and unconsciously spoiled that which he was avidly attempting to incorporate.

That he could "give" an orgasm to women, that they needed his penis, symbolically reassured him that he did not need them—that he had a giving organ superior to any breast. But the fact that a woman should then try to continue to be dependent on him evoked fear that she would want to rob him of what he had to give. Yet, in the middle of his desperate search for gratification of erotic longings to replace his need for love, this patient sensed his growing dissatisfaction and was aware, at one point, that he was actually searching for a relation with a person "underneath" the skin of women.

It was only by systematic examination of his oral demandingness and of his long dissatisfaction in the transference that the patient became aware of his tendency unconsciously to spoil and destroy what he most longed for, namely, understanding and interest on the part of his analyst and love as well as sexual gratification from women. Full recognition of his destructive tendencies toward the analyst and toward women led to gradual development of guilt, depression, and reparative trends. Finally, concern for his objects brought about a radical shift in his relation to the analyst, to his mother, and to the divorced woman whom (in acting out unconscious guilt) he had married during the course of his analysis.

Gradually he became aware of how much love and dedication he received from his wife and began to feel unworthy of her. He noticed he was becoming more interested in what went on inside her, that he could enjoy with her her moments of happiness, that he was becoming deeply curious about the inside life of another human being. He finally realized how terribly envious he had been of his wife's independent interests, of her friends, her belongings, her dresses, of the thousand little secrets he felt she shared with other women and not with him. He realized that by consistently depreciating her he had made her empty and boring for him and had made himself fearful lest he have to drop her as he had dropped other women before her.

At the same time, he experienced a dramatic change in his internal attitude during sexual intercourse. He described it as almost a religious feeling, a sense of overwhelming gratitude, humility, and enjoyment in finding her body and her person at the same time. He was now able to express this gratitude for her as a person in the form of physical intimacy while experiencing her body (now representing her total person) with a new excitement. In short, this patient was now able to experience romantic love linked with sexual passion for the woman he had been married to for over two years. His sexual life left him fully satisfied—a contrast to his old pattern of rapid disappointment and an immediate search for a new woman. Previously, he had sometimes masturbated compulsively after sexual intercourse; this masturbation pattern now disappeared.

A brief summary can scarcely convey the intensity and the many ramifications of this patient's unconscious envy and hatred of women. During adolescence he struggled constantly to control the awareness and the expression of this envy. Watching movies of World War II, he was incensed when actresses exhibited themselves before a large audience of cheering soldiers. He felt this was cruel and that the soldiers should have stormed the stage and killed the actresses. He brooded endlessly over the fact that women were aware of their breasts and genitals and that at night, when they took off their underclothes—those marvelous, soft garments which had had the privilege of lying close to a woman's body—they would throw them —treasures neglected and unavailable to him—on the floor.

One finds intense envy and hatred of women in many male patients. Indeed, from a clinical viewpoint, it seems the intensity of this dynamic constellation in men matches that of penis envy in women. With regard to this phenomenon, I find myself in agreement with those who, like Jones (1948), Melanie Klein (1945), Horney (1967), and Chasseguet-Smirgel (1970), have questioned the overriding importance given penis envy in both sexes in the early psychoanalytic literature. What distinguishes narcissistic personalities in men is not only the intensity of this configuration but the pathological devaluation of women (in the final analysis, devaluation of mother as a primary object of dependency).

Devaluation of female sexuality by these male patients, plus denial of their own dependency needs for women, contributes to their incapacity to sustain any deep personal and sexual involvement with them. Complete absence of sexual interest in women in the most severely ill patients; the frantic search for sexual excitement and sexual promiscuity, linked with an incapacity for establishing a more permanent relationship, in less severe ones; and a limited capacity for transitory infatuation in still milder cases represent the spectrum of narcissistic pathology of love life.

Transitory infatuations may be the beginning stage of a capacity for falling in love, but with an idealization limited to that of the cherished physical sexual attributes of the women to be conquered. What these patients are not able to achieve, however, is the more normal idealization linked with falling in love where the female genitality, as well as the individual woman, is idealized, and gratitude for her love and concern for her as a person develop into the capacity for a more stable relation. The sense of fulfillment that goes with falling in love is lost for them; at most, there may be the fleeting sense of fulfillment at having achieved a conquest.

The incapacity for falling in love and for maintaining a state of being in love is at times hidden beneath an externally stable relationship with a woman. One patient with a narcissistic personality structure thought he was happily married, although he had a difficult time explaining the early stages of his relationship with his wife. Only after years of analysis did he reveal that his wife had been just one of many "pick-ups." She was very attractive, and a number of friends and acquaintances had congratulated him on his friendship with her. Since her family could be very helpful to the development of the patient's political career, he felt she was an ideal woman with whom "to establish" himself and marry. On the surface, he treated her in a gentle, friendly, detached manner, but he ruthlessly neglected her deeper needs. He did not understand why she seemed unhappy when he was giving her all the material security she needed. In his daily behavior he expressed his unconscious wish to be the preferred child of an enslaved mother; any illness of hers annoyed him deeply because it interfered with his well-being; he was uninterested in what she did or thought; and he had very little, if any, sexual interest in her after they married.

Another patient expressed his envy and his fear of women by projecting onto them his own hungry, exploitative needs in the following fantasy: he imagined having an affair with a marvelous, perfect woman whom he would meet at a motel located on the highway. They would meet by chance, her having driven to the motel from one direction and he from the opposite one. They would spend a marvelous night together, and then he would get into his car and escape, while she would resume her trip in the opposite direction in her own car.

Envy of mother as the primary source of love and dependency is, of course, as intense in women as in men; and an important source of penis envy in women is their search for a dependent relation with father and his penis as an escape and liberation from a frustrating relation with mother. The oral components of penis envy are, therefore, extremely intense in women with a narcissistic personality structure, as are their vengeful devaluations of others. Whether the prognosis for psychoanalytic treatment of women with a narcissistic personality structure is more guarded than for men is an open question. Paulina Kernberg (1971) has published a case illustrative of a woman with narcissistic personality reflecting these mechanisms.

One narcissistic patient, a woman in her early twenties, was icily attractive, a trait typical of narcissistic women (in contrast to the warm, human coquettishness of hysterical personalities). She was able to replace one man after another as her slave. She exploited men ruthlessly. When they finally decided to leave her, she merely "missed" them, reacting with anger and vindictiveness, but without longing, mourning, or guilt. It is very important to differentiate this kind of incapacity to develop a full-fledged emotional relation from the apparent "uninvolvement" of masochistic women, who cannot have a complete relation with a man without having unconscious guilt feelings. At times, only analytic exploration permits this differential diagnosis, which is of crucial prognostic importance in psychoanalytic treatment: the prognosis for women having hysterical or depressive character structures with strong masochistic components is infinitely better than that for women with a narcissistic personality.

A PRIMITIVE TYPE OF INTENSE FALLING IN LOVE

The next stage on the continuum is the development of very intense love attachments (with primitive idealization) somewhat more enduring than the transitory involvements of narcissistic patients. All these are characteristic of patients with borderline personality organization without the typical structure of narcissistic personalities. Perhaps the most frequent type of this pathological falling in love is displayed by women with infantile personalities and borderline personality organization, who cling desperately to men idealized so primitively, so unrealistically that it is usually very difficult to get any real picture of these men from the patient's description of them. On the surface, such involvements resemble those of much better integrated masochistic women who submit to idealized, sadistic men, but there are characteristics distinguishing them. The following is a typical illustration.

The patient was an obese 18-year-old girl. She habitually took a variety of drugs, and her performance at school was gradually deteriorating in spite of a high I.Q. Her chronic rebelliousness caused her to be expelled from several schools and was expressed predominantly in violent scenes at home. In the hospital, she conveyed the impression of an impulsive, hyperactive, disheveled, and chronically dirty adolescent. Although she was at first accepted with open arms by a group of adolescents on her floor, she was gradually rejected by them because of her uncanny way of promoting suspicion and fights among the members of the group. She showed a haughty, controlling, negativistic attitude toward the staff, relieved only by transitory efforts to ingratiate herself with those she felt wielded the ultimate power over her daily life.

Her ruthless exploitation of most people contrasted sharply with her complete dedication and submission to a young man she had met in another hospital and to whom she daily wrote long, passionate love letters. He responded only occasionally, and then in a rather desultory manner; apparently, he was having some difficulties, never specified, with the law. In spite of careful efforts on the part of the patient's hospital physician to gain some realistic picture of this man, he remained a nebulous figure, although, according to the patient, he was a perfect, ideal, loving, "beautiful man."

In psychotherapy, the patient described glowingly intense sexual experiences with her boy friend, her sense of complete fulfillment in their relationship, and her conviction that if she could just escape with him and live a life isolated from the rest of the world she would be happy and normal. The patient had seen several psychotherapists previously, and she came to our hospital "prepared" to fight off efforts on the part of the staff to separate her from her boy friend. She believed these efforts to be motivated by their "narrow, moralistic, antisex" attitudes, which, in turn, reflected (in the patient's view) their submission to the demands of her own parents, who were "rigid, moralistic, restrictive members of the establishment."

It was true that forceful separation from the boy friend and direct criticism of her sexual life had been attempted by some staff members of the other hospitals, as well as of our own. However, when the psychotherapist said he understood she was happy with one area of her life in which she could obtain gratification but pointed out the striking contrast between her complete submission to and idealization of the boy friend and the ruthless behavior toward everybody else, including the therapist, the patient showed greater anxiety than she ever had during the many arguments about her sexual life.

She was able to forgive—or rather to rationalize—the boy friend's harsh, ruthless, exploitative, and depreciatory behavior, and yet remain highly sensitive, often even paranoid, about other people's slights or neglects. Only after having been rejected totally and obviously by the boy friend and having found another young man in our hospital with whom she repeated this same relation could she disengage from the first one. This she did so completely that after a few months it was hard for her even to evoke the first one's face.

This patient presented a predominance of splitting mechanisms and primitive idealization of an "all-good" object as a defense against generalized projection of her aggression onto multiple "all-bad" objects, whom she tried to control omnipotently, fight off, or escape from. This primitive idealization linked with splitting mechanisms is very different from the later type of idealization linked with the integration of previously split-off "good" and "bad" object relations and the concomitant development of the capacity for guilt, concern, depression, and the need for reparation. (Hartocollis [1964] has described the transference implications of "hospital romances," their defensive function in helping the patient avoid intense, ambivalent reactions toward the therapist, and the problems of hospital management of these situations.)

Paradoxically, the type of falling in love described in this patient has a better prognosis than the ephemeral infatuations of narcissistic personalities, notwithstanding that narcissistic personalities appear to be much more "reality oriented" than typical borderline patients without narcissistic personality structure. The pathological deterioration of internalized object relations in narcissistic personalities constitutes a structural complication that makes their treatment much more difficult than that of the usual borderline patient. For this reason, and in spite of the fact that the love relations of the kind mentioned in the case of the infantile girl are so determined by primitive idealization, they represent a higher point on the continuum I am tracing. And yet, if and when in the treatment of narcissistic personalities the pathological narcissistic structure can be undone and a higher level idealization (related to guilt, concern, and reparative trends) appears as part of falling in love, an important step forward has occurred.

Most of the cases mentioned so far (the most severe types of character pathology) presented a relative freedom of expression of genital activity despite the absence (or rather replacement) of total object relations. I have suggested (1967, Chapter 5) that a pathological condensation of pregenital and genital drive derivatives under the predominant influence of pregenital aggression is characteristic of borderline patients. Although impotence, premature ejaculation, and frigidity can be found in borderline patients, one frequently finds capacity for genital enjoyment and orgasm in the context of both heterosexual and homosexual genital and polymorphous perverse activity. A number of factors combine to bring about this apparent sexual freedom.

First, in both sexes the activation of genital zones and modes of interaction serve as attempts to escape from the frightening, frustrating relations centering on oral needs and dependency. It is as if an unconscious hope for oral gratification through sexual activity and for a kind of relation different from the frustrating pregenital one with mother fosters an escape into early sexualization of all relations. Second, insofar as splitting and related mechanisms predominate over repression and its related mechanisms, a premature development of oedipal conflicts (in the sense of a defensive flight into a premature sexualized relationship with the parental figures) can be expressed in conscious, although mutually dissociated, fantasies and activities.[1] Third, identity diffusion and other structural ego alterations determined by the predominance of splitting mechanisms also affect superego integration and bring about superego distortions, which interfere with the processes leading to normal repression of infantile polymorphous perverse trends and permit direct expression of oedipal wishes. Freud (1938) originally described the process of ego splitting in observing patients with perversions. One patient, for example, masturbated with fantasies of having intercourse with both her parents, although she was frigid with her boyfriend.

Paradoxically, it is when integration of internalized object relations takes place and total object relations are established that the normal triangular oedipal relations develop and infantile prohibitions against sexuality become paramount. At this point, genital strivings are repressed in the context of full-fledged oedipal relations, and genital inhibitions may develop.

THE MUTUAL INFLUENCES OF SEXUAL CONFLICTS AND THE CAPACITY FOR TOTAL OBJECT RELATIONS

At the next level of pathology of falling in love, a greater capacity for what may be called romantic idealization exists in the context of genital inhibition. The following cases illustrate these features.

A woman in her late twenties entered psychoanalytic treatment because of strong pressure from her father, a locally well-known industrialist. Her main symptoms and presenting problems were heterosexual promiscuity, alcoholism, and depressive reactions. She presented a rather typical depressive-masochistic character structure with hysterical features. When feeling lonely, she would pick up a man at a party, social gathering, or bar rather indiscriminately—as if she were available to whomever wanted her—and then live with him until he dropped her. Her easy availability to men was well known throughout the restricted social group of her upper-middle-class family, and it was the feedback her father was receiving, indicating that she was considered a prostitute by his social group, that led him to convince her to go into treatment. She had undergone several induced abortions, some of them under traumatically self-destructive circumstances. In sexual intercourse she was frigid, although occasionally she had been able to achieve some sexual excitement, particularly when she felt she was being humiliated by a man.

Her mother died when the patient was six years old. She described her father's second wife as controlling, domineering, and aggressive. The patient fought with the stepmother throughout her childhood and adolescence. She described her father as a warm, kind, but weak man, whose submission to his second wife she found maddening. She was the only child of the first marriage. There were several children from the second one, with whom she had always had a rather distant relation.

From the beginning of treatment, transference paradigms relating to oedipal struggles predominated. Over a period of three years, successive changes in the transference occurred, indicating that the analyst was representing clearly differentiated transference objects reflecting varying stages of her relations to her father, mother (or, rather, the idealized mother she had lost, including deeply repressed rivalry with her), stepmother, and half-siblings. What I want to stress, in other words, is the typical transference development of an ordinary or nonborderline character neurosis, which is in contrast to the typical part-object relations of borderline, and particularly narcissistic, patients; it is also in contrast to the stability of pregenital conflicts, particularly revolving around pregenital aggression, and the chronic devaluation of the transference object characteristic of narcissistic patients.

At first the patient saw the analyst as an agent of her father and stepmother. She felt he was a conventional and weak man, just like her father, who supposedly was under the control of her stepmother. Severe acting out of the transference occurred in the form of sexual promiscuity, of searching for weak men the patient could take away from other women (men who then dropped her in response to her inordinate demands on them). Working through of this transference paradigm was followed, during the second year of analysis, by focus on the self-defeating needs in her relations with men, particularly with the analyst, linked with deep, unconscious guilt feelings over her sexual activities and wishes, which represented oedipal strivings.

In exploring the patient's idealization of her mother—the image of a sweet, pure, wonderful woman—it turned out that the image of her stepmother as a hostile tyrant reflected the projection onto the stepmother of the patient's own image of herself in comparing herself with her real mother. The anger toward the stepmother had to do with projected guilt feelings because of the patient's oedipal competitiveness with her mother. Later on, the motivation for these guilt feelings toward her mother—and the defensive idealization of her—could be interpreted as derived from the patient's sexual wishes toward her father. Memories now emerged reflecting the patient's image of her father as having been quite seductive toward her during her childhood and adolescence. Actually, the father had made the patient the confidante of his relationships with other women during the patient's adolescence.

In the transference, the analyst was now seen as seductive and sexually teasing, and periods of intense sexual fantasies and longing involving the analyst alternated with periods of rage because of the analyst's supposed wishes to seduce the patient and then reject her. This transference paradigm gradually developed into generalized anger with men because of their "sexual superiority," and her fantasies in seducing men sexually now became linked clearly with penis envy. In inducing men to want her, she was attempting to compensate for her feeling that women need men because men are sexually complete.

In the third year of analysis, the wishes to have the analyst—and men in general—need her gradually changed into early dependent longings for her mother, whom she had experienced as cold and rejecting. She had turned to her father in an effort to receive sexual love from him to replace the lack of oral gratification from mother. The idealization of her mother, who had died at the height of the oedipal period, now appeared to be a defense, not only against oedipal guilt, but against earlier, orally determined rage against her.

The analyst was now seen as a mother image, cold and rejecting, and the patient developed strong wishes to be protected, cuddled, and loved by him as a good mother, who would reassure her against the fears about her bad mother. She developed sexual fantasies centering on her performing fellatio, related to the feeling that the orgasm of men represented symbolically the giving of love and milk, protection and nourishment. The desperate clingingness in her relations with men and her frigidity now came into focus as an expression of these oral longings toward men, an expression of her rageful wishes to control and incorporate them and her fear of letting herself experience full sexual gratification because that would mean total dependency and, therefore, total frustration by cruel "motherly" men.

It was at this stage of her analysis that the patient was able for the first time to establish a relation with a man who seemed a more appropriate love object than most of those she had previously chosen. (This relation actually developed into marriage sometime after the completion of her analysis.) Her capacity to achieve full sexual gratification with this man marked a dramatic change in her relation with him, with the analyst, with her family, and in her general outlook on life. I shall examine this episode of her analytic work more closely.

During the analysis, the patient became capable of achieving orgasm on a regular basis in intercourse with the man she later married. This occurred after working through the implications of the different transference paradigms reflected in her relation with him. To her surprise, she found herself crying the first few times after achieving a full orgasm, crying with a sense of embarrassment and, at the same time, of relief. She felt deeply grateful to him for giving her his love and his penis; she felt grateful that she could enjoy his penis fully, and at one point during intercourse had the fantasy that she was embracing a huge penis, spinning around it with a sense of exhilaration while feeling she was rotating around the center of the universe, the ultimate source of light. She felt his penis was hers, that she could really trust that he and his penis belonged to her.

At the same time, she was no longer envious that he had a penis and she did not. If he separated from her, she could tolerate it because what he had been giving her had become part of her inner life. Her new experience was something that belonged to her now and could not be taken away. She felt grateful and guilty at the same time for the love this man had given her while she had been, as she now realized, so envious and suspicious of him, so bent upon not giving herself fully to him to avoid his supposed "triumph" over her as a woman. And she felt she had been able to open herself up to enjoyment of her body and of her genitals in spite of the internal prohibitions stemming from the fantasied orders of her mother and stepmother. She had become free of the terror of becoming sexually excited with an adult man who treated her like an adult woman (and thus of breaking the oedipal taboo).

She also felt exhilarated at being able to enjoy her own genitals, and by being able to expose her body to her friend without the secret fear that her genitals were ugly, mutilated, and distasteful. She was able to say to him, "I cannot imagine what, if heaven exists, heaven could offer beyond this," referring to their sexual experience. She could enjoy his body, become sexually excited playing with his penis, which was no longer the hated instrument of male superiority and dominion. She now could walk on the street feeling she was equal to other women. She no longer needed to envy the intimacy of others, because she had her own intimate relation with the man she loved. But, above all, the capacity to enjoy sex jointly and to be fully aware she was receiving love from him while giving it to him—feeling grateful for it and no longer afraid of fully expressing her needs to depend upon him—was expressed in her crying after orgasm. As she dared to become dependent upon him, she felt more independent, more fulfilled and self-reliant. Experiencing a full orgasm, she could empathize with his orgasm, and she felt, in a strange way, that by accepting his penis and identifying herself with his orgasm, they had become one: there was no further need to envy him as a man.

I wish to stress the central feature in this case: the overcoming of penis envy. Both its oral roots (envy of the giving mother and the giving penis, together with fear over a hateful dependency upon it) and its genital roots (the childhood conviction of the superiority of male sexuality and men) were worked through in the context of a total object relation in which guilt over the aggression toward the object, gratitude for love received, and the need to repair guilt by giving love were all expressed together. This integration represents the achievement of the next stage of development on the continuum: namely, the integration of full genital sexuality into the capacity for total object relations.

This patient had been able to empathize with her friend, to have a real interest and concern for his life, and, while romantically idealizing some aspects of him, to have a rather realistic picture of his values and limitations in other areas. However, it was only now, with full achievement of sexual integration within their relation, that she was able to overcome deep-seated suspiciousness about him, needs to compete with him, and jealousy over those of his interests he did not share with her. Also, it was only now that she could fully enjoy having an independent life—enjoy numerous activities he could not participate in without feeling she was withholding or competing with him. The capacity to merge, to interchange their self-exeriences, as it were, and still to preserve their autonomy (all important prerequisites for a normal love relation) now developed spontaneously.

In the transference, this development was reflected in the patient's understanding that she no longer needed her fantasies that only the love of the analyst would give her a real sense of fulfillment as a woman and in her awareness that she could accept what the analyst offered without feeling sexually rejected or teased or humiliated by the fact that she opened her life fully to him while he kept his life from her. With her greater acknowledgment of her erotic, genital interest in the analyst and wish for a dependent relationship to him as a father figure, the patient's angry demandingness for sexual gratification from the analyst disappeared; and a sense of longing, mixed with sadness for the unrealistic nature of these longings, added a new dimension to the transference.

One might interpret the improved sexual relation with her friend as an acting out of the transference; indeed, such acting out elements were of course present, but combined with a realistic deepening of her relation to the friend and a process of growth and emotional maturing within her relation to both him and the analyst. Of particular interest was that the blending of erotic and tender strivings with a deepening awareness of the reality of the other person developed together with a sense of separateness and of the limited nature of all human engagements—in short, a mixture of longing and fulfillment and sadness in the relation with both the friend and the analyst. In this regard, the elements of concern, guilt, and reparation gave a mildly depressive quality to this patient's love relation.

In more general terms, it is as if the process of concern and guilt characterizing the earlier phase of integration of part object relations into total object relations (the above-mentioned blending of body surface erotism and personal relation) repeats itself as the capacity for a diffusely erotized total object relation becomes integrated with genital urges in the context of overcoming oedipal conflicts and inhibitions.

The following case concerns a man in his middle thirties who consulted me because of obsessive doubts about whether his fiancée was attractive or unattractive. To the first session he brought a suitcase containing oversized photographs of his fiancée, carefully sorted into those in which she appeared attractive to him and those in which she appeared unattractive. He asked the analyst whether he saw any difference in the two series of photographs. There was no difference at all with regard to the degree of attractiveness in the different photographs, so far as the analyst could tell; and, from what the patient later said, this was the same reaction he had received from friends to whom he had confided his difficulty. He later revealed that his fiancee appeared unattractive to him whenever she seemed sexually excited about him.

The patient presented a typical obsessive character structure, with strong reaction formations against aggression, a consistent overpoliteness, and an almost pedantic way of expressing himself. Of very high intelligence, he had already obtained an important position in his field in a local university but was handicapped in his work because he was shy and fearful of more senior colleagues and insecure regarding his students, whom he suspected of secretly making fun of him because of his "correct, conservative" ways.

His family consisted of a number of younger and older sisters and a domineering, nagging mother who controlled the household, according to the patient, with the help of her "female army" (his sisters.) His father was overtly tense and somewhat explosive but quite submissive to his wife. Throughout his childhood, the patient felt he lived in a house of women, full of secrets and places he could not enter, drawers he could not open, subjects he could not listen to. He was reared in an extremely religious atmosphere, where everything related to sex was considered dirty. In his childhood, his mother spied on him while he was having sex play with his younger sister's friends, and afterward she punished him severely.

The patient was very proud of his "moral purity" and quite shocked when the analyst failed to appreciate "as a moral achievement" the fact that the patient had had no sexual intercourse throughout his life, nor any sexual excitement about women with whom he had felt "in love." Later on, he admitted that there were women who had excited him sexually throughout his adolescence, generally women of lower socioeconomic status than he. He idealized and completely desexualized women of his own social group. He had never had any symptoms, he claimed, until he started dating his fiancée, about two years before consulting, and the obsessive doubt of whether she was attractive or repulsive developed as she was pressing for greater physical intimacy, such as kissing or caressing.

In the transference, his obsessive-compulsive perfectionism at first interfered seriously with free association and gradually became the major focus of analytic work in the first two years of analysis. Behind his perfectionistic submission to psychoanalysis lay an unconscious mockery of the analyst as supposedly powerful but actually weak and impotent—an unconscious reaction similar to the one the patient had toward his senior colleagues and that he projected onto his students (whom he saw as mocking him). Intense defiance of and rebelliousness against father figures gradually emerged in the transference and took the specific form of intense suspicion that the analyst was out to corrupt the patient's sexual morality (a wish the patient attributed to all psychoanalysts).

Later, the patient felt the analyst was also an agent of his fiancée, wanting to push the patient into her arms; he consulted a number of ministers about the dangers of psychoanalysis to sexual morality and to the purity of his relationship with his fiancee. After thus seeing the analyst as repeating father's superficially controlling but deeply submissive behavior to mother (the analyst being an agent of the fiancée), the transference gradually shifted into his perceiving the analyst as his mother, spying on him and pretending to be sexually tolerant in order to have him express his sexual feelings and then punish him. During the second and third years of analysis, this mother transference became predominant, and the same conflicts could be analyzed in his relation to his fiancée and in his general view of women as dangerous mothers who were out to tease young men, to provoke them into sexual behavior in order to later take revenge on them.

This transference paradigm shifted, in turn, to a still deeper level at which sexual excitement in connection with his sisters, and particularly his mother, came into the foreground, with deeply repressed fears of retaliation from father. At this level, the perception of a hostile mother was a displacement from his even more frightening perception of a hostile father. It became very clear that what he sometimes felt as unattractive in his fiancée were aspects of her skin, which appeared too "warm" and "hairy" to him and which became connected with memories of his mother's facial complexion and the impression he had as a child that the flushing of her face indicated sexual intimacy with his father. He also occasionally felt his fiancée had strong body odors, and again he connected this with the odors he had perceived during menstrual periods of his mother and sisters and his exciting and repulsive thoughts about menstrual napkins.

At that juncture, the characteristic neatness, politeness, and overconcern with cleanliness became the focus of the analytic work. These character traits now appeared to represent a reaction formation against sexual feelings of any kind; they also represented a quiet, stubborn protest against the "excited" and disorderly, overpowering mother. Finally, they represented his aspiration to become a neat little boy who would be loved by father if he renounced his competitiveness with father and with men in general.

Throughout the fourth year of his psychoanalysis, the patient began, for the first time, to feel sexual impulses for his fiancée. Previously, when he had found her attractive, she represented the idealized, pure, unavailable woman—a counterpart of the sexually exciting but repulsive mother image. During the fifth and final year of analysis, the patient started to have intercourse with his fiancée and, after a period of premature ejaculation (linked with fear of his genitals' being damaged in the vagina and a reactivation of paranoid fears of the analyst as the vengeful combined father-mother figure), his potency became normal. It was only then that the patient discovered he had always had a compulsive need to wash his hands frequently, because this symptom disappeared in the context of his sexual experiences with his fiancée. It is this latter episode of his analysis that I wish to focus on further.

The patient used to meet with his fiancée on Sunday mornings, originally to join his parents and other members of his family to go to church. Later on, the two met in his office rather than in his apartment—which was close to where his parents lived—and spent Sunday morning together instead of going to church. One Sunday morning the patient was able, for the first time in his life, as part of sexual play to suck her genitals and feel excited. He marveled at her reaching an orgasm this way. He was profoundly impressed that she could be so free and open with him. He realized how terribly prohibitive and frowning he had envisioned all women (mother) to be about sex. He also realized, with a feeling of exhilaration, that the warmth, humidity, odor, and taste of his fiancee's body and genitals excited rather than repulsed him, and his feeling of shame and disgust turned into sexual excitement and satisfaction. To his surprise, he did not have a premature ejaculation while having intercourse with her, and he understood this was related to his having lost—at least temporarily—the feeling of anger and resentment against her as a woman.

He realized, during the ensuing weeks, that his staying at his office and being involved sexually with his fiancée represented a rebellion against both his father and his mother and against those aspects of his religious convictions which represented a rationalization of superego pressures. This patient in his adolescence had had the strong fantasy that Jesus was watching him, particularly when he was spying on his sisters' girl friends as they were undressing. It was dramatic to observe how his attitude to religion changed and how he now began to perceive Jesus as being concerned not so much with whether human beings "behaved well" sexually as with the search for love and human understanding.

There were other changes in the life of this patient. As he was able to enjoy fully the sexual aspects of his relationship with his fiancée, his tastes in art changed; he could now enjoy the passionate style of some European expressionist painters, some contemporary literature, post-romantic music of the turn of the century: all these he had previously rejected as too turbulent, unclear, or messy.

The patient also became aware that those aspects in his fiancée which at times seemed disgusting to him represented, in his mind, aspects of his mother when she, during his childhood, had appeared sexually excited with his father. As these aspects of his fiancée receded in importance, he recognized other, more realistic features she shared with his mother, such as her cultural and national background. When his fiancée sang songs of her native region, he was deeply moved; the songs gave him the feeling of communicating with a part of his past—not with his mother as a person, but with the background from which she stemmed. He felt that in reaching such a total fulfillment in his relation with his fiancée he was also reaching a new bridge with his past, previously rejected by him as part of his hidden rebelliousness against his parents.

What I am trying to illustrate here is a higher level of idealization than both the primitive idealization characteristic of the predominance of splitting processes and the later idealization occurring in the context of guilt, concern, and reparative trends when total object relations are achieved. This new type of idealization represents the idealized identification, not with the body or even the person of the love object but with the values for which this person stands. Intellectual, aesthetic, cultural, and ethical values are included here; and I think this represents, in part, integration of the superego on a higher level, one linked to the new capacity for integrating tender and sexual feelings and to the definite overcoming of the oedipal conflict. At the same time, in this establishment of identifications with the love object involving value systems, a movement from the interrelation of the couple to a relationship with their culture and background is achieved, and past, present, and future are thereby linked in a new way.

FALLING IN LOVE AND REMAINING IN LOVE

The last two cases show in some detail the importance of resolving sexual inhibitions in the context of the resolution of oedipal conflicts in order to be able to deepen and fully develop a love relation. But they also illustrate the relation between the capacity for falling in love and that for remaining in love. Both patients had the capacity for falling in love but were not capable of changing a passionate involvement into a stable, yet passionate love relation. The first patient had fallen in love with several men but unconsciously had managed to have them terminate the relation because of her inordinate demands on them. The second patient had originally fallen in love with a girl who became his fiancée, but after an increasing degree of sexual intimacy his obsessive doubts about her attractiveness blocked the development of the relation.

These are, of course, well-known developments in neurotic patients and patients with relatively less severe types of character pathology. As their relationships deepen, unconscious conflicts reflecting predominantly oedipal struggles interfere with the continuity of the state of being in love. On the surface, this situation resembles that of narcissistic patients with transitory infatuations, but the difference is that non-narcissistic patients clearly are able to involve themselves in a deep, meaningful way with other human beings, including those with whom they fall in love. Thus, for example, the masochistic woman who developed promiscuous behavior was able to establish deep, appropriate loyalties with friends at work and relatively conflict-free social relations; the same held true for the man with the obsessive-compulsive neurosis. On the surface, the difficulty of these two patients might also resemble the primitive idealization of borderline patients in that the capacity for falling in love is not matched with the capacity for developing a lasting love relation (except with turbulent, highly neurotic features). There is, however, an impressive difference in the capacity for more realistic evaluation of the love object and in the toned-down, yet humanly deeper idealization that characterize nonborderline patients' falling in love.

Only relatively normal people have the capacity for falling in love and developing such a passionate attachment into a stable love relation. It requires the resolution of the conflicts along the continuum of developmental tasks highlighted in the examination of the pathology of each of these stages of development.

Balint (1948, p. 117) has suggested:

> What we call "genital love" is a fusion of disagreeing elements: of genital satisfaction and pregenital tenderness. The expression of this fusion is "genital identification," and the reward for bearing the strain of this fusion is the possibility of regressing periodically for some happy moments to a really infantile stage of no reality testing, to the short-lived reestablishment of the complete union of micro- and macrocosmos.

I would suggest a modification of Balint's formulation: The incorporation of pregenital trends in the form of tenderness, a crucial precondition for the capacity of mature falling in love, is a consequence of the integration of part object (absolutely good and absolutely bad) into total object relations, an integration that implies at least partial resolution of pregenital conflicts over aggression and the establishment of the capacity for tolerating ambivalence to love objects. This integration permits the incorporation of body-surface erotism into a total object relation. Later on, tenderness, which represents this incorporation, needs to expand into the capacity for full genital enjoyment, which, in turn, requires a sufficient resolution of oedipal conflicts. It is such a resolution in the context of the capacity for establishing total object relations that develops the capacity for both a full, deep, lasting, passionate relation and full genital gratification.

The capacity for sexual intercourse and orgasm does not by any means guarantee the capacity for being maturely in love—nor does the capacity for a total object relation without the resolution of oedipal conflicts and the related freeing from sexual inhibition. The capacity for falling in love indicates the achievement of important preconditions for the capacity for being in love: in the case of narcissistic personalities, it marks the beginning of the capacity for concern and guilt and some hope for overcoming deep, unconscious devaluation of the love object. In borderline patients, primitive idealization may be the first step toward a love relation different from the love-hate relation with their primary objects. This occurs if the splitting mechanisms responsible for this primitive idealization have been resolved and this love relation or one replacing it is able to tolerate and resolve the pregenital conflicts against which primitive idealization was a defense. In the case of neurotic patients and patients with relatively less severe character pathology, the capacity for falling in love should, if psychoanalytic treatment resolves the unconscious, predominantly oedipal conflicts, mature into the capacity for a lasting love relation.

REFERENCES

Arlow, J. A., Freud, A., Lampl-de Groot, J., and Beres, D. (1968). Panel discussion. *International Journal of Psycho-Analysis* 49: 506-512.

Balint, M. (1948). On genital love. In: *Primary Love and Psychoanalytic Technique*. New York: Tavistock, 1959, pp. 109-120.

Chasseguet-Smirgel, J. (1970). *Female Sexuality*. Ann Arbor: University of Michigan, pp. 1-3, 94-134.

Freud, S. (1938). Splitting of the ego in the process of defense. *Standard Edition* 23: 273-278.

Hartcollis, P. (1964). Hospital romances: some vicissitudes of transference. *Bulletin of the Menninger Clinic* 28: 62-71.

Horney, K. (1967). *Feminine Psychology*. London: Routledge & Kegan Paul.

Jones, E. (1948). The early development of female sexuality. In: *Papers on Psycho-Analysis*. Boston: Beacon Press, 1961, pp. 438-451.

Kernberg, O. (1967). Borderline personality organization. In: *Borderline Conditions and Pathological Narcissism*. New York: Jason Aronson, 1975, pp. 3-47.

———(1970). Factors in the psychoanalytic treatment of narcissistic personalities. In: *Borderline Conditions and Pathological Narcissism*. New York: Jason Aronson, 1975, pp. 227-262.

Kernberg, P. (1971). The course of the analysis of a narcissistic personality with hysterical and compulsive features. *Journal of the American Psychoanalytic Association* 19: 451-471.

Klein, M. (1945). The oedipus complex in the light of early anxieties. In: *Contributions to Psycho-Analysis, 1921-1945*. London: Hogarth Press, 1948, pp. 377-390.

Riviere, J. (1937). Hate, greed, and aggression. In: *Love, Hate and Reparation*, eds. M. Klein and J. Riviere. London: Hogarth Press, pp. 3-53.

eight

Mature Love: Prerequisites and Characteristics

In the previous chapter I described some intrapsychic prerequisites for falling in love and remaining in love and examined the consequences of failure to establish these prerequisites. I proposed that two major developmental stages must be achieved in order to establish the normal capacity for falling and remaining in love: a first stage, in which the early capacity for sensuous stimulation of erogenous zones (particularly oral and skin erotism) is integrated with the later capacity for establishing a total object relation; and a second stage, in which full genital enjoyment incorporates earlier body-surface erotism in the context of a total object relation, including a complementary sexual identification. I also described a continuum in the capacity for falling in love and remaining in love, illustrating this continuum with case material highlighting the particular prerequisites of various points along it. In elaborating my findings, I stressed that these points have diagnostic, prognostic, and therapeutic implications. The socially isolated, almost completely noninvolved narcissistic personality who comes for treatment because of impotence, conflicts over homosexual urges, or any other kind of sexual psychopathology has a poor prognosis. Narcissistic personalities who are at least able to establish promiscuous sexual relations, implying some involvement with others, have a somewhat better prognosis (I have earlier [1970] spelled out other prognostic considerations for narcissistic personalities).

The impulsive, chaotic, infantile personality functioning on a borderline level has a better prognosis than the narcissistic patient, although superficially his love life may seem disturbed, inappropriate, and immature. Sexual promiscuity on this structural level may reflect the rapid breakdown of the primitive idealization typifying his sexual involvements and the desperate search for another object with whom a primitively idealized relation can be reestablished. The very fact that such borderline patients are able to establish a relatively stable relation with another human being—in the context of which tender and genital feelings can be expressed—represents a real potential for emotional growth. This is often obscured by the extremely violent, destructive, inappropriate nature of most other, split-off interactions of these patients, who may utilize the idealized love relation to rationalize and externalize the responsibility of all other interpersonal conflicts. Typically, such patients accuse the rest of the world of being cold, selfish, hostile, conventional, and rigid; if everybody were like their idealized love object, there would, they think, be no problem. Psychotherapists may be tempted to see the idealized love relation only as acting out or as a defense against more realistic awareness of the patient's intrapsychic conflicts and relations with others, including the therapist, but this would be a mistake. The taking of the patient's statement at face value and considering this highly idealized love relation a normal development—particularly when the patient is an adolescent—would be the opposite mistake and would be detrimental, for it would feed into the patient's splitting operations and perpetuate his unawareness of his incapacity to evaluate the love relation and the love object realistically.

Patients at the next level of the continuum, characterized by the capacity for falling in love and for establishing a stable love relation, although under some degree of sexual inhibition, reflect oedipal conflicts as the overriding etiological factors. I stressed earlier (see Chapter 7) that, paradoxically, it is when integration of internalized object relations takes place and total object relations are established that the normal triangular oedipal relations develop and infantile prohibitions against sexuality become paramount. At this point, repression of genital strivings occurs in the context of full-fledged oedipal relations, and genital inhibitions may develop. Therefore, at this higher level of ego organization, a greater capacity for what may be called romantic idealization exists. Psychoanalytic treatment of these conditions has a generally good prognosis. It is probably because these conditions represent the most favorable indication for psychoanalysis and because psychoanalysis developed into the context of exploring them that it has so focused on genital primacy in connection with overcoming the oedipal complex and developing emotional maturity.

MATURE LOVE RELATIONS: A REVIEW OF SOME PSYCHOANALYTIC VIEWPOINTS

If we focus on the broader context of the entire spectrum of psychopathology, the concept of genital primacy appears in a new light. The capacity for sexual intercourse and orgasm does not guarantee sexual maturity, or even necessarily represent a relatively higher level of psychosexual development. Lichtenstein (1970) has recently examined this issue, particularly Jacobson's application of ego psychological principles in her presentation of psychosexual development. Lichtenstein observes that "clinical observations do not confirm a clear correlation between emotional maturity (i.e., the capacity to establish stable object relations) and the ability to obtain full satisfaction through genital orgasm (genital primacy) . . ." (p. 317). He suggests that sexuality is the earliest and most basic way for the growing human personality to experience an affirmation of the reality of his existence, but concludes that ". . . the concept of genital primacy in the classical sense can no longer be maintained" (p. 317).

Clinically one finds that the full capacity for orgasm in sexual intercourse is present both in severe narcissistic personalities and in mature people and that sexual inhibition is present both in the most severe type of narcissistic isolation and in relatively mild neuroses and character pathology. This apparently paradoxical situation can perhaps best be understood in terms of the structural implications for ego and superego functioning of the development of internalized object relations.

I have suggested earlier (Chapters 2 and 5, 1972) a model of development of the psychic apparatus that integrates instinctual, ego (including ego identity), and superego development in the context of stages of development of internalized object relations. This model implies that consecutive stages of development of internalized object relations determine the characteristics of instinctual life, of ego and superego integration, of predominant defense mechanisms and character traits, and degree and type of psychopathology; the model integrates the stages of libidinal and aggressive developments as component systems of the evolving constellations of internalized object relations. According to this viewpoint, the relative "freedom" of expression of sexual urges in interpersonal situations despite severe pathology of internalized object relations is due to the fact that libidinal trends have not been integrated with total object relations and hence can be expressed as split-off, instinctual derivatives at the service of pregenital needs in part-object relations. In contrast, it is precisely because genital tendencies have become integrated with total object relations at a time when object constancy has been achieved that they express in their inhibitions the conflicts with such specific (oedipal) objects.

What are the characteristics of a capacity for establishing a mature love relation?

Balint (1948) suggests that, in addition to genital satisfaction, a true love relation includes idealization, tenderness, and a special form of identification. He agrees with Freud (1912), however, that a good love relation is possible without any idealization, and that in many cases idealization hinders rather than helps the development of a satisfactory love relation. Regarding the "special form of identification," Balint suggests calling it "genital identification," within which the "interest, wishes, feelings, sensitivity, shortcomings of the partner attain—or are supposed to attain—about the same importance as our own" (p. 115). Balint's principal emphasis is on the element of tenderness; he suggests that tenderness derives from pregenital trends and that "the demand for prolonged, perpetual regard and gratitude forces us to regress to, or even never to progress from, the archaic infantile form of tender love" (p. 114). In short, he believes that what we call genital love is a fusion of genital satisfaction and pregenital tenderness and that genital identification is the expression of this fusion.

Rollo May (1969) stresses the importance of care as a precondition for being able to love in a mature way. Care, he says, "is a state composed of the recognition of another, a fellow human being like one's self; of identification of one's self with the pain or joy of the other; of guilt, pity, and the awareness that we all stand on the base of a common humanity from which we all stem" (p. 289). (He considers "concern" and "compassion" possible alternative terms. Indeed, his description of care is closely related to Winnicott's [1963] analysis of concern.)

May's description of the aspects of mature love stresses the relation between the capacity for tenderness and that for concern; he also puts the capacity for genital identification (in Balint's terms), that is, for full identification without losing one's identity in the love relation, in a central position. In addition, May underlines the presence of sadness in the love relation (I think this sadness derives from the consolidation of total object relations and from the reactivation of concern, guilt, and reparation) and the importance of the genital experience itself, which provides a shift in consciousness, a new union wherein there develops a oneness with nature—an aspect I examine in some of the case material in this chapter.

Wisdom (1970), in reviewing some of the basic findings and dilemmas in the psychoanalytic approach to the understanding of love and sex, suggests that Melanie Klein's theory of the depressive position accounts for some but not all of the fundamental components in adult love. He suggests that the normal idealization of love arises through neutralization of the bad aspect of the object by reparation rather than by keeping the idealized object wholly good by splitting off from what is bad (a difference, it seems to me, related to the difference between the idealization of the love objects of borderline patients and that of neurotic patients).

I shall now attempt to summarize my position and, in so doing, bring together various aspects of my clinical and metapsychological formulations. The first prerequisite for being in love is the full development of oral and body-surface erotism (in the broadest sense) and its integration, together with libidinally and aggressively determined pregenital part object relations, into total object relations. This integration implies the integration of internalized object relations "with opposite signs" (Chapter 2) and fulfills what Winnicott (1955, 1963) described as the prerequisite of a capacity for concern.

The achievement of this stage of development of internalized object relations brings about the transformation of body surface erotism into tenderness and of need-gratifying relationships into object constancy. Together with the capacity for mourning, guilt, and concern, it results in a deepening awareness of the self and of others, the beginning of the capacity for empathy and for higher level identifications (in Jacobson's [1964] terms, partial, sublimatory identifications). This links the development of the capacity for being in love with the capacity for and proneness to depression. Bak (1973), stressing the relation between being in love and mourning, has stated that being in love is an emotional state based on the separation of mother and child and directed toward overcoming this as well as later separations and losses of important objects. Bergmann (1971) has said that the capacity to love presupposes a normally developing symbiotic experience and individuation-separation phase. Wisdom (1970) has enumerated the aspects of falling in love related to the capacity for developing mourning and concern. Josselyn (1971) has suggested that parents who deprive the child of opportunities to mourn over the loss of loved objects contribute to the atrophy of the capacity to love.

The elements I would stress regarding the mourning processes involved in being in love are those of growing up and becoming independent, the experience of leaving behind the real objects of childhood at a time when the most intimate and fulfulling kind of love relation with another human being is established. In this process of separation from the real objects of the past, there is also a confirmation of the good relations with internalized objects of the past, as the individual becomes confident of his capacity for combining love and sexual gratification in a growth-promoting mutual reinforcement—in contrast to the conflict between love and sex in childhood.

The achievement of this stage permits the development of the capacity for falling in love, implying the capacity for tenderness, an idealization more sophisticated than that characteristic of primitive splitting in patients with borderline personality organization, and some capacity for identification and empathy with the love object.

The next stage of development is the full integration of genitality into the love relationship, achieved by resolving oedipal conflicts. This permits a further deepening of the mutual identification and of empathy, because a full sexual identity clarifies the reciprocal sexual roles and leads to a full awareness of social and cultural values and of nature and the inanimate world—an awareness that is both private and shared, and enhanced by sharing. Normal sexual identity is a consequence of, rather than a prerequisite for, normal identity formation. It cements ego identity and gives it depth and maturity.

The integration of genitality into the love relation permits the transmutation of falling in love into the state of being in love. It does so by providing the capacity for full sexual enjoyment, which, in turn, implies a full integration of pregenital erotism and genital trends. It also permits this transmutation by elevating the level of idealization beyond the implications of guilt, concern, and the need for reparation of the earlier stage into an idealization that includes the sublimation of oedipal trends into the love relation and the integration of value systems with an ideal expressed by the object. In other words, at this stage, tenderness expands into full sexual enjoyment, identification deepens with full sexual identification and empathy, and idealization becomes a mature commitment to an ideal representing what the loved person is or stands for, or what the couple, united, might become.

In this connection, I am suggesting that there exist different types of idealization and that they imply normal as well as pathological functions. I think that normal functions of idealization have been neglected because the more severe and pathological types of this mechanism have been lumped together with them. Broadly, I propose three levels of idealization: (1) A primitive level, characteristic of ego states that reflect a predominance of splitting mechanisms; this is found in the borderline personality organization and is associated with the most primitive form of falling in love, usually not leading to a capacity for remaining in love—that is, to a mature love relation. (2) An idealization linked to the establishment of the capacity for mourning and concern (the "depressive position"), with a more realistic awareness of and empathy for the object but still devoid of genital features. This level is characteristic of states of falling in love of the usual neurotic patient; and here the capacity for establishing a stable love relationship exists to some extent, although it is usually conflict ridden and unsatisfactory. (3) A normal idealization, achieved toward the end of adolescence or in young adulthood, which is based upon a stable sexual identity and a realistic awareness of the love object. It includes social and cultural in addition to personal and sexual ideals.

What I wish to stress is that a mature selection of the person one loves and with whom one wants to live one's life involves mature ideals, value judgments, and goals, which, added on to the satisfaction of the needs for love and intimacy, give a broader meaning to life. It may be questioned whether the term "idealization" still applies here; but, insofar as a person is selected who corresponds to an ideal to be striven for, there is an element of transcendence in such selection, a commitment that comes naturally because it is the commitment to the type of life that the relationship with that person represents.

Let us return to Balint's (1948) stress on genital satisfaction, idealization, tenderness, and a special form of identification—genital identification—as being the main components of a true love relation. Tenderness, I have implied, stems from the integration of oral and body-surface erotism with total object relations, a viewpoint compatible with Balint's analysis. Idealization, I have suggested, is an important component of love relations, but one has to differentiate levels of idealization and their functions in terms of levels of structural development. I agree with Balint that genital identification is an essential element of normal love relations. It includes the capacity for a full identification with one's own sexual role and the capacity for empathy with the complementary sexual role of the love object. In general terms, genital identification implies coming to terms with the heterosexual and homosexual identifications derived from preoedipal and oedipal conflicts. Careful analysis of the emotional reactions during sexual intercourse, particularly in patients who have reached a stage of working through the various levels of pregenital and genital conflicts as expressed in their sexual engagements, reveals the manifold, simultaneous and/or shifting, heterosexual and homosexual, pregenital and genital identifications activated in that context.

One aspect of these emotional reactions is the excitement and gratification derived from the orgasm of the sexual partner. This gratification corresponds to the gratification of such needs as the capacity to provide oral gratification or the reconfirmation of the identification with the oedipal figure of the same sex, which reflect heterosexual components. At the same time, the excitement accompanying the partner's orgasm also reflects an unconscious identification with that partner and, in normal heterosexual intercourse, a sublimated expression of homosexual identifications from both pregenital and genital sources. Sexual foreplay may also include identification with the fantasied or real wishes of the object of the other sex, so that passive and active, masochistic and sadistic, voyeuristic and exhibitionistic needs are expressed in the simultaneous reconfirmation of one's own sexual identity and tentative identification with the complementary one of the sexual partner.

Such an intense double identification during orgasm also represents a capacity for transcendence, for entering and becoming one with another person in a psychological as well as physical sense, and a reconfirmation of emotional closeness, linked to the activation of the ultimately biological roots of human attachment. In contrast to the primitive fusion of self- and object-images during the symbiotic phase of development (Mahler, 1968), the higher level fusion of orgasm is based upon and reconfirms one's own individuality, and particularly a mature sexual identification.

Thus, sexual identification with one's own and one's partner's complementary sexual roles implies a sublimated integration of heterosexual and homosexual identity components. This integrative function of intercourse and orgasm is also carried out in the polarity of love and hate, because the capacity for fully experiencing concern for the loved person (which underlies an authentic, deep human relationship) presupposes the integration of love and hatred, that is, the tolerance of ambivalence. It seems to me that such ambivalence, which continues as a feature of stable, meaningful human relations, is activated in sexual intercourse where sexual and aggressive excitement are blended. A meaningful sexual relationship, it seems to me, includes encounters in which the partner is utilized as a "pure sexual object"; sexual excitement may be maximal during such expression of the need to "use" and/or be "used" by the other person sexually. Mutual empathy and implicit collusion with such sexual expressions are counterparts to similar empathy and collusions in connection with violent anger, attack, and rejection in the relationship. The confidence that all of these conditions can be contained within an over-all loving relation—which also has periods of quiet, mutual contemplation and sharing of the participants' internal life—provides meaning in depth to human relations.

APPLICATIONS TO LOVE RELATIONS IN ADOLESCENCE

One general prerequisite for the capacity of normal adolescent falling in love is the achievement of ego identity, which reflects the capacity for total object relations (Chapter 2; Erikson, 1956). Actually, Erikson (1956) describes the achievement of intimacy as the first stage of adulthood, and he stresses the dependency of this stage upon the achievement of a sense of identity in adolescence. Although I agree that achievement of normal ego identity is a prerequisite for the achievement of intimacy—in the sense of a total object relation with a member of the opposite sex, including tenderness, full genital gratification, and human depth—I do not think that the establishment of ego identity is a universal issue in normal adolescence. I agree with Jacobson's (1964) statement that "serious identity problems appear to be limited to neurotics with specific narcissistic conflicts, and to borderline and psychotic patients" (p. 29).

On the basis of my work with patients presenting borderline personality organization and patients (borderline or not) presenting narcissistic personality structure, I think that ego identity is established gradually, throughout infancy and childhood, in the process of overcoming primitive ego organization in which splitting mechanisms and related operations predominate. Ego identity depends upon and reinforces the establishment of an integrated ego (with repression and related defensive operations as predominant mechanisms) in the context of integration of total object relations. The continuum of stages in the development of the capacity for falling and remaining in love represents an application of this conception to normal and pathological love relationships.

Normal adolescence typically presents identity crises but not identity diffusion—two concepts which deserve to be clearly differentiated (Erikson, 1956, 1959). An identity crisis involves a loss of the correspondence between the internal sense of identity at a certain stage of development and the confirmation provided by the psychosocial environment. Such a discrepancy threatens one's sense of identity as well as one's relationship to the environment and calls for their reexamination. In contrast, identity diffusion is a severe psychopathological syndrome typical of borderline personality organization (Chapter 5 and Jacobson, 1964). It is characterized by mutually dissociated ego states. This lack of integration extends to the superego and, even more fundamentally, the world of internalized object relations. A mutual relation exists between identity crisis and ego identity: the more stable a basic ego identity, the better is the individual equipped to deal with identity crises; and, likewise, the weaker the ego identity, the more serious becomes any environmental challenge to it.

Clinically, the differential diagnosis between identity crisis and identity diffusion requires a careful examination of an adolescent's behavior and subjective experience throughout his total life situation. Rebellious challenging of authority (harsh and inflexible challenge of traditional norms of behavior within home, school, and the social, cultural, and political environment) may coexist with behavior manifestations radically opposite to his professed rebellious convictions. Intense love relationships and loyalties may coexist with inconsiderate, neglectful, even ruthless and exploitative behavior. However, in carefully exploring the adolescent's relations to his different, apparently contradictory ego states and actions, one may find a basic sense of emotional continuity clearly differentiating the neurotic and normal adolescent from his more disorganized counterpart who exhibits identity diffusion. The following characteristics are particularly helpful in differentiating relatively benign emotional turmoil from the syndrome of identity diffusion: (1) the capacity for experiencing guilt and concern, and the genuine wish to repair aggressive behavior, which is recognized as such after an emotional outburst; (2) the capacity for establishing lasting, nonexploitative relations with friends, teachers, or other grownups, as well as a relatively realistic assessment of such persons in depth; (3) a consistently expanding and deepening set of values (regardless of whether these values conform to or are in opposition to the prevalent culture surrounding the adolescent). The absence of these capacities reflects a lack of integration of the self-concept, a lack of understanding in depth of others, and the predominance of primitive defensive operations—all characteristic of identity diffusion.

The practical implication of this differential diagnosis is that a reasonable certainty about the stability of an adolescent's established ego identity provides the basic reassurance that the turmoil and conflicts involved in his falling in love—and love relations in general—do not reflect the more serious psychopathology of borderline and narcissistic personality structures. The typical clinical manifestations of sexual conflicts in adolescence, such as the dissociation of tenderness from sexual excitement, the dichotomy of asexual idealized objects and of sexual devalued objects of the other sex, the coexistence of excessive guilt and impulsive expression of sexual urges, may represent the entire range from normal to severely neurotic conflicts and are a diagnostic challenge. In contrast, the presence of identity diffusion indicates serious psychopathology, and the sexual conflicts in this case constitute only the beginning of long-term interference with a normal love life.

Another aspect of normal adolescent falling in love, which may be helpful in distinguishing between normal and neurotic love relations in adolescence and their borderline and narcissistic counterparts, is this: the personal love relation produces an experience of transcendence—the adolescent acquires a new awareness of and feeling of kinship with his culture and with nature. The following cases illustrate this normal development.

A 17-year-old boy had been referred for treatment because of marked rebellious behavior at school. On examination he revealed a neurosis without serious character pathology. During treatment, he fell in love with a girl and developed a relation with her that lasted for about two years. In the course of this relation, he had his first experiences of sexual intercourse and reacted to them with a sense of happiness, gratitude to his girl, and pride. Two aspects of his feelings are particularly relevant at this point. One was his newly found relation with nature, and the other was his understanding of art and literature. Making long excursions with her to the countryside, he felt the two of them were alone together in a tiny capsule of self-contained happiness surrounded by the world of nature, which they were facing alone. At the same time, he felt he could sense the movement, the rhythm and permanence of nature, admire it, enjoy it, while sensing painfully that trees and grass and the sky also were self-contained, "closed off" in their own meaning, and had to be accepted as such.

The couple's romantic longing for nature now coincided with a sense of loneliness and yet of mutual sharing of their loneliness. He also felt that this same loneliness was expressed in his and his girl's bodies, the beauty of her face and her breasts and her legs, movingly close and gratifying, yet mysteriously distant and self-contained. Still, it was as if sexual intercourse and orgasm opened a bridge not only between their bodies but between their persons as well, and between the two of them and nature at large. A new feeling for music opened up for him, which he described as the most direct expression of what goes on inside a human being and impossible to put into words. I should like to stress the sense of personal oneness in all of this, of empathy with and longing for nature and art, and, at the same time, the painful yet strangely gratifying acceptance of loneliness and separation as the counterpart of the discovery of inner depths.

Another patient, an 18-year-old girl, was referred because of depression and consequent academic failure in the first year of college. Her psychiatric examination revealed relatively mild depressive-masochistic trends, with an over-all well-organized personality structure. She had fallen in love with a boy she met at college; but after six months he had left her, and this had triggered her depression. The psychiatric diagnosis was of a pathological mourning reaction, and the patient improved rapidly in the course of a few sessions geared mainly to psychological exploration of her presenting difficulties. Because of her rapid symptomatic improvement and the relative absence of serious character pathology, no further treatment was recommended. She returned to college, and follow-up information five years later revealed that she had continued functioning well, had married, and appeared to be leading a well-adjusted and satisfactory life.

The aspect I wish to focus upon here is how she felt about the little town where her love affair and its end had taken place, her experience of the motel where she and her boy friend met, the streets, the park, and the buildings they had visited together. She had been afraid of going back to all those places and having to face again, in each of them, the painful loss of her boy friend. But, in the course of her exploratory interviews, she decided to visit those places again and discovered that, painful as the consequent intensification of her mourning reaction was, there was also something reassuring in the permanence of the buildings, the room they had shared, the benches they had sat on, the whole world of inanimate objects that sustained the memories of moments spent together.

This is, of course, a quite typical experience when working through a mourning process, but I would like to stress the "coming alive" of inanimate objects—the background figures of human experience—illuminated by a love relation. This reaction to inanimate objects, as well as to nature and art, is intimately connected with the transcending aspect of a full love relation, in which the capacity for a total object relation and the capacity for genital enjoyment are integrated. Searles (1960) has examined the intimate relation between the experience of the nonhuman environment, on the one hand, and normal or psychopathological development, on the other. Frosch (1964, 1966) has clarified the mutual relations among reality experience, reality testing, and relation with reality and has suggested the concept of "reality constancy" as a psychic structure that arises in conjunction with the establishment of stabilized internal representations of the environment. He suggested (1966) that reality constancy is closely interwoven with object constancy but that reality constancy evolves beyond the limit of "love-object constancy." In agreement with Frosch, I would add that the capacity to experience in depth the nonhuman environment, to appreciate nature and art, and to experience one's self within a historical and cultural continuum are intimately linked with the capacity for being in love—not that these potentials cannot persist without being in love, but falling in love represents a developmental crisis powerfully favoring the deepening of these other potentials.

The painful mourning processes involved in the internal separation from (and/or acquisition of) inanimate objects belonging to persons who have been loved and lost highlight the more general expression of the investment in a room, a house, a neighborhood, a city linked with personal experiences of loving relations (centered, of course, on the relations with the parental figures). All this reflects a general process by which internal representations of the environment are bound in the context of the establishment of love-object constancy. The normal, protective function of the stability in the inanimate environment is thus intimately linked with the libidinal investment in other human beings and in the self. This is illustrated dramatically in the case of patients with pathological narcissism, where narcissistic loss or failure may bring about frightening experiences of estrangement from and loss of meaning of the inanimate world.

APPLICATIONS TO LOVE RELATIONS IN MIDDLE AGE

I shall now focus on some normal and pathological developments of love relations during adulthood, particularly on conflicts of women between the ages of 35 and 55. The conflicts mentioned here have their counterpart in men of this age, and I hope the symmetrical aspects of these conflicts will become evident. At this age, the children of married women become adolescents and old, unresolved, or latent conflicts regarding sexual identity and sexual fulfillment are activated in the parents as they struggle with the manifestations of these conflicts in their children. Anthony (1969) has described the parent's conflicts around envy of a child of the same sex who is developing his or her full sexual potential and is often more successful and freer in his or her sexual experiences; the unconscious seductiveness to and the jealousy of the sexual experiences of the child of the opposite sex; the strivings for and defenses against gratification of the parent's own unfulfilled sexual yearnings through their children.

Rangell (1955) has discussed how oedipal conflicts reemerge in the unconscious relations of parents with their children. For example, a father may project onto his son a reactivation of his own adolescent oedipal competitiveness and sexual rebellion, while identifying with his internal image of a revengeful, jealous father in dealing with him. For women in our culture, this conflict may be particularly difficult. Given the frequent inhibition of female sexuality during adolescence and the painful awareness on the part of a woman who has finally, after years of marriage, grown out of her own oedipally determined adolescent inhibitions, some envy and jealousy of her daughter, who may now be achieving what she, the mother, achieved only after many years of painful growth, are only natural. Obviously, the greater the mother's sexual inhibitions, the more painful will be the oedipal rivalry with the daughter. Another complication occurs because of the frequent compensatory aspects that love relations with the husband have for unresolved sexual conflicts. Hysterical women with sexual inhibition and deep-seated self-depreciation linked to castration anxiety and penis envy, for example, who identify themselves with an idealized husband unconsciously representing the penis they wished to achieve, may reach their late thirties and forties with a gradual realization of the exaggerated nature of that idealization of the husband, a painful loss of that compensatory identification with him, and a reactivation of a more direct expression of hostility to and competitiveness with the husband—and her now adolescent children. In more general terms, both persistence of unresolved sexual conflicts and their partial resolution after years of adult experience may create potential stress in the relations of the middle-aged woman with her adolescent daughter.

On a different level, a woman of this age group may develop a reactivation of the internal conflicts she had with her parents when she was an adolescent and they were middle aged. A woman in her late thirties and forties has to come to terms again with the conflicts, idealization, hatred, or hostile dependency upon the mother of her adolescent years. The combined impact of experiencing her own adolescent conflicts in relations to her children and her internal conflicts with her own parents in a painfully questioning self-examination at this point constitutes a life crisis. This critical moment may bring about either a significant increase in the reconfirmation of a woman's security and faith in herself and her resources, or it may cause a gradual deterioration of the equilibrium sustained throughout early adulthood and the development of chronic psychopathology. In other words, if a woman is capable of reconfirming her trust in her bodily integrity and attractiveness, in her internal values and capacity for fulfillment as a woman, if she can become deeply convinced that she is able, being what she is, to satisfy her own needs and respond to the sensual and tender needs of the man she loves, this may provide a new sense of internal freedom and of creativity. Women with this kind of conviction are able to express it unconsciously in their physical attractiveness, in what they have to offer a man, in their capacity for being independent and for structuring their life creatively in a growing attractiveness as a woman and as a human being. In contrast, the failure of this process may bring about chronic severe envy, competition, and rage at younger women; a desperate need to "look young" (missing an inner sense of erotic security and harmony); angry devaluation of sexual functions and of their bodies, attended by a general deterioration of their physical attractiveness and erotic relations with men; and a loss of the capacity for new investments in people, ideas, and work. The influence of women's emotional attitudes to their sexual lives on their physical appearance, well-being, and general attractiveness cannot be overestimated.

The potentially healthy and creative aspects of the conflicts of women of this age group stem from the normal development of a sense of internal security and from broadening sources of self-esteem in women who are successful in their married lives. Women who have been able to bring up children with success, to direct a home in ways which realistically reconfirm their unconscious identification with—or triumph over—their mother image and, particularly, who have had years of gratifying sexual experiences thus gradually work through the remnants of oedipal fears and inhibitions. This permits, in turn, an increasing sexual gratification, further contributing to resolution of conflicts around castration anxiety and penis envy. In a good marriage, the mutual support and dependence of husband and wife foster a resolution of fears, of pathological idealization, and of resentment against the other sex. The children's reaching adolescence not only activates a mother's conflicts with them but also gives her more free time and leisure and the possibility for resuming her own professional, cultural, and work interests, which had to be dropped during the childbearing years. Thus, the reactivation of the woman's adolescent conflicts in the confrontation with adolescent daughters normally occurs under circumstances much more favorable than those in which she first experienced these conflicts. Of course, opposite forces are at work too; particularly when hostile dependency on mother (with preoedipal as well as oedipal factors) has not been overcome, problems in identification with an aging mother may exacerbate all other conflicts regarding sexual identity. One patient, who had had a relatively satisfactory sexual life in the early years of her marriage, found herself, to her surprise, reacting with shame and disgust to sexual intercourse when her daughter became an adolescent. She had the fantasy that she was now behaving like a ridiculous, lecherous old woman who was making a fool of herself in the eyes of her daughter—the relation she had had with her own mother.

It is very helpful to explore carefully, in every case of a woman in her late thirties or forties in which psychoanalytic treatment is contemplated, what her attitude is to her own sexual functioning and sexual needs, particularly regarding the extent to which there is a genuine awareness of and wish to resolve sexual inhibitions as part of an effort to increase the mutual gratifications of a sexual relation with a man. The tendency to brush over this entire area as "no longer so important" or deep-seated convictions that a better sexual functioning is only a "necessary price" to pay for becoming more attractive to a man have more ominous implications for women of this age than for women who start their treatment in early adulthood. In contrast, a willingness to question old convictions that reflect deeply ingrained resentment of and hostility to men may illustrate a genuine wish to change.

A history of having genuinely fallen and remained in love is prognostically favorable, in contrast to essentially narcissistic cases in which there is very flimsy, if any evidence of past genuine states of having been in love. Again, a genuine interest in men as a source of human as well as sexual gratification, without a predominance of dependent, clinging, or exploitative features, separates the better functioning neurotic, particularly hysterical and masochistic cases, from the more ominous infantile, borderline, and, particularly, narcissistic cases. A realistic acceptance, on the part of a woman who has never been married or who is divorced, of the limited opportunities for remarrying and of the possibility of having to obtain gratification in depth from less conventional relations with men should be explored before the transference implications of these issues overshadow the real life goals (Ticho, 1972). Last, the degree of investment in work or a profession, in the education of the children, in the cultural and intellectual values that make life worthwhile in spite of the conflicts, inhibitions, and problems in the area of sex and love relations are of great diagnostic and prognostic significance. The search for a marriage as an escape from an independent, autonomous stand and commitments in life is much more omninous now than in cases whose treatment starts shortly after adolescence. At times, characterological structures serving to deny dependency needs and including reaction formations against sexual inhibition may emerge as sexual freedom, a personal ideology of casualness about sexual engagements, or a commitment to ideological affirmations of women's social and sexual independence of men. More ominous are cases of severe narcissistic personality. These may present a facade of possessing freedom for sexual enjoyment and apparent stability in the relation with a man. Only gradually do they permit us to discern their lack of capacity for investments in depth and their generally reserved prognosis. In all cases, the risk that analysis—particularly with a male analyst—may become a replacement for life itself needs to be carefully evaluated.

From a clinical viewpoint, the potential of women of this age group both for great improvement in general functioning and for serious decompensation of chronic psychopathology may cause us either to underestimate the possibilities of psychoanalytic treatment in some cases or to be overly optimistic about prognosis in other cases, where 10 or 20 years of apparently good adult adjustment were followed by an only recent deterioration. The following cases illustrate the unfinished elaboration of conflicts stemming from adolescence, the influence of cultural disadvantages for women, the spiraling consequences of narcissistic and infantile features, and the potential for surprising improvement in some instances.

Case 1: A 40-year-old woman architect was seen because of a chronic deterioration of her relationship with her second husband. The diagnosis was narcissistic personality. She had been a brilliant, popular student, had dated since age 14, and had married at age 20. She had always admired her powerful father and expected her bright and successful husband to emulate him. She dropped her own profession because of what she experienced as unbearable competition with men. Unconsciously, she interfered with her husband's work and, after a gradually failing business situation, managed to get her husband and her father involved in chronic triangular fights. The patient was divorced at age 35, went back to work, became quite successful, but was very lonely and felt her three daughters needed a father. At age 37, she married a man who was also bright, active, and successful. Struggles similar to those she had had with her first husband ensued. During the diagnostic study, prior to a decision being made about treatment, the second husband finally left her, after violent scenes in which she reacted with rage to any efforts he made to assert himself. The patient could not accept treatment because, in her need to maintain an image of perfection of herself, she saw it as a humiliating defeat and shameful giving-in to the "world of men."

The patient grew increasingly despondent, was unable to work, and became convinced that all men were out to get her. She experienced a brief depressive episode, followed by a chronic and anhedonic withdrawal into noncompetitive routine work below her capacities and experience. The children, who before adolescence had taken her side, gradually turned against her, and she so resented their independence that she ended up practically alone.

Case 2: A 35-year-old woman with severe frigidity finally divorced her husband after years during which they both conducted extramarital affairs. She was also frigid in her extramarital experiences and finally accepted the fact that her husband could not be blamed for her frigidity. After the divorce, she entered psychoanalytic treatment and resumed her studies in preparation for a profession that would help her take care of her children and assure her own future. Her basically hysterical-masochistic personality structure was modified sufficiently for her to gradually establish satisfying tender, as well as sexual, relations with men she met at the university and later at work. In her early forties, she married a man with whom she had established a satisfactory intellectual, human, and sexual relation. One major concern during her treatment was her fear of influencing her own daughters with her negative internal attitudes about sex and of being forced by "destiny" to repeat her own mother's behavior with her daughters. The strong, loving investment in her daughters, in spite of her oedipal rivalries with them, was a major positive factor in carrying her through times of intense negative transference as her penis envy and revengeful anger against men was elaborated in the analysis.

Case 3: A 42-year-old woman musician had had a series of long-lasting, deep, but masochistic and eventually frustrating affairs with men, in the course of which it seemed as if she had been left again and again by the men she loved. She entered treatment after becoming aware of her own participation in destroying the relation with a man who wanted to marry her. The basically masochistic relations with men were worked through. A major issue was that of her angry disappointment with herself for having "wasted" so many years of her life in what she now saw as drifting relations and, particularly, her regret at not having had children. Menopause, occurring during analytic treatment, provided an important focus around which she could explore the realistic mourning over lost opportunities for having a child. Her ingrained conviction that her sexual life and attractiveness were coming to an end served to rationalize her internal prohibitions against establishing a better relation with a man. Her deep commitment to her art and the combination of cultural sophistication, physical attractiveness, and enjoyment of her work were all important factors in the successful outcome of treatment. A crucial stage occurred when she finally came to terms with having to accept relations with men different from those of her adolescent fantasies.

Case 4: A 37-year-old woman had lived for 15 years with a husband she depreciated and her small children, with whom she had very little involvement. She became depressed when her lover, a distinguished politician with whom she had carried on an affair for almost 10 years, asked her either to divorce her husband and marry him or to terminate the affair. She developed chronic anxiety and depression. Several efforts at psychiatric treatment failed because of her haughty derogation of therapists, whom she suspected of being ruthless exploiters and before whom (all males) she felt humiliated as a woman for having to submit to "opening herself up." The diagnosis revealed a basically narcissistic personality structure. The breakdown of her apparently satisfactory life situation disrupted the precarious equilibrium maintained by her being in control of the two men without being really involved with either one.

Case 5: A 35-year-old woman entered treatment for obesity, sadomasochistic sexual relations with her husband, and a chronic hostile dependency upon her own mother. Of high intelligence, she had dropped out of college to get married just before obtaining her degree. From the beginning of the analysis, it was evident that she expected the psychoanalyst to serve as an ever-giving penis-breast, providing her with love, food, and sexual gratification; she appeared to be aspiring to a symbiotic union with him. She divorced her husband in the course of analysis and tried to blackmail the analyst into a position of giving her orders and taking care of her daily life by refusing to improve (indicated particularly through overeating). This treatment ended in failure, as happens with some women with infantile or narcissistic personality structure who enter treatment at midlife as a last resort; after their habitual characterological attempts to control the immediate environment fail, they try to gratify infantile dependent needs in the analysis using it as a replacement for their usual external life.

In working with a woman of this age group, the analyst must explore very carefully the general quality of the patient's object relations and the particular conflicts regarding her feminine identification, including the conscious and unconscious attitudes to her own sexuality, body, and men. There is a danger of overgeneralization in treating this age group, which does need individualized prognosis: for example, the analyst unwittingly may be agreeing that "life has passed by," that a woman in her forties has to face the loss of her physical attractiveness, that available partners are few, and that she has serious limitations in competing for work. To assume all this may feed into the rationalization of otherwise treatable character pathology. Patients with good object relations and with a general willingness to face their sexual conflicts without excessive recrimination because of the years lost may have a surprisingly good prognosis with psychoanalysis. In particular, hysterical personality structures with masochistic features, if there is not excessive secondary rationalization of the pathological character structure and of sexual inhibition, may have a much better prognosis than is indicated by their "tragic" list of long-standing disappointments and failures over many years. In contrast, women with borderline personality organization, whose compensation during early adulthood is being lost, create many more serious therapeutic problems and have a poorer prognosis than adolescent and young adult borderline cases. Perhaps the most serious group is that of women with narcissistic personalities, whose narcissistic gratification, stemming from physical attractiveness, youth, wealth, and social success, gradually fades and whose basic psychopathology thus has a generally grave prognostic outlook.

If the psychoanalyst reaches the conclusion that a woman of this age group, in spite of her past failures and her feelings of hopelessness and unattractiveness, does have basic values which, given a characterological modification, will permit her realistic gratifications in the future, he should then provide a treatment setting and strategy which assures that analysis will not be used as a replacement for life itself.

Some analysts' conventionalized and narrow views regarding female sexuality may play into these patients' unconscious efforts to convince their psychoanalysts that (given these patients' age and life situation) it does not make much difference whether or not they resolve their sexual inhibitions and conflicts. Any such unconscious submission of the analyst to primitive, sadistic superego pressures within the patient—rationalized with the culturally determined handicaps and sexual uncertainty of women in our society—may militate against the full working through of sexual inhibitions and the freeing of the capacity for a full relation with a man—particularly in those patients who, because of their generally good development of internalized object relations, may have a much better prognosis than that traditionally assumed for character pathology of many years duration.

Neutrality (in a technical, psychoanalytic sense) depends, I think, upon a shared background of culturally determined assumptions on the part of the analyst and the patient; and the problem of a woman's position in society may be one area in which the analyst has to be particularly attuned to the possibility of his identification with a traditional cultural outlook that places women in an inferior role and supports their acceptance of that role. Therefore, the analyst must be especially wary of an implicit stand that overvalues the conventional adjustment of women to society or underestimates a woman's potential to develop new, nonconventional patterns of adaptation.

I have emphasized that a continuity exists between the normal states of falling in love and remaining in love. It is usually possible, if one examines in depth the level of development of internalized object relations of the patient who claims that he is in love, to arrive at a fairly accurate prediction regarding the extent to which he will be able to establish such a continuity. It is true, of course, that, from a simple descriptive viewpoint, falling in love does not say much about the capacity for remaining in love.

This continuity between falling in love, remaining in love, and a stable, affectionate relationship does not imply, it seems to me, a guarantee of the couple's staying together. The very fact that the precondition for such a deep and lasting relation between two people is the achievement of a capacity for depth in relation to one's own self as well as to others—for empathy and understanding which opens the deep pathways of the unspoken multiple reactions among human beings—creates a curious counterpart. As someone becomes more capable of loving in depth and better able realistically to appreciate someone else over the years as part of his or her personal and social life, he or she may find others who, realistically, could serve as an equally satisfactory or even better partner. Emotional maturity is thus no guarantee of nonconflictual stability for the couple. A deep commitment to one person and the values and experiences of a life lived together will enrich and protect the stability of the relationship, but, if self-knowledge and self-awareness are deep, at the cost of activating from time to time a longing for other relations (the potential of which may be a realistic assessment) and repeated renunciations. But longing and renunciation also may add a dimension of depth to the life of the individual and the couple; the redirection of longings and fantasies and sexual tensions within the couple's relationship may likewise bring an additional, obscure, and complex dimension to it. All human relationships must end, and the threat of loss, abandonment, and, in the last resort, of death is greatest where love has most depth; awareness of this also deepens love.

REFERENCES

Anthony, E. J. (1969). The reactions of adults to adolescents and their behavior. In: *Adolescence: Psychosocial Perspectives*, eds. G. Caplan and S. Lebovici. New York: Basic Books, pp. 54-78.

Bak, R. C. (1973). Being in love and object loss. *International Journal of Psycho-Analysis* 54: 1-8.

Balint, M. (1948). On genital love. In: *Primary Love and Psychoanalytic Technique*. London: Tavistock, 1959, pp. 109-120.

Bergmann, M. S. (1971). Psychoanalytic observations on the capacity to love. In: *Separation-Individuation*, eds. J. B. McDevitt and C. F. Settlage. New York: International Universities Press, pp. 15-40.

Erikson, E. H. (1956). The problem of ego identity. *Journal of the American Psychoanalytic Association* 4: 56-121.

———(1959). Growth and crises of the healthy personality. In: *Identity and the Life Cycle (Psychological Issues, Monograph 1)*. New York: International Universities Press, pp. 50-100.

Freud, S. (1912). On the universal tendency to debasement in the sphere of love (contributions to the Psychology of Love II). *Standard Edition* 11: 178-190.

Frosch, J. (1964). The psychotic character: clinical psychiatric considerations. *Psychiatric Quarterly* 38: 81-96.

———(1966). A note on reality constancy. In: *Psychoanalysis: A General Psychology*, eds. R. M. Loewenstein, L. M. Newman, M. Schur, and A. J. Solnit. New York: International Universities Press, pp. 349-376.

Jacobson, E. (1964). *The Self and the Object World*. New York: International Universities Press.

Josselyn, I. M. (1971). The capacity to love: a possible reformulation. *Journal of the American Academy of Child Psychiatry* 10: 6-22.

Kernberg, O. (1972). Early ego integration and object relations. *Annals of the New York Academy of Sciences* 193: 233-247.

———(1975b). *Borderline Conditions and Pathological Narcissism*. New York: Jason Aronson.

Lichtenstein, H. (1970). Changing implications of the concept of psychosexual development: an inquiry concerning the validity of classical psychoanalytic assumptions concerning sexuality. *Journal of the American Psychoanalytic Association* 18: 300-318.

Mahler, M. S. (1968). *On Human Symbiosis and the Vicissitudes of Individuation. Vol. 1: Infantile Psychosis*. New York: International Universities Press.

May, R. (1969). *Love and Will*. New York: Norton.

Rangell, L. (1955). The role of the parent in the Oedipus complex. *Bulletin of the Menninger Clinic* 19: 9-15.

Searles, H. F. (1960). *The Nonhuman Environment*. New York: International Universities Press.

Ticho, E. (1972). Termination of psychoanalysis: treatment goals, life goals. *Psychoanalytic Quarterly* 41: 315-333.

Winnicott, D. W. (1955). The depressive position in normal emotional development. *British Journal of Medical Psychology* 28: 89-100.

———(1963). The development of the capacity for concern. *Bulletin of the Menninger Clinic* 27: 167-176.

Wisdom, J. O. (1970). Freud and Melanie Klein: psychology, ontology, and weltanschauung. In: *Psychoanalysis and Philosophy*, eds. C. Hanly and M. Lazerowitz. New York: International Universities Press, pp. 327-362.

nine

Toward an Integrative Theory of Hospital Treatment

The purpose of this chapter is to formulate an integrative set of theoretical propositions providing a common frame of reference for the different treatment modalities in the psychoanalytic hospital. Such a theoretical structure should also permit the establishment of clearer boundaries among the various therapeutic modalities utilized in the hospital so that they can be optimally geared to an individual patient's needs. This frame of reference also may contribute to decreasing the traditional tensions between administrators and clinicians by providing a conceptualization of their actual professional and functional interdependence.

THE CONCEPT OF STRUCTURAL CHANGE IN THE LIGHT OF OBJECT-RELATIONS THEORY

In psychoanalytic theory, the term "structural intrapsychic change" (in the direction of clinical improvement) refers to changes in the relationships among ego, id, superego, and external reality. In clinical terms, this means changes in impulse-defense configurations, that is, in the defensive structures which determine the boundaries among ego, superego, and id. Such changes require, according to psychoanalytic theory, interpretation and resolution of these defenses so that unconscious conflicts may become conscious and be resolved in consciousness. Such conflict resolution, in turn, modifies the impulse-defense equilibrium in the direction of more effective ego functioning, brings about a broadening of the sphere of the mature ego, greater ego autonomy, and better gratification of instinctual needs, as well as of reality demands.

From this theoretical viewpoint, structural intrapsychic change requires psychoanalysis or psychoanalytic psychotherapy. Such changes as do occur in patients within a hospital setting would be predominantly behavioral changes rather than structural intrapsychic changes. Nonanalytic psychotherapy and other hospital treatment devices would hardly be able to modify unconscious intrapsychic conflict. Indeed, one finds many patients whose behavior changes in response to social pressures within the hospital but then reverts to previous patterns once they leave the hospital system.

A modified formulation of intrapsychic structure and of structural intrapsychic change, which incorporates recent findings regarding severely regressed (particularly borderline and psychotic) patients, opens the possibility of obtaining change in these structures by means of particular therapeutic functions of the hospital as a social system. This modified conception is an application of psychoanalytic object-relations theory (Guntrip, 1961; Sutherland, 1963; Jacobson, 1964; Chapter 2). I will briefly summarize the main aspects of psychoanalytic object-relations theory as presented in Chapters 1, 2, and 5. This theory proposes, in essence, that the basic units of the intrapsychic structures are constellations of self-images, object-images, and affect-dispositions which reflect particular internalized object-relations represented by such self-object-affect units. These units of internalized object relations coalesce into more complex psychic structures (such as the ideal self and ideal objects), and these structures, in turn, finally give the ego, the superego, and the id their definite forms.

The earliest intrapsychic units of this kind are undifferentiated self-object representations linked with primitive, overwhelming affect dispositions of either a pleasurable or a painful, frightening nature (Jacobson, 1964). All pleasurable internalized experiences condense into a primitive self-object representation determining the ego core; all unpleasurable ones also condense and are then first "expelled" (as a primitive "non-me") and later projected. These are the earliest libidinally and aggressively invested internalized object relations. At a later stage of development, self- and object representations are sorted out from each other in both pleasurable and painful constellations. This separation of self- from object-representations and the maturation and development of perceptive and cognitive functions influence each other and contribute to the delimitation of boundaries between self and outside world (ego boundary).

The next stage of development consists of an integration of libidinally and aggressively invested self-representations culminating in an integrated self-concept and an integration of object-representations (originally of a multiple, primitive, fantastic kind) into constellations of object-representations resembling ever more closely—and permitting the realistic perception of—real, external objects (parental figures, siblings, etc.). The integration of self-representations brings about a contrast between a realistic perception of the self (real self) and idealized fantasy formations of the self (which, in turn, integrate into the ideal self). Integration of realistic object-representations contrasts real object-representations with idealized ones representing parental figures of a magical, all-need-gratifying kind (ideal objects).

A condensation of the ideal self and ideal objects determines the ego ideal, which will form part of the superego. A remnant of primitive, condensed self-object images invested with aggression and projected outside determine persecutory parental images because they distort the perception of early frustrating experiences into persecutory fantasies. Internalization of such persecuting, primitively conceived objects (particularly of the parental forbidding and punishing functions) determines sadistic forerunners of the superego. The ego ideal and these sadistic forerunners become integrated as the early superego. Later they expand with internalization of more realistic parental demands and prohibitions (Jacobson, 1964).

The integrated self-concept and the related increasingly realistic, libidinally invested object-representations together constitute ego identity, a basic organizer of the ego. Thus, the self (or integrated self-concept) becomes the center of the world of internalized object relations, a world constituted by the self plus the totality of object-representations. The self is part of the ego; that part of the ego not related to the world of internalized object relations is represented by the totality of nonpersonified ego functions and structures. Ego integration establishes a firm repressive barrier against internalized self- and object-images linked with intolerable or forbidden sexual and aggressive needs, for which the id acts as the consolidating reservoir. Thus, psychic development culminates in the establishment of the definite structures of the mind as described by Freud (ego, superego, and id).

This theory of intrapsychic structure has important consequences for the conceptualization of structural intrapsychic change and the role of hospital treatment in achieving such structural change.

First, the substructures which jointly determine the over-all psychic structures are no longer to be viewed simply as impulse-defense configurations but rather as dynamic structures, each involving an impulse-defense configuration in the context of an internalized object relation.

Second, structural change occurring after consolidation of an integrated superego, ego, and id is radically different from structural change in patients who have not achieved such integration. In the case of neurotic patients and patients with neurotic character pathology, where ego, id, and superego are integrated (although involved in pathogenic conflicts and defensive operations), the activation of any particular object relation within the treatment situation simultaneously expresses conflicts between these over-all intrapsychic structures. The defensive mechanisms in these conflicts center on repression and related mechanisms (the classical mechanisms of defense of the ego, superego, and id). Under these circumstances, much preliminary interpretive work needs to be done if the patient is to reach the point of structural change, because defensive operations (such as pathological character traits) are secondarily integrated into and protected by the over-all psychic structure involved. In addition, because of the abstraction and depersonification of internalized object relations within the ego and the superego, reactivation of these relations in the therapeutic situation takes time.

In contrast, in patients with borderline character pathology or psychoses, the ego and the superego remain unintegrated (with projection of personified superego nuclei) and the ego functions have been infiltrated by primitive instinctual derivatives. This infiltration derives from the predominance of a different set of defense mechanisms from those centering on repression in better integrated patients. At the level of borderline personality organization and in the psychoses, there is a predominance of splitting and related primitive defensive operations (such as projection, projective identification, primitive idealization, denial, omnipotence, and devaluation), which have in common their defense of the psychic apparatus against conflict by dissociation of contradictory primitive ego states. Each of these dissociated primitive ego states reflects a primitive internalized object relation, a basic unit of self- and object-image, and a corresponding primitive affect disposition relatively unintegrated and hence easily activated in the interpersonal field (Kernberg, 1967). There thus exists in the patient's interactions in the hospital a potential for rapid development of new relationships representing primitive object relations. This affords the opportunity for a diagnosis of the pathogenic conflicts involved because the patient's interpersonal relationships in the hospital reflect quite directly these primitive intrapsychic dispositions.

In addition, from this viewpoint, one might consider two levels of internalized object-relations: (1) a basic level, characterized by multiple self- and object-representations corresponding to primitive fantasy formations linked with primitive impulse derivatives; and (2) a higher level, characterized by sophisticated, integrated self- and object-representations linked with higher levels of affect dispositions; all of these higher-level object relations reflect more accurately the early childhood experiences and conflicts between the individual and his real parental figures and siblings.

These two levels of object relations differentiate ordinary transference—the transference neurosis in standard psychoanalytic cases—from the primitive transferences in borderline and psychotic conditions. Primitive transferences may evolve into—but are not equivalent to—transference psychosis. Transference psychosis is characterized by loss of reality testing in the transference situation. Clinically, this is reflected in delusional thoughts involving the therapist, possible appearance of hallucinations in the treatment hours, activation of primitive, overwhelming affective reactions in the transference, and the patient's loss of a sense of separate identity from the therapist. The dynamic mechanisms of this loss of reality testing in borderline patients are different from those in psychotic patients (Kernberg, 1975b, Chapter 5). Primitive transferences, regardless of whether they decompensate into transference psychosis or not (that is, of whether the patient has or has not lost reality testing) are different from the sophisticated transferences typical of transference neurosis. In transference neurosis a more realistic dyadic, oedipal-triangular, or sibling relationship is mobilized, while in the case of primitive transferences, primitive object relations are activated with multiple self- and object-images representing the deepest layers of the mind. These primitive multiple object relations are of a fantastic nature and do not reflect actual past interactions with the parents (as do the higher-level transference reactions of transference neurosis); rather they reflect early fantasy structures, fantastic relationships with object-representations which are normally submerged within the structure of more realistic transference dispositions in the context of an integrated ego and superego.

As stated before, this conceptualization has important theoretical and clinical implications for hospital treatment. In the psychoanalytic treatment of neurotic patients and patients with higher-level character pathology, transference neurosis develops gradually, and primitive object relations emerge in the transference only after the working through of higher-level psychic structures and defenses. In contrast, in the hospital patients are seen who suffer from severe character pathology, borderline personality organization, or psychotic reactions. In all of these cases, primitive levels of structural development predominate, and primitive object relations are immediately activated intrapsychically and interpersonally. Thus it is possible to observe directly and (under certain conditions) gradually influence intrapsychic conflict by means of an understanding, confronting, (technically) neutral hospital team, which can clarify and consistently influence the primitive object relations activated in the interpersonal field. The hospital team may both communicate their observations to the psychotherapist, and to reflect directly to the patient the nature of the distortions in his interactions with them. In this process, external reality is reinforced, thus providing a protective structure in addition to a diagnostic tool. The concept of a neutral hospital atmosphere derives from Anna Freud's (1946) concept of the technical neutrality of the psychoanalyst and his attitude equally distant from id, superego, external reality, and acting ego; neutrality in this regard implies a potential alliance with the observing ego of the patient.

PSYCHOANALYTIC THEORY OF SMALL GROUPS AND THE ACTIVATION OF PRIMITIVE OBJECT RELATIONS IN THE SOCIAL FIELD

Insofar as the hospital represents a society organized around more or less structured processes, the patient is faced with participation in a setting which reinforces in varying degrees the activation of primitive object relations. There is impressive clinical evidence that, regardless of the degree of maturity and psychological integration of the individual, small, closed, unstructured groups (as well as large groups with minimal structure and no clearly defined task relating that group to its environment) tend to bring about an immediate regression toward the activation of defensive operations and interpersonal processes that reflect primitive object relations.

In other words, a potential exists in all of us for activation of primitive levels of psychological functioning when the ordinary social structure is lost, when ordinary social roles are suspended, and when multiple objects are present simultaneously in an unstructured relationship (thus reproducing in the interpersonal field a multiplicity of primitive intrapsychic object relations). Our theoretical understanding of why this surprising development takes place in groups is still insufficient, but the fact that it does occur—particularly in individuals with severe character pathology, borderline conditions or psychotic syndromes—makes the hospital an impressive diagnostic (and potentially therapeutic) tool. It can aid in understanding primitive levels of internalized object relations and modifying them in a controlled social system. However, there must be sufficient flexibility, or lack of structuralization within the hospital milieu, if such regression is to occur. A highly regimented hospital routine may block this regression and obscure its full observation. It may also foster pathological dependency and apathy in certain patients (as well as in staff), thus artificially increasing their regression.

Such immediate activation of primitive levels of functioning does not occur in a dyadic relationship such as a standard psychoanalysis or individual psychoanalytically oriented psychotherapy. Although severely regressed patients develop primitive transferences rather soon even in individual psychotherapy and psychoanalysis, this is not true for less regressed patients, who usually take quite a long time before reaching a similar level of primitive object relations in individual treatment. Yet, such less regressed patients may immediately present an activation of primitive levels of functioning in group situations.

There exists a potential in everybody for an activation of both higher-level object relations leading to transference neurosis in individual treatment and primitive-level object relations leading to regressive situations in groups. However, the more severely regressed the patient, the more the activation of primitive object relations spills over into the individual treatment setting as well and the more his intrapsychic problems contaminate immediately the social field of the group. It may well be that the primitive transference dispositions that can be observed in the early hours of psychoanalysis in many patients and that then go underground for a time reflect the predisposition to activate primitive object relations under conditions of uncertainty and role diffusion similar to those which are maximal in group situations.

An additional implication of these two levels of activation of internalized object relations is that the higher dyadic-triangular level occurs particularly in individual therapeutic relationships, while the lower or "groupish" level occurs particularly in unstructured group situations. This conceptualization permits the development of a theory of treatment combining individual and group modalities to deal simultaneously with different levels of intrapsychic conflicts, with the combination of these two modalities in different proportions or at different times, according to the nature of the individual patient's psychopathology. However, the psychological processes activated in individual and group therapeutic processes overlap, and (as will be mentioned later) the use of a combination of individual and group therapies in many cases is still controversial.

Another hypothesis implicit in all that has been said is that the potential for activation of primitive object relations may be much stronger in neurotic and normal persons than psychoanalytic exploration within a dyadic situation (the standard psychoanalytic situation) may indicate. It may well be that because the relationships within the family setting represent social structures which reinforce dyadic and triangular object relations they protect the psychic apparatus from its regressive potential for activation of multiple fantastic object relations.

Following Erikson (1956) we have defined introjection, identification, and ego identity as a progressive sequence in the process of internalization of object relations (Chapter 1). Introjection represents the most primitive type of internalization of the self-, object-, and affect-components of the basic intrapsychic units mentioned before. Identification represents a higher-level introjection, within which both self- and object-representations are more elaborate, delimited, and precise; the affect disposition linking the self- and object-representations is more toned down, differentiated, less diffuse and intense than in the case of introjection. Identification presupposes a higher level of development of the perceptive and cognitive abilities of the child, to the point of recognizing the role aspects of interpersonal interaction. Role implies a socially recognized function carried out by the object or by both participants in the interaction.

Introjections coalesce with similar, later ones, gradually develop, and then are integrated into identifications. In turn, identifications are reshaped by later ones, then combine and are integrated into an over-all ego identity. Introjections form the core of related identifications. It may well be that the potential for regression from a certain identification to the underlying more primitive introjection is quite prevalent, and that the role enactments of ordinary interpersonal relationships protect the higher-level identifications from such a regression. Also, there may be a normal potential for reestablishment of a certain identification after some temporary regression to a component introjection. This might explain, in part, the rapid regression that occurs in certain group situations and the rapid recuperation from such regression: groups may induce such regression by eliminating the usual role reinforcement of normal interpersonal interactions.

The role aspects of the relationships between infant and mother and among the child, its parents, and its siblings may obscure the "groupishness" (potential for regression in groups) in all of us. The individual relationship between psychoanalyst or psychotherapist and patient may contribute to activation of such dyadic and triangular infantile and childhood relationships and determine a situation in which the primitive level of internalized object-relations only becomes available after the working through of higher-level psychic structures and defenses. Again, a general implication is that treatment might take place simultaneously on a "dyadic" (individual therapy) and on a "group" level and simultaneously tap different levels of development and structuralization of intrapsychic life.

Even highly trained, relatively healthy and mature professionals in the behavioral sciences present activation of primitive emotional processes in unstructured group situations. Developments in group-dynamics experiences and readily available observations regarding group processes in professional organizations related to the behavioral sciences (obviously, in all human organizations) make it clear that, in certain group situations without precise role definitions or a clear-cut external task, primitive defenses, primitive object relations, and, even more interestingly, deep personal conflicts may come to the surface rapidly. This is a further illustration of the potential for regression in unstructured group situations in all of us, which is different (in the speed of production and recovery) from the regressive moves in a standard psychoanalytic situation. In non-borderline patients in a dyadic psychotherapeutic relationship, regression occurs to object-relations of the childhood oedipal level, or to pregenital levels of development in the dyadic, triangular, and sibling family setting; regression may occur to primitive object relations and early defensive structures of the ego, but this latter type of regression usually takes a long time. In contrast, the regression in group situations is very rapid, leads immediately to defensive operations and object relations of the primitive, early level, and is transitory in the sense that recovery is rapid outside the group setting.

Bion's analysis of the regressive phenomena that occur in small groups when their task structure ("work group") fails is relevant here (Bion, 1959; Rioch, 1970). He described the development of certain basic emotional reactions within the group ("basic-assumptions group"), reactions which exist potentially at all times but are activated particularly at times of breakdown of the task group. He described the "fight-flight" assumption, the "dependent" assumption, and the "pairing" assumption as the predominant constellations of the basic-assumptions group.

In the "dependent" group, the members perceive the leader as omnipotent and omniscient, while they consider themselves inadequate, immature, and incompetent. The idealization of the leader on the part of the members is matched by their desperate, greedy, but futile efforts to extract knowledge, power, and goodness from him.

The failure of the leader to live up to such an ideal of perfection is met first with denial, then with a rapid, complete devaluation of him and a search for substitute leadership. Thus primitive idealization, projected omnipotence, denial, envy, and greed and defenses against them characterize the dependent group. Members feel united by a common sense of need, helplessness, and fear of an outside world they dimly experience as empty or frustrating.

The "fight-flight" group is united against vaguely perceived external enemies as well as to protect the group from any infighting. Any opposition to the "ideology" shared by the majority of the group cannot be tolerated, and the group easily splits into subgroups which fight each other. Frequently, one subgroup becomes subservient to the idealized leader while another subgroup attacks that subgroup or is in flight from it. The group's tendency to forcefully control the leader, or to experience itself forcefully controlled by him; to experience "closeness" in a shared denial of intragroup hostility; and to project aggression onto an outgroup are all prevalent. In short, splitting, projection of aggression, and "projective identification" are predominant, and the search for nurture and dependency on the part of the dependent group is replaced by conflicts around aggressive control, with prevalent suspiciousness, fight, and dread of annihilation.

In the "pairing" group, a couple (frequently but not necessarily heterosexual) symbolizes the hopeful expectations of the group that the selected pair will "reproduce itself"—thus preserving the current threatened identity and survival of the group. The fantasies experienced about this selected pair expresses the group's hope that, by means of magical "sexual" union, the group will be saved from the conflicts related to both the dependent and fight-flight assumptions. In the pairing group, in short, generalized intimacy and sexual developments are experienced as a potential protection against the dangerous conflicts around dependency and aggression (which, we may add, have a pregenital character, in contrast to the genital one of the pairing group). What is particularly striking is that the defensive mechanisms activated within the basic-assumptions group correspond to the defensive operations characteristic of primitive internalized object-relations. Indeed, impulses, defenses, and object relations of that primitive level of intrapsychic development become evident in the basic-assumptions group.

Main (1957) in analyzing the group reaction of nursing staff involved in the treatment of predominantly borderline and some psychotic patients ("special" cases) in the hospital, found that these patients managed to activate group phenomena in this nurses' group similar to those of Bion's basic-assumptions group. The implication is that regressed (particularly borderline) patients may, under certain conditions, activate their intrapsychic object relations in the interpersonal relations among the staff of the hospital: the patient induces in his social field a reenactment of the conflicts within his intrapsychic world. The combination of massive projection, omnipotent control, denial, primitive idealization, and, above all, splitting of staff reflects both the intrapsychic mechanisms involved and the behavioral means by which staff relationships are distorted by the patient's intrapsychic world. Stanton and Schwartz (1954), in turn, have demonstrated how splits and covert conflict in the interpersonal and social fields of the hospital may intensify intrapsychic conflict and disorganization in the "special" (borderline and in some cases psychotic) patients mentioned above. In short, the patients' intrapsychic conflicts and the potential cleavages and stresses within the social system of the hospital are reciprocally reinforcing.

All of this provides evidence about the rapid activation of primitive levels of defensive operations in the context of primitive internalized object relations in certain groups, as well as in social and administrative situations within the hospital. The question may now be raised, Granted that such an activation of early intrapsychic, object-relations-determined structures occurs in the interpersonal field, what is the therapeutic (in contrast to the merely diagnostic and educational) potential of such an activation?

Psychoanalytic exploration of the patient's interpersonal field within the hospital may greatly contribute to the diagnosis of his intrapsychic conflicts and may be utilized therapeutically in two ways: (1) in psychoanalytic group therapy which directly interprets to the patients as a group the activation of primitive conflicts within the group as a whole; and (2) in the hospital therapy, that is, in the approach of the hospital therapist who interprets to the patient as an individual the total interpersonal situation which the patient has created around himself and how this interpersonal situation reflects his conflictual, intrapsychic object relations. The working-through process in these two therapeutic situations is different. In psychoanalytic group therapy (following, as has been implied, the orientation of Bion [1959], Ezriel [1950], and Sutherland [1952]), the working through occurs not from the viewpoint of the individual patient's genetic development but from the viewpoint of the historical development of the group as a whole. The working through of the deeper layer of object relations on the part of each individual patient occurs in repetitive cycles, in a "disorderly" fashion from the individual's point of view but not from the point of view of the total group history. The intensity and potential clarity of the controlled social situation of the small group are the strength of this psychoanalytic group approach.

The examination of the individual patient's evolving deployment of primitive object relations in the social field of the hospital may be better accomplished by the hospital therapist's systematic examination with the patient of his interpersonal experiences in the hospital. These interpersonal experiences include all of the patient's interactions with hospital staff and with other patients. The hospital therapist integrates the many observations of staff in their interactions with the patient. As team leader of the staff involved with the patient's treatment, he facilitates the development of an integrating understanding of the patient's impact on the total social system of the floor or section and communicates this understanding to the patient.

This examination of the patient's total impact on the social system requires a "neutral" hospital milieu, that is, a staff attitude basically equidistant from the different intrapsychic and external agencies involved in the patient's conflicts and, overall, an atmosphere of friendliness, relative tolerance, interest, and intellectual alertness. This atmosphere is in contrast to two extremes: (1) the hospital run with a barracks strictness which interferes with the full development of the patient's pathological object relations, and (2) the hospital so unstructured that a complete examination of the patient's interpersonal field becomes impossible. This atmosphere also fosters free and open communication and interactions between all staff members and the patient and encourages staff to use their specific technical skills, their psychological understanding, and their personalities in maximizing the patient's opportunities for meaningful human relations in the hospital.

In addition, it is possible to combine such group- and hospital-therapy approaches with a more standard psychoanalytic or psychoanalytically oriented individual therapy, within which a systematic development of transference analysis leading to the crystallization of higher-level object relations and conflict resolution would become the main task, in the context of the dyadic patient-therapist relation. Chapter 6 summarizes the modified psychoanalytic procedure that I have proposed as treatment of choice for patients with borderline personality organization.

Psychoanalytic exploration of the patient's interactions in the total social field of the hospital (hospital therapy), within a small, closed, unstructured group (psychoanalytic group therapy), and in individual psychotherapy or psychoanalysis cannot be, in clinical practice, as sharply delimited from each other as implied above. Primitive levels of object relations will develop, even rapidly, within the individual treatment setting of borderline and psychotic patients; transference analysis, the examination of the patient's interactions within the small group, and examination of his interactions in the hospital at large will necessarily overlap. However, an additional frame of reference may contribute further to the delimitation of the functions of all these different treatment modalities. I am referring here to A. K. Rice's systems theory of organization, which treats the individual, the group, and the social organization as a continuum of open systems (Miller and Rice, 1967; Rice, 1963, 1965, 1969).

A SYSTEMS-THEORY APPROACH INTEGRATING PSYCHOANALYTIC OBJECT-RELATIONS AND SMALL-GROUP THEORIES WITH A THEORY OF HOSPITAL ADMINISTRATION

Open systems are characterized by exchanges with the environment which are defined by input, conversion, and output phases. Rice proposes that the individual, the group, and the social institution may be seen as such open systems, and that properties common to the functions and structure of open systems may be applied to all three. The practical implication is that a common set of laws may be established regulating individual, group, and institutional functioning, and, particularly, that the boundaries between individual, group, and institution, and between the institution and its environment can be examined in an integrative frame. What follows is a brief summary of the pertinent aspects of Rice's theories.

All open systems carry out tasks in their exchange with the environment. A task which an open system must carry out to survive is called a primary task. In a given system, there may be several primary tasks which may constitute constraints on one other. In general, all task performance is limited by constraints; and, in order to carry out a task successfully, a system must have a definition of the task, an understanding of the processes necessary to carry it out, and a view of the constraints limiting task performance. Each system must include a control function which will permit the analysis of the environment, the internal reality of the system, and the executive organization of task performance within such a reality. Because by definition open systems must carry out exchange with the environment to survive, this control function must be at the boundary between the system and its environment. The primary task of any open system involves exchange with the environment and its control function must determine and preserve the boundary of the system. Breakdown of system boundaries implies breakdown of control of the open system, and this, in turn, brings about breakdown in carrying out the primary task, thus threatening the survival of the system. This theory may be applied to patients, groups, and the hospital as a social system.

In the case of the psychic life of an individual, the ego may be conceived as the control function, ego boundaries as the boundaries defined and protected by ego functions, and the person's intrapsychic world of object relations as the inner space or inner world of the system. Rice (1969) proposes that in the mature individual the ego function mediates the relationship between the external and the internal worlds and thus takes a "leadership" role in relation to the individual and exercises a "management" control function. The primary task of the individual is to satisfy the instinctual and object-oriented needs of his internal world by means of interactions with his social environment, adapting to and creatively modifying his interpersonal world in terms of his intrapsychic needs and, in turn, elaborating intrapsychic needs in terms of external reality. Psychopathology may be seen as a breakdown (in varying degrees) of the control function (ego), with the consequent breakdown of both adaptation to the environment and gratification of basic intrapsychic needs.

In the case of the group, the group leader may be seen as the control function; the primary task of the group is that which determined its existence in the first place; and the activation of primitive object relations within the group structure (Bion's "basic assumptions group") represents the internal world of object relations of the group (Rice, 1969). From the viewpoint of hospital treatment, groups may be classified into three general types: (a) task groups, which are organized to carry out a task involving interchange with the environment (work projects, study groups, etc); (b) group-dynamics groups, in which the task consists of learning experimentally about the psychodynamics of group behavior; and (c) psychotherapeutic groups, in which the task is the examination of psychological developments within the group for the purpose of treating the psychopathology of the group members.

The following considerations regarding the leadership of these three types of groups always refer to functional leadership, which is derived from a series of activities or achievements related to group tasks. This concept is in contrast to the concept of leadership as a personality attribute or of the leader as a charismatic figure. In other words, functional leadership is contrasted to leadership linked to personality structure. Functional leadership may be carried out by an individual or by a group of individuals, and it may shift within the task group in response to shifting requirements.

The leader of the task group has to be able to define the task, carry out or delegate responsibility for the different phases and subdivisions of the task, and evaluate performance in examining the relationship between the internal and external worlds of the group (measuring task performance or conversion by the differences between input and output). He also must be able to detect and utilize the emotional constellations (basic assumptions) of the group, which will remain more and more in the background as task performance improves. Reduction of task performance (because of excessive constraints or poor leadership) activates basic group assumptions and basic group leadership and challenges the task group leader.

In the group-dynamics group, the consultant leads the group in the task of observing its own behavior and learning from it. The nature of this task greatly intensifies the development of the basic-assumptions group, the need for the consultant to interpret the assumptions insofar as they become resistance to learning, and the need to maintain an optimal balance between experiencing and observing on the part of the entire group membership.

The therapist of a psychotherapeutic group is the leader for the task of psychological exploration, with techniques similar to those of group dynamics but with the additional goal of linking learning about primitive object relations and the related defensive mechanisms activated in the group with the respective intrapsychic conflicts of the group members.

In the case of the hospital as an organization, hospital administration represents the leadership or management carrying out the control functions of the system. For the psychoanalytic teaching hospital, the primary tasks of the system are patient care, education, and research. The creation and protection of an optimal social atmosphere within the hospital to permit the development and examination of intrapsychic, interpersonal, intragroup, and intergroup processes for therapeutic purposes are specific tasks of the psychoanalytic hospital which especially call for functional, task-oriented leadership. The therapeutic community is a special organization within the hospital or within sections of the hospital; it is geared to an open examination of all the social processes occurring within the hospital or section, for the purpose of maximizing the therapeutic opportunities for (1) individual treatment (individual psychotherapy or psychoanalysis, and hospital therapy), (2) group treatment (group therapy and task groups), and (3) group-dynamics experiences (for educational purposes and for the development of leadership among the hospital staff). The therapeutic community will be examined further later on.

In summary, the primary task of the individual is to negotiate with the environment so as to fulfill the needs that stem from his own internal world; his control function, including boundary control, is the ego. In the case of the group, the primary task is that for which the group has become organized, and its control function is the group leader or group leadership. The equilibrium between the group focusing on the task (task group) and the group focusing on the activation of primitive object relations in its social field (basic-assumptions group) depends on the extent to which the task is clear and defined, the adequacy of task leadership, and the examination of the basic assumptions that are either included in the task or taken into consideration as task constraints. In the case of the hospital, the primary task is to carry out the purposes for which the hospital has been established, and the control function is represented by hospital administration. Consideration of the emotional needs of hospital staff is a basic constraint on task performance, just as basic group assumptions are a basic constraint on the task or work group. In the case of the psychoanalytic hospital, focusing on the emotional life within the social field of the hospital becomes a primary therapeutic function, and the therapeutic community is one task system for carrying out this function. This is the great advantage of a therapeutic community: a basic constraint (the emotional needs of groups within the hospital) becomes a major task objective (the study of emotional conflicts as a learning experience in conflict management and emotional growth).

Within this model, psychopathology may be conceptualized as breakdown of the control function, failure in carrying out the primary task, and threat to the survival of the system: in the case of the individual, we see breakdown of the ego and emotional catastrophe; in the case of the group, breakdown of group leadership and paralysis in basic assumptions; in the case of the hospital, breakdown of administration, failure to carry out the task, and loss of morale. Breakdown of boundary control is the main manifestation of breakdown in the control function; loss of ego boundaries is a primary cause of loss of differentiation between self and nonself and a basic characteristic of the psychoses.

AN INTEGRATIVE CONCEPTUALIZATION OF TREATMENT MODALITIES WITHIN THE HOSPITAL

In this conceptualization, treatment may be defined as the introduction of a "consultant" (therapist) into the system. The consultant's primary task is to diagnose the nature and causes of the breakdown in the control function; to facilitate reestablishment of boundary control; and to accomplish an adequate redefinition both of the primary task and its constraints and of the organizational means and structures required to carry it out. The consultant needs to be an expert in the field in which the breakdown occurs (individual, group, or organization). He must be sufficiently outside the system to be able to examine its internal workings and external environment objectively. The consultant needs to negotiate with the system the nature and limits of his task, renegotiating it as he himself redefines the nature and limits of his task. The consultant, in interacting with the system in conflict, establishes a task system of its own; this system needs, in turn, a definition of its primary task and of its boundaries. The main boundary of the consultant is the time boundary: a consultant without a clearly defined time boundary tends to become confused with the control function of the system (individual, group, or organization).

Applying this conceptualization to ("formal") individual psychotherapy, we might say that the psychotherapist acts as a consultant to the patient, diagnosing his control function (ego), the nature, causes, and extent of its breakdown, diagnosing also the nature of the internal world (internalized object relations) and the environment and the nature of the transactions which would be necessary to satisfy the patient's internal needs within his given environment. In short, the psychotherapist focuses on both the control function and the internal world of the patient. Insofar as they tend particularly to activate the higher level of internalized object relations, individual psychotherapy and psychoanalysis activate the patient's potential for dyadic, oedipal-triangular, and sibling relationships (transference neurosis). However, as we have seen, in borderline and psychotic patients, individual psychotherapy also directly activates primitive object relations, together with remnants of the control function (ego), directly negotiating such primitive object relations in a fragmented, disorganized way. From this viewpoint, individual psychotherapy of borderline and psychotic patients may be conceived as a clarification, within each of the fragmented ego states that are activated in the transference, of the patient's relationship with reality and of the particular object relations activated at that point. Clarification becomes interpretation of the patient's perceptions and the realistic aspects of the treatment hours simultaneously with interpretation of his primitive internalized object relations in the transference. In the case of severely regressed psychotic patients, the disintegration of the ego may interfere with the minimal work needed to separate internal needs from reality perception; in these cases, a shift in the psychotherapeutic task to a predominant focus upon the control function (ego) may be the first stage of treatment until sufficient observing ego is present to participate in the therapeutic task of sorting out reality from intrapsychic needs.

In group psychotherapy, the focus is predominantly on primitive object relations and related defensive operations as they become activated in the basic-assumptions group. In psychoanalytic group psychotherapy, the focus is primarily on the internal world of object relations, with less emphasis on the nature of the individual patient's control function (ego). The implication is that, in contrast to individual psychotherapy, which may be indicated for all patients along the continuum of psychosis-borderline-neurosis, analytic group psychotherapy is most indicated where the patient's control function is stable enough to be able to participate in the examination of the basic group assumptions, that is, in the case of neuroses and borderline conditions. Group dynamics is not a therapeutic modality as such and would be reserved for staff trained as experts in the treatment of individual, group, and therapeutic community modalities (and as experts in organizational leadership).

Concentration on boundary control between groups sharply focuses the qualities and deficiencies of group leadership (Rice, 1965). The therapeutic community examines patient, staff, and combined patient-staff leadership, including that of hospital administration. Sociological research in the hospital in recent years has stressed the therapeutic value of such an open examination of leadership, authority, and power struggles within the hospital (Rubenstein and Lasswell, 1966).

The therapeutic community and individual hospital therapy operate at a similar level of simultaneous examination of internal object relations and the control function (ego). Insofar as the therapeutic community utilizes group methods and thus activates the basic-assumptions group, it contributes to the activation of primitive object relations and may examine them and the related defenses as developments in the social field; insofar as it is geared to task performance (that is, to the negotiation of the needs of task performance of different groups within the hospital) and to the intergroup relationships that entails (particularly staff-patient relationships), the focus of the therapeutic community is on the control function as well.

However, the therapeutic community requires sufficient individual control function (ego) for participation in the stressful community examination of breakdown and correction of intergroup boundaries, thus excluding the more severely regressed psychotic patients. In contrast, the therapeutic community might be an ideal model for somewhat less regressed psychotic patients and for those with borderline conditions in which the control function (ego), though deficient, is still available.

Individual hospital therapy may be compared to the therapeutic community in that it also focuses predominantly on the individual's control function (ego), that is, on the extent to which the patient is able to negotiate his intrapsychic needs within the interpersonal environment of the hospital. Insofar as the hospital therapist communicates to the patient the effects of the patient's behavior on the interpersonal field in the hospital and the intrapsychic implications of the distortions thereby created, the hospital therapist also focuses upon the patient's internal world of object relations. However, insofar as the hospital therapist focuses upon the here and now of the patient's interactions in the hospital (in contrast to transference analysis within "formal" individual psychotherapy), issues of control and of multiple boundary relationships with other patients, staff, and task systems predominate. The hospital therapist represents the entire hospital to the patient, in the same way that the therapeutic community reflects the hospital or section social system and permits its examination by the entire group of patients. The hospital therapist may not be able to carry out such a complex task with severely regressed psychotic patients who are seriously withdrawn or isolated from the social life of the hospital. In contrast, in this function the hospital therapist is of maximal use to the borderline patient who needs a "consultant" to clarify his interactions within the hospital social system.

The hospital therapist carries out a particular boundary function between the hospital as a social system and the individual patient as an open system. Insofar as the hospital therapist makes decisions concerning the patient's life, he really shifts from a consultant's role to an auxiliary ego role, that is, he becomes the "management" of the patient. This implies abandonment of neutrality in a technical sense, at the risk of losing the monitoring capacity to evaluate the patient's ego resources for carrying out management functions himself. However, this radical change in the hospital therapist's role is necessary, particularly for patients with little motivation for change. Groups or social organizations without the will to survive would die; it is an aspect of the medical—indeed humanitarian—ethic that we "take over" for a patient whose control function has broken down and who would, psychologically (and sometimes physically), die if we did not move in. The hospital therapist, therefore, really becomes a "hospital administrator" in the case of severely regressed psychotic patients; this may also be true, to a lesser extent, for some borderline patients.

By definition, task groups within the hospital minimize the activation of primitive object relations (basic assumptions) in their members and maximize the potential for task leadership, cooperation, task orientation, and reality orientation in patients. Therefore, they directly reinforce the individual's control function (ego). Task groups seem ideally indicated for psychotic and borderline patients but are not so necessary in the treatment of neurotic patients. Roughly speaking, one might classify task groups in the hospital by professions (Brocher, 1970): the nursing profession would specialize in the establishment of family-living task groups, the activities department in the establishment of work and recreational task groups, the social worker in the establishment of social reintegration and rehabilitation task groups.

In summary, hospital treatment could be formulated as the simultaneous diagnosis and treatment of the patient's control function and his internal world of object relations. Analytic group psychotherapy would examine deeply the intrapsychic world of object relations; it is indicated for patients with a strong control function (particularly patients functioning on a neurotic level) and to a lesser extent for patients on a borderline level. Task groups which focus far more on the control function then on the internal world of object relations would be most clearly indicated for patients with serious deficits in their control functions, such as psychotic and borderline patients. Individual psychoanalytic psychotherapy or psychoanalysis would be indicated for the entire range of psychiatric patients (with the exception of specific or individual contraindications), in that it deals with different levels of object relations and the corresponding problems in the control function (ego). The therapeutic community, with a strong emphasis on the control function rather than the internal world of object relations—but with a sharp focus on the reality of interpersonal interactions in the hospital—appears ideally indicated for the less regressed psychotic patients and particularly for borderline patients. Hospital therapy is similar in its approach and indications to the therapeutic community and would naturally combine with it. The hospital therapist as a hospital administrator would reflect the particular need for taking over in the case of severely regressed psychotic patients (and some borderline patients), functioning in this case (in contrast to all other "consultant" functions of individual therapist, group therapist, therapeutic community leader, and hospital administrator) as an auxiliary ego.

The implication of this examination of different treatment modalities in terms of Rice's open-system theory, psychoanalytic object-relations theory, and psychoanalytic theory of small groups is that group therapy, individual therapy, therapeutic community, hospital therapy (and management), and task groups may be integrated in a common theoretical frame and, in varying proportions, are part of the treatment of hospitalized psychotic and borderline patients. In general terms, severely regressed psychotic patients require hospital management (including medication), individual psychoanalytic therapy in some cases, and task groups as the main modalities of treatment; borderline patients require individual psychoanalytic therapy, therapeutic community and/or hospital therapy, and task groups. However, in practice the differentiation of treatment modalities cannot be made as sharply as within such an ideal model. Classifying patients into neurotic, borderline, and psychotic conditions is certainly not sufficient for the purpose of treatment indication: for any particular patient this would depend upon highly individualized judgments.

The combination of individual and group psychotherapy for neurotic patients is controversial because of the danger of transference splitting and transference acting out; the opinions about this are divided, and the advantages and disadvantages of single or combined modalities needs much further research. Individual psychoanalytic psychotherapy and psychoanalysis seem ideally geared to focusing on dyadic and triangular relationships in depth over the entire range of psychopathology. Group psychoanalytic psychotherapy and group dynamics tend to activate rapidly primitive levels of object relations and pathological character defenses of the individual which might need a long time to become fully exposed in the individual treatment situation. Individuals who have undergone psychoanalysis first and group experiences later have been able to reconfirm findings from their own psychoanalysis within the group situation after brief periods of time. Yet I do not think any group experience permits the full range of integration of emotional learning available in psychoanalysis.

separated sharply from the patient's ego. Although for clinical purposes they may be separated, the internal world of object relations and the control function (ego) have common roots. It may well be that satisfactory development of the earliest dyadic relationship between infant and mother is a prerequisite for the establishing of a basic ego core, of basic trust, and the related capacity for a therapeutic alliance (Winnicott, 1954; Zetzel, 1966). The relationship between internalization of object relations and the development of the ego and psychic structures in general has already been examined (Chapter 2): psychoanalytic object-relations theory constitutes a basic theoretical tool in this analysis.

The implication of everything that has been said so far is that the hospital as a social system may provide various therapeutic structures which activate in different proportions the patient's control function and internal world of object relations.

It is important to stress the human, personal element in the therapeutic process. The therapist (consultant) cannot help the patient grow as a human being without authentic respect and concern for him. And one crucial aspect of the patient's learning process in treatment (managerial skill) is the development of concern for himself, as well as the capacity for establishing an authentic relationship with the therapist. Thus the patient is influenced both by what the therapist does and what the therapist is (Ticho, 1971). The therapist's availability as a real person, as somebody willing to understand and to help—a good, real object in contrast to the patient's transference distortions—is crucially important in the treatment. In this connection, the patient-therapist unit might be described as a higher-order unit of object relations: a higher-order self, a higher-order affect of hope and anticipation of help, a higher-order helpful object (Myerson, 1971). Only within this conceptualization may treatment be formulated as the learning of "managerial skills" in order to understand one's self, one's boundaries, one's internal needs, one's environment, and one's life tasks; only in this way can structural intrapsychic change be formulated as improvement in the control function (ego) and in the capacity of the patient to carry out his primary task (the expression of his intrapsychic needs in ways that are adaptive to his environment).

With these reservations, psychological treatment may be conceptualized as a particular form of (conscious and unconscious) learning for leadership of one's own self.

A CLINICAL ILLUSTRATION

One patient with chronic paranoid schizophrenia presented an idealization of a primitive father image conceived as a tyrannical, cruel, omnipotent suppressor of both sex and violence. The patient feared and yet admired this image of his father, and saw him as an indispensable protection against the outbreak of uncontrollable violence in himself and others. In the hospital, the patient presented periods of relative "integration" (with little thought disorganization and rather "appropriate" behavior on the ward) during which he meekly submitted to staff, identified himself consciously with political groups of the extreme right, had homosexual fantasies (linked to his submission to powerful men), and was terrified of women. At such times, he saw the director of the hospital service as a tyrant whom he admired and paid homage to. This submissiveness had an almost mocking quality to it; and he angrily defended the need for "law and order" on the ward, demanding punishment for all aggressive behavior of other patients. At other times, he was "disorganized"—that is, he presented a marked thought disorder, became openly aggressive with authority figures, approached in seductive ways women with "motherly" features, and, indeed, was not sure whether these women were his mother. In other words, primitive rebellion against oedipal father figures and sexual seductiveness toward mother images was acted out in the context of psychotic regression.

After some time, conflicts which replicated these problems developed among the staff on the service. Conflicts developed particularly among staff directly in charge of this patient's treatment, but eventually spread over the service at large, as this patient became a "special case." A psychiatric resident experienced one senior staff consultant as a dangerous tyrant who would punish him if he disagreed with the consultant's recommendation. Subtle competition simultaneously developed among other senior male consultants around the figure of the (apparently) "submissive" female staff member who was a special counselor to the patient. The entire staff perceived this woman counselor as a kind of reluctant, somewhat passive, but crucial judge of this case, and the male staff members involved eagerly sought her favorable opinion. At the same time, more generalized sexual and aggressive acting out was occurring among patients on the service. All this seemed related to the "testing" of a new service director, with fears shared by staff and patients alike about whether he would become a harsh, tyrannical suppressor of sex and violence, or a dangerous "libertarian" who would cause a chaotic diorganization of the service because of general loosening of impulse control. At one point, the staff's fantasies and fears regarding the new service director became condensed with the competition of senior consultants for the "favors" of the female staff member involved in the patient's treatment. The service director was now seen as the male figure who, in effect, had established a personal "pairing" with this woman counselor, thus triumphing over the other male consultants, and there was widespread fear that the new director would impose his ideas tyrannically over the treatment team of this patient. These fantasies were eventually shared by patients and staff alike, as patients expressed in community meetings their wishes for and fears of a strong father figure who would control sex and violence which would otherwise destroy the social fabric of the service.

The analysis of the patient's contributions to these fantasies shared by groups of patients and staff permitted both a reduction in anxiety and conflicts among staff and a sharper focus on the intrapsychic dynamics of the patient, all of which led to a more integrated and focused combination of psychotherapy and hospital milieu treatment for him.

In the psychotherapy, the patient was confronted with his fear about his aggression and sexual excitement and his fantastic conviction that either all his impulses were suppressed or he would kill his father and rape his mother. In the hospital milieu approach, he was permitted some expression of his anger, and the more primitive and destructive aspects of it were controlled by staff while pointing out to him that this was not done in punitive or retaliatory fashion. More contacts with female patients were implicitly fostered in his daily program of activities, while his more primitive, seductive behavior toward some women was discouraged. This example illustrates: (1) activation in the patient's object relations in the hospital of regressive condensation of oedipal conflicts with pregenital conflicts around aggression; (2) reciprocal activation of latent conflicts among the hospital staff in the interactions with the patient; and (3) therapeutic utilization of the understanding reached by hospital staff of these dynamics. The analysis of the distortions of the social structure permitted first a decrease in hospital conflicts, and then the utilization of a better understanding of the patient in his overall psychotherapeutic and milieu treatment.

The treatment modality implied in this example is geared to avoid and to repair the damaging influences on the treatment of individual patients of covert conflicts within the various echelons of the hospital administration and to utilize, diagnostically and therapeutically, the negative effects of the patient's intrapsychic conflicts on the social structure of the hospital. The proposed treatment modality requires, it must be stressed, an optimal, open examination both of the total social field surrounding the patient's treatment and of the reciprocal effects of the patient's intrapsychic life and this social field. All this information, made available to the psychotherapist, may then be incorporated into the psychotherapy, as well as directly utilized by the hospital treatment team at large. Such a treatment approach requires the establishment and protection of a functional, in contrast to an authoritarian, administrative hospital structure. Many of the criticisms that have been directed against the intensive treatment of regressed patients within a hospital setting have been directed against old-fashioned, overcrowded, understaffed, primitive treatment settings which do not reflect what a contemporary, psychoanalytically oriented hospital treatment approach may add to intensive psychotherapy. This brings us to another assumption regarding the therapeutic functions of the psychoanalytic hospital; namely, that the administration of the hospital itself may be utilized for purposes of learning about managerial and leadership functions and preconditions.

FUNCTIONAL HOSPITAL ADMINISTRATION AS A MODEL AND PRECONDITION FOR THE THERAPEUTIC COMMUNITY

The staff may learn about management at the individual, group, and organizational levels by open examination of the administrative system of the hospital, and hospital management may understand the therapeutic needs of the psychoanalytic hospital from the viewpoint of Rice's theory of administration. In this conceptualization, psychoanalysis and psychoanalytic psychotherapy become a particular theory and technique of "management consultation," and psychoanalytic object-relations theory (including the psychoanalytic theory of small groups) links the understandings of the internal world of the individual, the group, and the organization in a common frame of reference. Administrative theory, insofar as it concerns itself with the analysis of the control function and with the leadership of organizations, groups, and individuals, may be integrated conceptually with the psychotherapeutic approaches of the hospital. Hospital administration has to provide functional (task-oriented) leadership to create an open social atmosphere conducive to examining the administrative process itself. The norms, expectations, and values which the administrator communicates in his relationships with staff are likely to be recommunicated by staff to patients; lack of authenticity in staff-staff relationships will foster and legitimize similar behavior in patient-patient and patient-staff relationships, especially those involving the exercise of authority (Dolgoff, 1971).

Failure of hospital management implies a breakdown in the boundary functions of the hospital, in its capacity for carrying out the primary task, and therefore, also, to a greater or lesser extent, of all task systems within the hospital (including staff, patient, and staff-patient task groups). The deterioration of task groups activates basic-assumptions conditions within groups and in intergroup relationships to such an extent that primitive conflicts, primitive defensive operations, and the loss of task leadership all come about and make open, rational examination of the hospital as a social system impossible. Therefore, the therapeutic potentials of individual and group activities are reduced. In contrast, with efficient hospital administration and maintenance of functional task leadership, all task systems throughout the hospital may function adequately, and partial breakdowns in intraorganizational task systems can be localized, diagnosed, and treated. The preservation of task boundaries and of task leadership maximizes open examination of the hospital as a social system and mobilization of the therapeutic potentialities of such an examination.

Effective hospital management requires adequate definition by the hospital administration of the primary task (or tasks) of the hospital, definition of the constraints, and establishment of priorities and constraints on a functional basis. Hospital management needs adequate control over hospital boundaries, which implies stable, fully delegated authority regarding all hospital functions from the hospital board to the director or managing team. Such stable, clearly defined, authority needs to be delegated, in turn, by the hospital administration to hospital staff in a stable, clearly delimited, unambiguous way along functional, task-determined lines. Hospital administration, in order to carry out the boundary-control functions of the hospital, must provide adequate representation of the external environment to the hospital staff and must communicate the internal needs of the hospital to the external environment with which the hospital relates in carrying out its task. In the case of the psychoanalytic hospital, strict administrative boundaries should be matched by wide-open professional doors (open examination of all professional issues), so that changing needs, demands, and constraints from the environment can be explored, analyzed, and incorporated into the decision-making process. Such an administrative structure should involve opportunities for learning about administration by means of open examination of its functioning for all hospital staff (although in varying degrees and in accordance with the specific professional functions of hospital staff).

The therapeutic community is an organized social structure within the hospital, centering on the community meeting of patients and staff; it too requires meaningful, stable, delimited delegation of authority from hospital administration to staff and from staff to patients. As an organization, it should afford open interchange between staff and patients in the process of carrying out their respective functions within their respective delegated authority.

The therapeutic community is the comprehensive organization of the social system for psychotherapeutic purposes within the hospital or a hospital section (Jones, 1968; Caine and Small, 1969; Edelson, 1967; Falck, 1969). The community meeting is only one of its aspects, although a very crucial one. The community meeting includes all staff and all patients who form part of the social system included in the therapeutic community. The total authority invested in the therapeutic community must be necessarily less than that invested in the administrative head of the hospital or section; the community meeting permits public recognition of the extent and limits of this authority and what further delegation of this authority may be made to particular component systems of the community.

Delegation of authority in professional matters should not be done on an ideological, pseudo-democratic basis but on a functional one (Zaleznik, 1970). For example, authority regarding medical matters has to go to the physicians of the community. If authority is delegated regardless of the professional expertise, skills, experience, and motivation of staff and patients, role diffusion, ambiguities, and breakdown of task systems will occur. This may have very regressive, demoralizing, and, ultimately, antitherapeutic effects.

The primary task of the therapeutic community is the treatment of patients and not the expression of an equalitarian ideology (Falck, 1969; Zaleznik, 1970). All explorations of group conflicts, of task requirements and constraints, and of interpersonal difficulties and characterological problems of individual patients should have a therapeutic function. The design, organization, and actual carrying out of tasks by individuals and groups, by staff, patients, and staff-patient task forces should also have an ultimate therapeutic purpose. The functions of the therapeutic community may thus be grouped into: (1) analysis and strengthening of the control function of individual patients, groups, and the total community; and (2) analysis and modification of the internal world, the intrapsychic and interpersonal object relations of patients as individuals and as group members.

These functions may be carried out within the community meeting or may be delegated to groups, task forces, or individuals within the community. For example, "group-living meetings" may be designated to examine and resolve conflicts between individual patients, groups of patients, or patients and staff: as long as these meetings deal with the here and now only (and do not attempt to explore transference implications in terms of their genetic origins), they represent therapeutic community functions delegated to a particular subsystem of the community. "Floor meetings" may deal with concrete tasks of daily life in the hospital, again representing one delegated function of the therapeutic community.

Group-living meetings, floor meetings, and other meetings may, of course, be organized regardless of whether a therapeutic-community model exists at the hospital or section. The advantage of the therapeutic-community model is that it incorporates, by definition, the total social field of the patients' interactions in the hospital or sections. It includes in its realm formal and spontaneous groups and overt and covert stress and conflict in the social system; above all, it permits a functional definition of roles and tasks for staff and patients alike, and in this way maximizes the functional (as opposed to hierarchical) organization of the hospital or section (Falck, 1969). Functional organization, in turn, permits optimal openness of exploration of the social field for the therapeutic purposes mentioned above.

Patient government meetings, staff meetings, and joint patient-staff meetings should be geared to exploring tasks and task constraints within the hospital, particularly task constraints created by the development of basic-assumptions groups within hospital group processes. The traditional philosophy of the therapeutic community implies that open communication, democratization, full information sharing, and open confrontation of conflicts have therapeutic values: we can now examine these assumptions in the light of the hypotheses formulated earlier regarding hospital administration.

Patient organization may indeed be a helpful therapeutic agent in that patients as a group may function as a "normal," effective social system (Falck, 1969) and, by means of such effective functions, improve the control function (ego) of individual patients and their capacity for interpersonal relationships. However, effective functioning of patient groups requires adequate patient leadership, clear task definition, and stable and unambiguous authority vested in such patient leadership. If the tasks carried out by patients are trivial rather than meaningful, if delegation of authority from staff to them is ambiguous or if patient leadership is ineffective, regression of the patient group to a basic-assumptions group, as well as ineffectiveness and failure, will develop; thus, patient groups may in some circumstances become antitherapeutic agents promoting hopelessness, passivity, cynicism, and despair. The democratization of social functions within the hospital may be therapeutic insofar as it is opposed to an authoritarian power structure (Rubenstein and Lasswell, 1966), which usually goes hand in hand with nonfunctional hospital administration. However, democratic decision-making may or may not coincide with (or bring about) functional, task-centered leadership. Staff and patients have different functions, authority, and expertise: efforts to deny this reality by means of "democratic" political procedures may lead to role diffusion, breakdown in task performance, and abandonment of task-determined leadership and individual responsibility.

Patients do have the capacity for helping each other as individuals and as groups; however, for groups to be helpful they must be task-centered—and so must their relationships with other groups within the hospital. In the last analysis, effective leadership within all therapeutic group structures, including the therapeutic community, depends upon authority delegated from the hospital administration. Dissociation of leadership of the therapeutic community from hospital leadership can only lead to failure of the therapeutic community. Not everything that goes on in therapeutic community meetings is therapeutic; not everything that is democratic means effective decision-sharing; and not everything that is open communication means improvement in intrapsychic and interpersonal relationships. One must acknowledge actual differences between staff and patients with regard to skill and expertise; an optimal balance has to be achieved between open communication and the right of privacy (within an open-communication system in which confidentiality cannot be guaranteed).

If the therapeutic community is geared to active problem-solving within the social system of the hospital, it has to be directed by active, task-oriented leadership. If the therapeutic community is seen only as a large group-dynamics exercise in which basic assumptions can be explored at the expense of carrying out realistic tasks, aimlessness, unproductivity, hopelessness, and cynicism may soon ensue. Contradictions in the administrative structure of the hospital or section between formal and informal aspects of the hospital social system, between a "pseudo-psychoanalytic" hospital philosophy (Novotny, 1971) and manipulation of patients on the part of staff will soon come out in the open if the therapeutic community (and particularly the community meeting) functions effectively. If ventilation of these problems is not then coupled with adequate means for bringing about change, the community meeting will become simply a griping session (not only for patients but for staff as well). Open examination of conflicts needs to be coupled with tools to solve them: it is the experience of successful task performance which gives meaning to the open examination of task constraints. For such experiences to occur, the therapeutic community needs to be clearly differentiated from group-dynamics experiences. (As earlier mentioned, group-dynamics experience is essentially not a therapeutic but an educational tool.) The actual leader of the therapeutic community must be willing and able to assume administrative authority and to assure himself of such delegated authority from the hospital administration.

SUMMARY

A conceptual model for a philosophy of treatment within the psychoanalytic hospital has been outlined. This model attempts to integrate several theories: (1) a theory of intrapsychic structure and of structural change derived from psychoanalytic object-relations theory; (2) a theory of activation of primitive object relations and related primitive defensive operations within small, unstructured groups and of reciprocal reinforcement in such groups of the intrapsychic and the interpersonal fields; (3) a theory of two general levels of activation of intrapsychic object relationships, a higher (dyadic-triangular) one predominantly activated in individual psychotherapeutic relationships and a lower (primitive) one particularly activated in nonstructured groups; (4) a theory of organizations as open systems, focusing on the issue of control function (leadership or management) and internal needs (an internal world) at the level of the individual, the group, and the hospital; (5) a theory ranging therapeutic modalities (including individual, group, and community methods) according to selective activation of problems in the control functions and/or problems in the expression of internal needs, and an application of this range to the prescription of treatment modalities for psychotic and borderline patients; (6) a theory of hospital administration (including therapeutic community models) derived from the theory of the organization as an open system mentioned above.

REFERENCES

Bion, W. R. (1959). *Experiences in Groups*. New York: Basic Books.

Brocher, T. (1970). Personal communication.

Caine, R. M. & Small, D. J. (1969). *The Treatment of Mental Illness*. New York: International Universities Press.

Dolgoff, T. (1971). Personal communication.

Edelson, M. (1967). The sociotherapeutic function in a psychiatric hospital. *Journal of the Fort Logan Mental Health Center* 4: 1-45.

Erikson, E. H. (1956). The problem of ego identity. *Journal of the American Psychoanalytic Association* 4: 56-121.

Ezriel, H. (1950). A psychoanalytic approach to the treatment of patients in groups. *Journal of Mental Science* 96: 774-779.

Falck, H. (1969). Personal communication.

Freud, A. (1946). *The Ego and the Mechanisms of Defense*. New York: International Universities Press, pp. 30-32.

Guntrip, H. (1961). *Personality Structure and Human Interaction*. London: Hogarth Press.

Jacobson, E. (1964). *The Self and the Object World*. New York: International Universities Press.

Jones, M. (1968). *Social Psychiatry in Practice*. Baltimore, Maryland: Penguin Books.

Kernberg, O. (1967). Borderline personality organization. In: *Borderline Conditions and Pathological Narcissism*. New York: Jason Aronson, 1975, pp. 3-47.

———(1975b). *Borderline Conditions and Pathological Narcissism*. New York: Jason Aronson.

Main, T. F. (1957). The ailment. *British Journal of Medical Psychology* 30: 129-145.

Miller, G. A., and Rice, A. K. (1967). *Systems of Organization*. London: Tavistock Publications.

Myerson, P. G. (1971). Personal communication.

Novotny, P. (1971). The pseudo-psychoanalytic hospital (Notes on the institutionalization of Countertransference Acting Out Patterns). *Bulletin of the Menninger Clinic* 37: 193-210.

Rice, A. K. (1963). *The Enterprise and its Environment*. London: Tavistock Publications.

———(1965). *Learning for Leadership*. London: Tavistock Publications.

———(1969). Individual, group and intergroup processes. *Human Relations* 22: 565-584.

Rioch, M. J. (1970). The work of Wilfred Bion on groups. *Psychiatry* 33: 56-66.

Rubenstein, R., and Lasswell, H. D. (1966). *The Sharing of Power in a Psychiatric Hospital*. New Haven & London: Yale University Press.

Stanton, A. A., and Schwartz, M. S. (1954). *The Mental Hospital*. New York: Basic Books.

Sutherland, J. D. (1952). Notes on psychoanalytic group therapy: I. therapy and training. *Psychiatry* 15: 111-117.

———(1963). Object relations theory and the conceptual model of psychoanalysis. *British Journal of Medical Psychology* 36: 109-124.

Ticho, E. (1971). Personal communication.

Winnicott, D. W. (1954). Metapsychological and clinical aspects of regression within the psycho-analytical set-up. In: *Collected Papers*. New York: Basic Books, 1958, pp. 278-294.

Zaleznik, A. (1970). Personal communication.

Zetzel, E. R. (1966). The analytic situation. In: *Psychoanalysis in the Americas*, ed. Robert E. Litman. New York: International Universities Press, pp. 86-106.

Bibliography

Abraham, K. (1920). Manifestations of the female castration complex. In: *Selected Papers on Psycho-Analysis*. London: Hogarth Press, 1927, pp. 338-369.

———(1921-1925). Psycho-analytical studies on character-formation. In: *Selected Papers on Psycho-Analysis*. London: Hogarth Press, 1927, pp. 370-417.

Anthony, E. J. (1969). The reactions of adults to adolescents and their behavior. In: *Adolescence: Psychosocial Perspectives*, eds. G. Caplan and S. Lebovici. New York: Basic Books, pp. 54-78.

Arlow, J. A., and Brenner, C. (1964). *Psychoanalytic Concepts and the Structural Theory*. New York: International Universities Press.

Arlow, J. A., Freud, A., Lampl-de Groot, J., and Beres, D. (1968). Panel discussion. *International Journal of Psycho-Analysis* 49: 506-512.

Arnold, M. B. (1970a). Brain function in emotion: a phenomenological analysis. In: *Physiological Correlates of Emotion*, ed. P. Black. New York: Academic Press, pp. 261-285.

———(1970b). Perennial problems in the field of emotion. In: *Feelings and Emotions*, ed. M. B. Arnold. New York: Academic Press, pp. 169-185.

———, and Gasson, J. A. (1954). Feelings and emotions as dynamic factors in personality integration. In: *The Nature of Emotion*, ed. M. B. Arnold. Baltimore: Penguin Books, 1969, pp. 203-221.

Bak, R. C. (1973). Being in love and object loss. *International Journal of Psycho-Analysis* 54: 1-8.

Balint, M. (1948). On genital love. In: *Primary Love and Psychoanalytic Technique*. London: Tavistock, 1959, pp. 109-120.

Bergmann, M. S. (1971). Psychoanalytic observations on the capacity to love. In: *Separation-Individuation*, eds. J. B. McDevitt and C. F. Settlage. New York: International Universities Press, pp. 15-40.

Bion, W. R. (1959). *Experiences in Groups*. New York: Basic Books.

———(1967). *Second Thoughts: Selected Papers on Psychoanalysis*. London: Heinemann.

Blanck, G., and Blanck, R. (1972). Toward a psychoanalytic developmental psychology. *Journal of the American Psychoanalytic Association* 20: 668-710.

Boyer, L. B., and Giovacchini, P. L. (1967). *Psychoanalytic Treatment of Schizophrenic and Characterological Disorders*. New York: Jason Aronson, pp. 208-335.

Bowlby, J. (1966). *Maternal Care and Mental Health*. New York: Schocken Books.

———(1969). *Attachment and Loss, Vol. I: Attachment*. New York: Basic Books.

Brenner, C. (1974a). On the nature and development of affects—a unified theory. *Psychoanalytic Quarterly* 43: 532-556.

———(1974b). Depression, anxiety, and affect theory. *International Journal of Psycho-Analysis* 55: 25-32.

Brierley, M. (1937). Affects in theory and practice. In: *Trends in Psychoanalysis*. London: Hogarth, 1951, pp. 43-56.

Brocher, T. (1970). Personal communication.

Brody, E. B., and Lindbergh, S. S. (1967). Trait and pattern disturbances. In: *Comprehensive Textbook of Psychiatry*, eds. A. R. Freedman and H. I. Kaplan. Baltimore: Williams & Wilkins, pp. 937-950.

Caine, R. M., and Small, D. J. (1969). *The Treatment of Mental Illness*. New York: International Universities Press.

Cannon, W. B. (1927). The James-Lange theory of emotion. In: *The Nature of Emotion*, ed. M. B. Arnold. Baltimore: Penguin Books, 1969, pp. 43-52.

Castelnuovo-Tedesco, P. (1974). Toward a theory of affect. *Journal of the American Psychoanalytic Association* 22: 612-625.

Chasseguet-Smirgel, J. (1970). *Female Sexuality*. Ann Arbor: University of Michigan, pp. 1-3, 94-134.

Cleckley, H. (1964). *The Mask of Sanity*, 4th ed. Saint Louis: Mosby, pp. 362-401.

Deutsch, H. (1942). Some forms of emotional disturbance and their relationship to schizophrenia. *Psychoanalytic Quarterly* 11: 301-321.

Dicks, H. V. (1967). *Marital Tensions*. New York: Basic Books.

Dolgoff, T. (1971). Personal communication.

Easser, B. R., and Lesser, S. R. (1965). Hysterical personality: a reevaluation. *Psychoanalytic Quarterly* 34: 390-405.

Edelson, M. (1967). The sociotherapeutic function in a psychiatric hospital. *Journal of the Fort Logan Mental Health Center* 4: 1-45.

Eissler, K. R. (1953). The effect of the structure of the ego on psychoanalytic technique. *Journal of the American Psychoanalytic Association* 1: 104-143.

Engel, G. L. (1963). Toward a classification of affects. In: *Expression of the Emotions in Man*, ed. P. H. Knapp. New York: International Universities Press, pp. 266-299.

Erikson, E. H. (1950). Growth and crises of the healthy personality. In: *Identity and the Life Cycle*. New York: International Universities Press, 1959, 1: 50-100.

———(1956). The problem of ego identity. *Journal of the American Psychoanalytic Association* 4: 56-121.

———(1959). Identity and the life cycle. *Psychological Issues*, New York: International Universities Press 1: 1-171.

———(1963). *Childhood and Society*. Second Edition. New York: Norton.

Ezriel, H. (1950). A psychoanalytic approach to the treatment of patients in groups. *Journal of Mental Science* 96: 774-779.

Fairbairn, W. D. (1952). *An Object-Relations Theory of the Personality*. New York: Basic Books.

———(1963). Synopsis of an object-relations theory of the personality. *International Journal of Psycho-Analysis* 4: 224-225.

Falck, H. (1969). Personal communication.

Fenichel, O. (1941). *Problems of Psychoanalytic Technique*. Albany: Psychoanalytic Quarterly.

———(1945). *The Psychoanalytic Theory of Neurosis*. New York: Norton, pp. 268-310, 324-386, 463-540.

Frank, J. D., et al. (1952). Two behavior patterns in therapeutic groups and their apparent motivation. *Human relations* 5: 289-317.

Freedman, D. A. (1972). On the limits of the effectiveness of psychoanalysis—early ego and somatic disturbances. *International Journal of Psycho-Analysis* 53: 363-370.

Freud, A. (1936). *The Ego and the Mechanisms of Defense*. New York: International Universities Press, 1946, pp. 30-32.

Freud, S. (1908). Character and anal erotism. *Standard Edition* 9: 167-175. London: Hogarth Press, 1959.

———(1910). A special type of choice of objects made by men. *Standard Edition* 11: 163-175. London: Hogarth Press, 1957.

———(1912). On the universal tendency to debasement in the sphere of love (contributions to the Psychology of Love II). *Standard Edition* 11: 178-190. London: Hogarth Press, 1957.

———(1915a). Repression. *Standard Edition* 14: 141-158. London: Hogarth Press, 1957.

———(1915b). The unconscious. *Standard Edition* 14: 159-215. London: Hogarth Press, 1957.

———(1917-1918). The taboo of virginity (contributions to the Psychology of Love III). *Standard Edition* 11: 192-208. London: Hogarth Press, 1957.

———(1923). The ego and the id. *Standard Edition* 19: 13-66. London: Hogarth Press, 1961.

———(1926). Inhibitions, symptoms and anxiety. *Standard Edition* 20: 87-156. London: Hogarth Press.

———(1927). Fetishism. *Standard Edition* 21: 235-239. London: Hogarth Press, 1961.

———(1931). Libidinal types. *Standard Edition* 21: 215-220. London: Hogarth Press, 1961.

———(1938). Splitting of the ego in the process of defence. *Standard Edition* 23: 273-278. London: Hogarth Press, 1964.

———(1940). An outline of psycho-analysis. *Standard Edition* 23: 139-171. London: Hogarth Press, 1964.

Friedlander, K. (1947). *The Psycho-Analytical Approach to Juvenile Delinquency*. New York: International Universities Press, pp. 183-187.

Fromm-Reichman, F. (1959). Psychoanalysis and Psychotherapy. *Selected Papers*. Chicago: University of Chicago Press.

Frosch, J. (1964). The psychotic character: clinical psychiatric considerations. *Psychiatric Quarterly* 38: 81-96.

———(1966). A note on reality constancy. In: *Psychoanalysis: A General Psychology*, eds. R. M. Lowenstein, L. M. Newman, M. Schur, and A. J. Solnit. New York: International Universities Press, pp. 349-376.

———(1970). Psychoanalytic considerations of the psychotic character. *Journal of the American Psychoanalytic Association* 18: 24-50.

Giovacchini, P. L. (1963). Integrative aspects of object relationships. *Psychoanalytic Quarterly* 32: 393-407.

Glover, E. (1956). *On the Early Development of the Mind*. New York: International Universities Press.

Greenson, R. R. (1958). On screen defenses, screen hunger, and screen identity. *Journal of the American Psychoanalytic Association* 6: 242-262.

Guntrip, H. (1961). *Personality Structure and Human Interaction*. London: Hogarth Press.

———(1968). *Schizoid Phenomena, Object Relations and the Self.* New York: International Universities Press.

———(1971). *Psychoanalytic Theory, Therapy, and the Self.* New York: Basic Books.

Hartmann, H. (1939). *Ego Psychology and the Problem of Adaptation.* New York: International Universities Press, 1958.

———(1948). Comments on the psychoanalytic theory of instinctual drives. *Psychoanalytic Quarterly* 17: 368-388.

———(1950). Comments on the psychoanalytic theory of the ego. In: *Essays on Ego Psychology.* London: Hogarth Press; New York: International Universities Press, 1964, pp. 113-141.

———(1955). Notes on the theory of sublimation. In: *Essays on Ego Psychology.* New York: International Universities Press, 1964, pp. 215-240.

———, Kris, E., and Loewenstein, R. (1946). Comments on the formation of psychic structure. *Psychoanalytic Study of the Child* 2: 11-38. New York: International Universities Press.

———, and Loewenstein, R. (1962). Notes on the superego. *Psychoanalytic Study of the Child* 17: 42-81.

Hartocollis, P. (1964). Hospital romances: some vicissitudes of transference. *Bulletin of the Menninger Clinic* 28: 62-71.

———(1974). Origins of time: a reconstruction of the ontogenetic development of the sense of time based on object-relations theory. *Psychoanalytic Quarterly* 43: 243-261.

Heimann, P. (1943-44). Certain functions of introjection and projection in early infancy. In: *Developments in Psycho-Analysis,* ed. Klein et al. London: Hogarth Press, 1952, pp. 122-168.

———(1966). Comments on Dr. Kernberg's paper (Structural derivatives of object relationships). *International Journal of Psycho-Analysis* 47: 254-260.

———, and Valenstein, A. (1972). The psychoanalytic concept of aggression: an integrated summary. *International Journal of Psycho-Analysis* 53: 31-35.

Holder, A. (1970). Instinct and drive. In: *Basic Psychoanalytic Concepts of the Theory of Instincts, Vol. III,* ed. H. Nagera. New York: Basic Books, pp. 19-22.

Horney, K. (1967). *Feminine Psychology.* London: Routledge & Kegan Paul.

Jacobson, E. (1953). On the psychoanalytic theory of affects. In: *Depression.* New York: International Universities Press, 1971, pp. 3-47.

———(1954). Contribution to the metapsychology of psychotic identifications. *Journal of the American Psychoanalytic Association* 2: 239-262.

———(1957a). Denial and repression. *Journal of the American Psychoanalytic Association* 5: 61-92.

———(1957b). Normal and pathological moods: their nature and functions. In: *Depression*. New York: International Universities Press, 1971, pp. 66-106.

———(1964). *The Self and the Object World*. New York: International Universities Press.

———(1966). Differences between schizophrenic and melancholic states of depression. In: *Depression*. New York: International Universities Press, 1971, pp. 264-283.

———(1971). *Depression*. New York: International Universities Press.

Joffe, W. G., and Sandler, J. (1965). Notes on pain, depression, and individuation. *Psychoanalytic Study of the Child* 20: 394-424.

Johnson, A. M., and Szurek, S. A. (1952). The genesis of antisocial acting out in children and adults. *Psychoanalytic Quarterly* 21: 323-343.

Jones, E. (1948). The early development of female sexuality. In: *Papers on Psycho-Analysis*. Boston: Beacon Press, 1961, pp. 438-451.

Jones, M. (1968). *Social Psychiatry in Practice*. Baltimore, Maryland: Penguin Books.

Josselyn, I. M. (1971). The capacity to love: a possible reformulation. *Journal of the American Academy of Child Psychiatry* 10: 6-22.

Kernberg, O. (1963). Discussion of the paper, Object relations theory and the conceptual model of psychoanalysis by John D. Sutherland, M.D. *British Journal of Medical Psychology* 36: 121-124.

———(1965). Countertransference. In: *Borderline Conditions and Pathological Narcissism*. New York: Jason Aronson, 1975, pp. 49-67.

———(1967). Borderline personality organization. In: *Borderline Conditions and Pathological Narcissism*. New York: Jason Aronson, 1975, pp. 3-47.

———(1968). The treatment of patients with borderline personality organization. In: *Borderline Conditions and Pathological Narcissism*. New York: Jason Aronson, 1975, pp. 69-109.

———(1969). A contribution to the ego-psychological critique of the Kleinian school. *International Journal of Psycho-Analysis* 50: 317-333.

———(1970). Factors in the psychoanalytic treatment of narcissistic personalities. In: *Borderline Conditions and Pathological Narcissism*. New York: Jason Aronson, 1975, pp. 227-262.

———(1971). Differential diagnosis and treatment. In: *Borderline Conditions and Pathological Narcissism*. New York: Jason Aronson, 1975, pp. 153-183.

———(1972). Early ego integration and object relations. *Annals of the New York Academy of Sciences* 193: 233-247.

———(1974). Further contributions to the treatment of narcissistic personalities. In: *Borderline Conditions and Pathological Narcissism*. New York: Jason Aronson, 1975, pp. 263-314.

———(1975a). Normal and pathological narcissism: structural and clinical aspects. In: *Borderline Conditions and Pathological Narcissism*. New York: Jason Aronson, 1975, pp. 315-342.

———(1975b). *Borderline Conditions and Pathological Narcissism*. New York: Jason Aronson, 1975.

———(1975c). Cultural impact and intrapsychic change. In: *Adolescent Psychiatry*, Volume 4, eds. H. C. Feinstein and P. Giovacchini. New York: Jason Aronson, 1975, pp. 37-45.

Kernberg, P. (1971). The course of the analysis of a narcissistic personality with hysterical and compulsive features. *Journal of the American Psychoanalytic Association* 19: 451-471.

Klein, M. (1934). A contribution to the psychogenesis of manic-depressive states. In: *Contributions to Psycho-Analysis, 1921-1945*. London: Hogarth Press, 1948, pp. 282-310.

———(1940). Mourning and its relation to manic-depressive states. In: *Contributions to Psycho-Analysis, 1921-1945*. London: Hogarth Press, 1948, pp. 311-338.

———(1945). The Oedipus complex in the light of early anxieties. In: *Contributions to Psycho-Analysis, 1921-1945*. London: Hogarth Press, 1948, pp. 377-390.

———(1946). Notes on some schizoid mechanisms. In: *Developments in Psychoanalysis*, eds. M. Klein, P. Heimann, S. Issacs, and J. Riviere. London: Hogarth Press, 1952, pp. 292-320.

———(1952). Discussion of the mutual influences in the development of ego and id. *Psychoanalytic Study of the Child* 7: 51-53.

Knapp, P. H. (1963). Introduction: emotional expression—past and present. In: *Expression of the Emotions in Man*, ed. P. H. Knapp. New York: International Universities Press, pp. 3-15.

Knight, R. P. (1953). Borderline states. In: *Psychoanalytic Psychiatry and Psychology,* eds. R. P. Knight and C. R. Friedman. New York: International Universities Press, 1954, pp. 97-109.

Kohut, H. (1971). *The Analysis of the Self.* New York: International Universities Press.

Laughlin, H. P. (1956). *The Neuroses in Clinical Practice.* Philadelphia: Saunders, pp. 394-406.

Leeper, R. W. (1970). The motivational and perceptual properties of emotions as indicating their fundamental character and role. In: *Feelings and Emotions,* ed. M. B. Arnold. New York: Academic Press, pp. 151-185.

Lichtenberg, J. D., and Slap, J. W. (1973). Notes on the concept of splitting and the defense mechanism of the splitting of representations. *Journal of the American Psychoanalytic Association* 21: 722-787.

Lichtenstein, H. (1970). Changing implications of the concept of psychosexual development: an inquiry concerning the validity of classical psychoanalytic assumptions concerning sexuality. *Journal of the American Psychoanalytic Association* 18: 300-318.

Lorenz, K. (1963). *On Aggression.* New York: Bantam Books.

MacLean, P. D. (1967). The brain in relation to empathy and medical education. *Journal of Nervous and Mental Diseases* 144: 374-382.

———(1969). The hypothalamus and emotional behavior. In: *The Hypothalamus,* eds. W. Haymaker, E. Anderson and W. J. H. Nauta. Springfield, Ill.: Charles C Thomas, pp. 659-678.

———(1972). Cerebral evolution and emotional processes: new findings on the striatal complex. *Annals of the New York Academy of Sciences* 193: 137-149.

Madison, P. (1961). *Freud's Concept of Repression and Defense.* Minneapolis: University of Minnesota Press.

Mahler, M. S. (1968). *On Human Symbiosis and the Vicissitudes of Individuation. Vol. 1: Infantile Psychosis.* New York: International Universities Press.

———(1971). A study of the separation-individuation process and its possible application to borderline phenomena in the psychoanalytic situation. *Psychoanalytic Study of the Child* 26: 403-424.

———(1972). On the first three subphases of the separation-individuation process. *International Journal of Psycho-Analysis* 53: 333-338.

———(1973). Personal communication.

Main, T. F. (1957). The ailment. *British Journal of Medical Psychology* 30: 129-145.

May, R. (1969). *Love and Will*. New York: Norton.

Mayman, M. (1963). Personal communication.

McDougall, W. (1928). Emotion and feeling distinguished. In: *The Nature of Emotion*, ed. M. B. Arnold. Baltimore: Penguin Books, 1969, pp. 61-66.

Menninger, K. (1938). *Man Against Himself*. New York: Harcourt Brace.

———, and Mayman, M. (1956). Episodic dyscontrol: a third order of stress adaptation. *Bulletin of the Menninger Clinic* 20: 153-165.

———, Mayman, M., and Pruyser, P. (1963). *The Vital Balance*. New York: Viking.

Miller, G. A., Gallanter, E., and Pribram, K. H. (1960). *Plans and the Structure of Behavior*. New York: Holt, Rinehart & Winston.

———, and Rice, A. K. (1967). *Systems of Organization*. London: Tavistock Publications.

Miller, J. G. (1969). Living systems: basic concepts. In: *General Systems Theory and Psychiatry*, eds. W. Gray, F. J. Duhl, and N. D. Rizzo. Boston: Little, Brown, pp. 51-133.

Modell, A. H. (1968). *Object Love and Reality*. New York: International Universities Press.

Moore, B. E. (1968). Some genetic and developmental considerations in regard to affects. Reported by L. B. Lofgren. *Journal of the American Psychoanalytic Association* 16: 638-650.

———(1973). Toward a theory of affects: the affect in search of an idea. Reported by P. Castelnuovo-Tedesco. *Journal of the American Psychoanalytic Association* 22: 612-625.

Morgane, P. J. (1972). Panel discussion. *Annals of the New York Academy of Sciences* 193: 302-304.

Mullahy, P. (1952). *The Contributions of Harry Stack Sullivan*. New York: Hermitage House.

———(1953). A theory of interpersonal relations and the evolution of personality. In: *Conceptions of Modern Psychiatry*, ed. H. S. Sullivan. New York: Norton, pp. 239-294.

———(1955). *Oedipus, Myth and Complex*. New York: Grove Press.

Murphy, L. (1963). From a report presented to Topeka Psychoanalytic Institute Research Seminar, May 15, 1963. (Unpublished).

———(1964). Adaptational tasks in childhood in our culture. *Bulletin of the Menninger Clinic* 28: 309-322.

Myerson, P. G. (1971). Personal communication.

Novey, S. (1959). A clinical view of the affect theory in psychoanalysis. *International Journal of Psycho-Analysis* 40: 94-104.

Novotny, P. (1971). The pseudo-psychoanalytic hospital (Notes on the Institutionalization of Countertransference Acting Out Patterns). *Bulletin of the Menninger Clinic* 37: 193-210.

Nunberg, H. (1955). *Principles of Psychoanalysis.* New York: International Universities Press.

Olds, J. (1960). Differentiation of reward systems in the brain by self-stimulation techniques. In: *Electrical Studies on the Unanesthetized Brain,* eds. Ramey and O'Doherty. New York: Harper and Row, pp. 17-51.

Parsons, T. (1964a). Social structure and the development of personality: Freud's contribution to the integration of psychology and sociology. In: *Social Structure and Personality.* London: The Free Press, pp. 78-111. Also in: *Psychiatry,* 1958, 21: 321-340.

———(1964b). The superego and the theory of social systems. In: *Social Structure and Personality.* London: The Free Press, pp. 17-33. Also in: *Psychiatry* 1952, Vol. 15, No. 1.

Peto, A. (1967). On affect control. In: *The Psychoanalytic Study of the Child.* New York: International Universities Press, 1971, 22: 36-51.

Prelinger, E., Zimet, C. N., Schafer, R., and Levin, M. (1964). *An Ego-Psychological Approach to Character Assessment.* Glencoe: Free Press.

Pribram, K. H. (1970). Feelings as monitors. In: *Feelings and Emotions,* ed. M. B. Arnold. New York: Academic Press, pp. 41-53.

———(1971). *Languages of the Brain.* New Jersey: Prentice-Hall, Inc.

Rangell, L. (1955). The role of the parent in the Oedipus complex. *Bulletin of the Menninger Clinic* 19: 9-15.

Rapaport, D. (1953). On the psychoanalytic theory of affects. In: *The Collected Papers of David Rapaport,* ed. M. M. Gill. New York: Basic Books, 1967, pp. 476-512.

———(1960). *The Structure of Psychoanalytic Theory.* New York: International Universities Press.

———, Gill, M. M., and Schafer, R. (1945-1946). *Diagnostic Psychological Testing,* 2 Vols. Chicago: Year Book Publishers.

———, and Gill, M. (1959). The points of view and assumptions of metapsychology. In: *The Collected Papers of David Rapaport,* ed. M. Gill. New York: Basic Books, 1967, pp. 795-811.

Reich, A. (1953). Narcissistic object choice in women. *Journal of the American Psychoanalytic Association* 1: 22-44.
Reich, W. (1933). *Character Analysis.* New York: Noonday Press, 3rd ed., 1949.
Rice, A. K. (1963). *The Enterprise and its Environment.* London: Tavistock Publications.
———(1965). *Learning for Leadership.* London: Tavistock Publications.
———(1969). Individual, group and intergroup processes. *Human Relations* 22: 565-584.
Rioch, M. J. (1970). The work of Wilfred Bion on groups. *Psychiatry* 33: 56-66.
Riviere, J. (1937). Hate, greed and aggression. In: *Love, Hate and Reparation,* eds. M. Klein & J. Riviere. London: Hogarth Press, pp. 3-53.
Rosenfeld, H. (1963). Notes on the psychopathology and psychoanalytic treatment of schizophrenia. In: *Psychotic States.* London: Hogarth Press, 1965, pp. 155-168.
———(1964). On the psychopathology of narcissism: a clinical approach. *International Journal of Psycho-Analysis* 45: 332-337.
———(1965). *Psychotic States: A Psychoanalytic Approach.* New York: International Universities Press, pp. 13-127; 155-168.
Ross, N. (1975). Affect as cognition: with observations on the meanings of mystical states. *International Review of Psycho-Analysis* 2: 79-93.
Rubenstein, R., and Lasswell, H. D. (1966). *The Sharing of Power in a Psychiatric Hospital.* New Haven & London: Yale University Press.
Sandler, J. (1960). On the concept of the superego. *Psychoanalytic Study of the Child* 15: 128-162.
———(1972). The role of affects in psychoanalytic theory, physiology, emotion and psychosomatic illness. *A Ciba Foundation Symposium,* London, April.
———, and Rosenblatt, B. (1962). The concept of the representational world. *Psychoanalytic Study of the Child* 17: 128-145.
———, Holder, A., and Meers, D. (1963). The ego ideal and the ideal self. *Psychoanalytic Study of the Child* 18: 139-158.
Schachter, S. (1970). The assumption of identity and peripheralist-centralist controversies in motivation and emotion. In: *Feelings and Emotions,* ed. M. B. Arnold. New York: Academic Press, pp. 111-121.

Schafer, R. (1968). *Aspects of Internalization*. New York: International Universities Press.

Schmale, Jr., A. H. (1958). Relationship of separation and depression to disease. *Psychosomatic Medicine* 20: 259-277.

Schur, M. (1966). *The Id and the Regulatory Principles of Mental Functioning*. New York: International Universities Press.

Searles, H. F. (1960). *The Nonhuman Environment*. New York: International Universities Press.

———(1965). *Collected Papers on Schizophrenia and Related Subjects*. New York: International Universities Press.

Segal, H. (1964). *Introduction to the Work of Melanie Klein*. London: Heinemann; New York: Basic Books.

Shapiro, D. (1965). *Neurotic Styles*. New York: Basic Books.

Spitz, R. (1945). Diacritic and coenesthetic organizations: the psychiatric significance of a functional division of the nervous system into a sensory and emotive part. *Psychoanalytic Review* 32: 146-161.

———(1965). *The First Year of Life*. New York: International Universities Press.

———(1972). Bridges: on anticipation, duration, and meaning. *Journal of the American Psychoanalytic Association* 20: 721-735.

Stanton, A. A., and Schwartz, M. S. (1954). *The Mental Hospital*. New York: Basic Books.

Stone, L. (1954). The widening scope of indications for psychoanalysis. *Journal of the American Psychoanalytic Association* 2: 567-594.

Stross, L. (1966). Personal communication.

Sullivan, H. S. (1953). *The Interpersonal Theory of Psychiatry*. New York: Norton.

Sutherland, J. D. (1952). Notes on psychoanalytic group therapy. I. therapy and training. *Psychiatry* 15: 111-117.

———(1963). Object relations theory and the conceptual model of psychoanalysis. *British Journal of Medical Psychology* 36: 109-124.

———(1966). Psychoanalytic object-relations theory applied to the analysis of psychological tests. Presented to the Topeka Psychoanalytic Society, April 1966. (Unpublished).

———(1969). Psychoanalysis in the post-industrial society. *International Journal of Psycho-Analysis* 50: 673-682.

———, and Gill, H. S. (1970). The object relations theory of personality. In: *Language and Psychodynamic Appraisal*. The Tavistock Institute of Human Relations, pp. 8-18.

Ticho, E. (1971). Personal communication.

———(1972). Termination of psychoanalysis: treatment goals, life goals. *Psychoanalytic Quarterly* 41: 315-333.

Tinbergen, N. (1951). An attempt at synthesis. In: *The Study of Instinct*. New York: Oxford University Press, pp. 101-127.

Tomkins, S. S. (1970). Affect as the primary motivational system. In: *Feelings and Emotions*. ed. M. B. Arnold. New York: Academic Press, pp. 101-110.

van der Waals, H. G. (1952). Discussion of the mutual influences in the development of ego and id. *Psychoanalytic Study of the Child* 7: 66-68.

———(1965). Problems of narcissism. *Bulletin of the Menninger Clinic* 29: 293-311.

Weisman, A. D. (1958). Reality sense and reality testing. *Behavioral Science* 3: 228-261.

Will, O. (1961). Psychotherapy in reference to the schizophrenic reaction. In: *Contemporary Psychotherapies*, ed. M. I. Stein. New York: Free Press, pp. 128-156.

———(1967). Schizophrenia: the problem of origins. In: *The Origins of Schizophrenia*, ed. J. Romano. Proceedings of the First Rochester International Conference on Schizophrenia, pp. 214-227.

Winnicott, D. W. (1954). Metapsychological and clinical aspects of regression within the psycho-analytical set-up. In: *Collected Papers*. New York: Basic Books, 1958, pp. 278-294.

———(1955). The depressive position in normal emotional development. *British Journal of Medical Psychology* 28: 89-100.

———(1960). Ego distortion in terms of true and false self. In: *The Maturational Processes and the Facilitating Environment*. New York: International Universities Press, 1965, pp. 140-152.

———(1963). The development of the capacity for concern. *Bulletin of the Menninger Clinic* 27: 167-176.

Wisdom, J. O. (1963). Fairbairn's contribution on object-relationship, splitting and ego structure. *British Journal of Medical Psychology* 36: 145-159.

———(1970). Freud and Melanie Klein: psychology, ontology, and weltanschauung. In: *Psychoanalysis and Philosophy*, ed. C. Hanly and M. Lazerowitz. New York: International Universities Press, pp. 327-362.

Yankelovich, D., and Barrett, W. (1970). *Ego and Instinct*. New York: Random House.

Young, P. T. (1961). Affective processes. In: *The Nature of Emotion,* ed. M. B. Arnold. Baltimore: Penguin Books, 1969, pp. 222-237.

Zaleznik, A. (1970). Personal communication.

Zetzel, E. R. (1966). The analytic situation. In: *Psychoanalysis in the Americas,* ed. Robert E. Litman. New York: International Universities Press, pp. 86-106.

———(1968). The so-called good hysteric. *International Journal of Psycho-Analysis* 49: 256-260.

CREDITS

Chapter 1

Reprinted from *International Journal of Psycho-Analysis*, 47: 236-253, 1966.

Chapter 2

Presented at the Annual Meeting of the American Psychoanalytic Association, Washington, D.C., May 1971. Published here for the first time.

Chapter 3

Presented at the Royden Astley Memorial Symposium on Narcissism, Pittsburgh, Pa., September 1973. Published here for the first time.

Chapter 4

Published here for the first time.

Chapter 5

Reprinted from the *Journal of the American Psychoanalytic Association*, 18: 800-822, 1970.

Chapter 6

Presented at the 1975 Edward S. Strecker Award Lecture, Philadelphia, Pa., November 1975. Reprinted from Strecker Monograph Series XII, 1975 and the *Journal of the National Association of Private Psychiatric Hospitals*, Winter 1975.

Chapter 7

This chapter is an expanded and modified version of a paper appearing in the *Journal of the American Psychoanalytic Association*, 22: 486-511, 1974.

Chapter 8

Reprinted from the *Journal of the American Psychoanalytic Association*, 2: 743-768, 1974.

Chapter 9

This chapter is an expanded and modified version of a paper appearing in *The Annual of Psychoanalysis*, 1: 363-388, 1973.

Index

Made in United States
North Haven, CT
03 June 2022